KARDEL

ADOLF HITLE
BEGRÜNDER
ISRAELS
(ADOLF HITLER -
FOUNDER OF
ISRAEL)

Gevidmet der Meistverfolgten unserer Zeit: der Wahrheit
(Dedicated to the most persecuted of our time - The Truth)

ISRAEL IM KRIEG MIT JUDEN
(ISRAEL IN WAR WITH JEWS)

VARLEGER
(PUBLISHER)

i

A hardocover edition of this book was originally printed
by a Publisher of Marva, 1211 Genf, Case 254,
Switzerland, © Copyright 1974 Kardel ISBN 3 85800 001 9

Translated by the Oficyna Wydawnicza "Fulmen",
Warszawa © Copyright 1996 Fulmen ISBN 83 86445 020 5
and in Poland is already sold out.

This introductory edition was translated by the Publisher,
Modjeskis' Society Dedicated to Preservation of Cultures,
P.O. Box 193, San Diego, CA 92038,
© Copyright 1997 Modjeskis' Society ISBN 09657523-0-5
and is also available for distribution under the address of
this Society.

All rights to said editions are preserved, as well as
translation rights into other languages by the Society
combined with interested entities.

- Unabridged fourth edition available now at the
  RÜGGEBERG Publishing House;
- Translated into foreign languages;
- Filmed in Eastern Europe;
- Commented by many, like the,

"Neue Politik", Hamburg:
  "The Author deserves a commendation for as he once
  was an intrepid soldier, also now fearlessly pushes
  matters forward while the others, not much brave
  former soldiers, are presently subserviently silent."

"Akemi Sakamoto", Tokyo:
  "Apparently the Taboo is still alive."

"Nuernberger Zeitung", Nuernberg:
  "It keeps tension. Moreover, the Author enormously
  dug through intimacies."

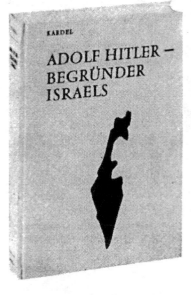

KARDEL

ADOLF HITLER –
BEGRÜNDER
ISRAELS

Das verfolgte Buch

- bei RÜGGEBERG vierte unveränderte Auflage erhältlich.

In die Weltsprachen übersetzt.

In Osteuropa verfilmt.

„Lob verdient der Verfasser dafür, daß er als einstmals tapferer Soldat nun so unerschrocken wie früher an Dinge herangeht, die andere ehemalige Soldaten, damals kaum weniger tapfer, heute unterwürfig verschweigen".

„Neue Politik", Hamburg

„Das Tabu ist anscheinend bis jetzt noch nicht ausgestorben".

„Akemi Sakamoto", Tokyo

„Nicht ohne Spannung. Außerdem sind die Intimkenntnisse des Verfassers enorm."

„Nürnberger Zeitung", Nürnberg

«Die Augen sind gewöhnlich glänzend, beide Lider sind schwer und geschwellt. Der Lymphsack unter dem Auge ist gewöhnlich voller und weiter vorstehend als bei Nichtjuden. Das hohe Wangenbein bedingt in der Regel die hohle Wange, die zum jüdischen Ausdruck beiträgt, während die Nase, von vorn gesehen, nur durch die weiche Beweglichkeit der Nasenflügel, dieses Hauptmerkmal der jüdischen Nase, unterschieden werden kann. Die Oberlippe ist gemeinhin kurz und die untere steht vor, was dem Gesicht einen etwas sinnlichen Ausdruck gibt.»

Die «Jewisch Encyclopaedia», das zwölfbändige jüdische Nachschlagewerk fur alle Fragen des Judentums, über das «eigentümliche Wesen des jüdischen Aussehens.»

Typical signs of Jewish features are: Eyes are usually shiny and both eye lids are heavy and swollen. The lymphbag under the eyes is usually fuller and stands out more than on Gentiles. The high cheekbone as a rule creates a sunken cheek. The nose can only be differentiated by its slightly moving nose wings when viewed from the front during breathing. The upper lip is short and the lower lip stands out and this gives the face a sensual expression." Source: Twelve volumes "Jewish Encyclopedia" on all questions pertaining Jewry and the Jewish curious nature and notions.

Adolf Hitler, with high probability a grandson of the Jew Frankenberger. Driven by his boundless hatred towards his own kinsmen, this man brought to reality his Vienna's youth dream to settle the European Jews in the Orient.

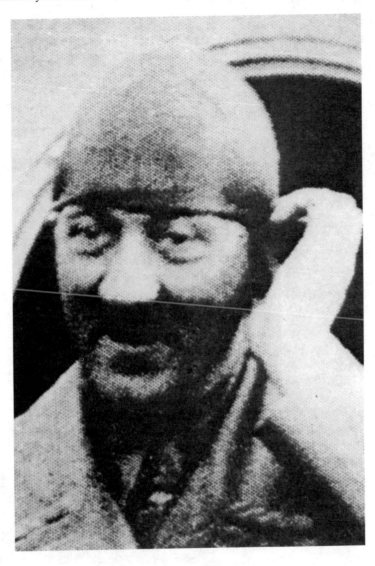

Adolf Hitler, mit an Sicherheit grenzender Wahrscheinlichkeit Enkel des Juden Frankenberger. Der Mann verwirklichte rastund rücksichtslos, getrieben von seinem masslosen Hass auf das eigene Blut, seinen Wiener Jünglingstraum, die europäischen Juden im Vorderen Orient anzusiedeln.

The main supporters of fulfilling the "Work of Masters" were Reinhard Heydrich, predominantly Jewish (above) and the full Jew Adolf Eichmann (below). As the organizer of the Jewish emigration prior to the Second World War Eichmann traveled to the country which today is Israel. "The only reason for the name change to 'Eichmann' was to get away from the ancestors name and from the history of Jewish people", wrote the Jewish names researcher G. Kessler in Leipzig, 1935.

Haupterfüllungsgehilfen bei diesem «Werk des Herrn» wurden der überwiegend jüdische Reinhard Heydrich (oben) und der volljüdische Adolf Eichmann (unten). E. bereiste als Leiter der jüdischen Auswanderung vor dem zweiten Weltkrieg das heutige Israel. «Einziger Sinn des Namens Eichmann war die Losreissung der Namensträger von ihren Vätern und von der Geschichte ihres Volkes», schrieb 1935 in Leipzig der jüdische Namensforscher G. Kessler.

CONTENTS

PREFACE

Hennecke Kardel dedicated his work to "THE MOST PERSECUTED IN OUR TIME - THE TRUTH", which is not quite right, for throughout the past 2000 years the "TRUTH" with the "Holy Bible" is courageously marching on but the people are not seeking it. If they were, they would not be glorifying errors which impede evolution of the human mind.

Kardel's work illustrates to what sacrifices human beings are willing to go if driven by a "superior" ideology. It shows people with their creative and destructive faculties used almost at the same time, climaxing in the "THIRTY YEAR WAR OF IDEOLOGIES", and as the Author correctly observed, it is the "SAME TIME" in the history of mankind.

Americans should know it best for their "SAME TIME" commenced 200 years ago with a short disruption by the Civil War. Americans - not segregated by religious orientation like Jews, who introduce themselves as such everywhere. It is a good sign that a German Jew Dietrich Bronder in his book "Bevor Hitler Kam" ("Before Hitler Came") (POST. r.71) has revealed to what extent the Israelites' dream of subduing the world influenced social life of Teutons (Germans) during their 1000 year history (some say 500 year), branded by Lucy S. Dawidowicz as the "WAR AGAINST JEWS" (POST. r.72)

D. Bronder undoubtedly sent a message to the Israeli-Judaites that the biblical dream after the "THIRTY YEAR WAR OF IDEOLOGIES" is impossible to materialize. The message is also a memento to those who are praying "Next Year In Jerusalem", for those prayers keep their children separate from other cultures in their own kindergartens and elementary schools. No wonder then when they later discover with astonishment that the Gentiles do not accept them. (POST. r. 99)

Just a few titles of the bibliographical sources, marked POSTSCRIPT (POST.), reference (r.), or footnotes (n.) permit one to obtain a good picture about what the brilliant (literally) minds during the last 500 years have been preoccupied with while the rest of the World, since Christopher Columbus and Nicolaus Copernicus, is going from false gods to the Jeffersonian "Nature's God".

The Publisher tries to implement Jefferson's intuition in a separate booklet under the title "NATURE'S GOD" by converging science with beliefs. For after acceptance of the theory of evolution by the Holy See, the humankind in the third Millennium A.D. should enrich its intuition and lay a new foundation for the "Nature's God" via sciences. The booklet is available from the Publisher upon request.

Publisher

INTRODUCTION

In 1973, on an Atlantic island, the author ran across a staff officer with whom and together with other men from a dozen of European nations, he besieged Leningrad some thirty years earlier. At the outbreak of the First World War, his parents, Jews of Vienna, while on an oceanic voyage were impounded and later settled on this island.

After first few drinks in a Casino have loosened their tongues, the author asked him: "Amigo, being a full Jew how can you wear these three medals and decorations with the swastika on your chest?" "Well", came back the answer in a beautiful Viennese jargon: "why don't you start scratching on Hitler yourself? Then you will see that a Vienna Jew like me will appear."

When a small Italian freighter came over, two weeks later the author stepped on land in Buenos Aires. Out of a million Jews residing in that city he spoke at the lunch table or in the cafeteria with many, and at one evening drink in the region of Chaco, he heard from a so called war criminal a similar sigh: "Hitler an Austrian mixed Jew? Oh, dear Lord. After all, the Eichmann of Linz, who has been caught here, was a pure Jew."

Finally, after an anti-Zionist and a very educated Jewish Lady in the Andes, threw herself into rage: "And this Ben Gurion is 'Hitler segundo', the second Hitler", the traveling author decided really to "scratch on Hitler," and to answer the pervasive question: "Is there any connection between Hitler's unclear origin, and the foundation of the State of Israel, which did not exist for two thousand years, and suddenly three years after Hitler's death came into being again?

One must believe very strongly in the ability to wipe vigorously such a question off the table, like Maser, a German pastor known as a celebrated researcher of Hitler's persona: all the ancestors of this very unique individual in the world's history, a concentration of cunningness, energy and intelligence, have been derived from old fashioned circles, which were deeply rooted in the Austrian forests with nothing else in between. The uncertain black spot in the life of his born-out-of-wedlock Jewish grandfather, Frankenberger, was cleared for sure by three illiterate men Romeder, Breiteneder, and Paukh, and by a document signed with three "X" marks but without the required signature of a very careful village pastor. And did not Hitler, after he became Fuehrer, explain to his legal advisor Hans Frank, a son of a Bamberg's Jewish lawyer, that he learned from his grandmother Schicklgruber that her son Alois, Hitler's father, without any doubt originated from an affair with the Jew Frankenberger? Why then, for fourteen years Frankenberger paid faithfully for the support of the born-out-of wedlock Alois? Noticeable in this Hitler's story about his grandmother is the fact, that Madame Schicklgruber died many years before he was born.

Maser, who is certain that the "last word" about Germany's Leader has not yet been said, comes to a conclusion: "Since the end of the great victories in the snows of Moscow, and the simultaneous entry of the U.S. into the war (winter 1941-42), Hitler knew that the only reason he ordered people to fight and die, was to prolong his decision of committing suicide." [1] It was far from it. Exactly at that moment the war turned into a two front campaign. Therefore he was going to lose.

Then Hitler called his most trustful Chief of Police, Reinhard Tristan Eugen Heydrich (Heydrich's father's name was Suess and SS-Chief Himmler claimed that Suess had "overcome the Jew within himself"),[2] and sanctioned him to finally solve the Jewish question, for one should realize that only by the destruction of Jews an old dream of "creation of a home place for the Jewish nation" a few years later could come true.

One year later a new expert on Hitler, Mr.Fest, strongly contradicted Mr.Maser's research results: "Obviously Maser cannot defend his thesis although he presented it as evidence. Anyway all his arguments are doubtful in a similar way."[3] After such a quite correct statement, for Mr.Fest the complex matter suddenly became simple: "In this context the question of Hitler's grand fatherhood is actually of a secondary rank."[4] For the researcher Fest from that moment on the entire question of Hitler's Jewish origin "is a subject of subordinate interest."[5] Let us protest now! Impartiality is a very bad form of devaluation of any research work. Anyone who does not want to know in detail about Hitler's half Jewish "alcoholic" father, whom he dragged home from the "ugly, shameful, stinky and smoky bars",[6] and who does not want to know about Hitler's endlessly psychotic hatred toward his kinsmen, will understand little about history of the twentieth century, about the creation of the State of Israel, and about oncoming events which will make us hold our breaths until the end of this century.

The unloved and probably hated father and born-out-of-wedlock grandfather are the two main figures necessary to properly understand this Adolf Hitler. Hitler's experiences with Jews in Vienna (as being mostly noted); in the First World War and during the Soviet Munich, for him are undesirable attestations and details of dirt, too.

After one and a half century it is very unlikely for anyone to be able to prove that the Jew Frankenberger was Hitler's grandfather on his father's side. However, it is certain that Hitler knew about the child support paid by Frankenberger, and the fear that Frankenberger could have been his grandfather never left him. This fear dominated all of his life and undoubtedly motivated his actions.

Unlike other historians, the author does not overestimate preserved documents by the Defense Services or other Offices. Between 1933 and 1945 various entities put away or suppressed many documents, or created false ones for misleading purposes. In his healthy state of mind the author evaluated personal impressions and memories of credible witnesses, even if they were of old age, Jewish, or the so called war criminals. The reader will find all of this confirmed in the content of the author's investigation. Bibliographical index of the most suppressed, bought out, or destroyed books, besides making up of his own mind, is witnessing all the past events with full credibility.

Once a New York Judge became very angry at the end of a long lasting trial: "I can do without your 'Thank You, Your Honor'," yelling at the just acquitted woman. "In the evidence of this case there is only one missing piece which would convict you, you damn husband murderer!" The author is not however of this type of diligence.

Before 1933 much was written in the country, as well as abroad, about Hitler's probable Jewish origin, and his close connections with half-bred Jews of the opposite sex were a subject of fun and joyful criticism. However, after his assumption of power the country people became cautious and those abroad more distinguished. After 1945 the re-educators of the German people were not inclined to talk about Jews' participation in the Jewish misfortune.

As to the treatment of Hitler's Vienna youthful dream of making the Jewish State of Israel out of Arabic Palestine, and Europe free of Jews, with Jewish full or partial participation in their misfortune, both sides have the entire matter intentionally hushed up. Hence, the old Nazis with the young Zionists, could be called NAZIONISTS.

There is no doubt that Hitler wasn't a National Socialist. However, his lofty idea, which derived from the graves of the First World War, betrayed him and with the help of his inborn sophistry made him a servant to his hatred of his kinsmen and Jewish complexes.

The ideology of national socialism isn't and doesn't have to be anti-Jewish. This was proven in 1973 by the Argentina's experience. Peron, who was called by his people back to power, loudly said what he is about, and his shirted thugs painted on the walls: "Socialismo nacional!". And his most important Prime Minister of Economy Ber Gelbard, tried to pull out the state's cart driven by the military from a public enemy swamp. Gelbard was a Jew, born in Poland.

The unfortunate encounter of Hitler's psychotic hatred towards his kinsmen and the Jewish lead Soviet dictatorship of Munich, right after the First World War formed out of the national socialism in Germany an ideological variation of racism.

For the destruction of Jews' existence - as it occurred in reality - it was difficult to find effective helpers who were not of Jewish origin. In the East three officials were at hand. They were partly Jewish, if not predominantly Jewish: Heydrich, Frank and Rosenberg.

Pictures of the three main criminals - Hitler, Heydrich and Eichmann, with their unobjectionable semitic eyes, noses and mouths, were presented for the author's scrutiny. They consciously or unwillingly participated in the foundation of Israel. At the time these pictures were taken they were matured in their forties.

At the bier the first one said to the second: "As the Leader of the Party and of the German Reich I will give you, my lovely friend Heydrich, the second German after me, the biggest honor I have to give you: the German Order of Highest Degree."[7]

The reader might look unsuccessfully for a book which long ago disappeared from the market. It was an extraordinary and instructive investigation conducted by a German Jew Dietrich Bronder, a high school teacher. Its title is: "Before Hitler Came". It was printed in 1964 and is about who was who in the Hitler's apparatus: "Of Jewish descent, or being related to Jewish families were: the

Leader and Reichschancelor Adolf Hitler; his representatives the Reichsminister Rudolf Hess; the Reichsmarshall Hermann Goering; the Reichsleader of the NSDAP Gregor Strasser, Dr.Josef Goebbels, Alfred Rosenberg, Hans Frank, Heinrich Himmler; the Reichsminister von Ribbentrop (who pledged close friendship with the famous Zionist Chaim Weizmann, the first head of the State of Israel who died in 1952); von Keudell; field commanders Globocnik (the Jewish destructor); Jordan and Wilhelm Hube; the great SS-Leaders Reinhard Heydrich, Erich von dem Bach-Zelewski and von Keudell II, who also were active in the destruction of Jews. Next came Hitler's bankers and before 1933 supporters: Ritter von Stauss (Vice-president of the NS-Parliament); von Stein; the General Field Marshall and Secretary of State Milch; the Under-Secretary of State Gauss; the physicist and old Party members Philipp von Lenhard and Abraham Esau; the very old party-member Hanffstaengel, NSDAP's newspaper Chief of Foreign Department (later on an advisor to President D.E.Roosevelt) as well as professor Haushofer."[8] (Inset: all of them were members of the secret Thule Order/ Society) This list is not complete. If you devote a little time to these findings of the relation between Hitler's sick hatred towards his kinsmen, with his henchmen on one side, and the creation of the State of Israel on the other, then you should satisfy your curiosity. Nevertheless the author as well as the publisher will be thankful for any new evidence which might emerge.

INCONSTANT AND TRANSITORY, WITH FATHER AND MOTHER

On a humid and cold afternoon of April 20, 1889 a cry was heard from the "Inn of Pommer" in Braunau on the River Inn. On the first floor, a young wife of a fifty year old Imperial Royal Customs Officer of Austria-Hungary had borne a son. This cry was bound to become considerably stronger throughout the first half of our century and shall end no earlier than he, who was born on this day and shot himself through his vociferous mouth in the ruins of the State Chancery in Berlin, 1945.

His lifelong discontent and his constant rage have their origin -it can be said - in an obviously unfortunate mixture of two nations. First, one, then the other believing that they were chosen by God or Providence: Jews and Germans - "No one else but you I want to put above all other nations."

His proud father of that day was out of wedlock and for forty years carried his mother's maiden name Schicklgruber.

One evening he grumbled through the mustache to his Customs colleagues: "As of tomorrow you shall call me Hitler."

Some other time, three old illiterate men were sent to the village pastor near their hometown and one after another swore that the man who died twenty years earlier was Johann Georg Hiedler, "the one who married Madame Schicklgruber", and before he died, he always wanted to adopt Alois, Adolf Hitler's father. This remarkable statement was documented by the honorable pastor, and by the three men from the forest who had confirmed this by subscribing the document with "X" marks [9]. Then the Customs Officer changed the Hiedler name (sometimes called Huettler) into the common Jewish name Hitler. Therefore on that April 20 the newborn citizen received the name Hitler. And he was called Adolf, or later mainly by girls, Wolf (Volve), and still later plainly and simply: "Mein Fuehrer" ("My Leader").

The half Jewish General Governor of Poland, Hans Frank, Hitler's lawyer during the war (who was hung in Nuremberg), shortly before his execution revealed that he knew about Hitler's Jewish origin. About this it was written in the book "In the Face of the Gallow." (see reference 42)

To the Hitler's researcher Maser, a pupil of the communist Niekisch, Frank's death cell confession was meant to counteract any future anti-Catholic arguments: "How come before the execution he made such a heavy-weighted allegation? Probably under a tough care of the American military Catholic priest Sixtus O'Connor in Nuremberg he ostensively presented himself as a remorseful and religious person in order to distance, in the future, all Catholics from the multi-million murderer Adolf Hitler, and thus to inflict upon the Jews restlessness, insecurity and consciousness of guilt." And there are people who take this Maser's wild speculation seriously.

Adolf's father, the Customs officer Alois Hitler, originated from the Austrian forests, close to the Czechoslovakian border, where even a fox and a hare live in peace together. He studied to be a shoemaker, but did not pursue this trade for long. However, at age of eighteen, he joined a promising financial enterprise in

Vienna which ran quite well. He was an intelligent lad whose frequent promotions changed his position. Kindheartedly he boarded thirteen year old niece, Klara Poelzl, who also came from his village. Later, when his second wife was dying, he got Klara pregnant and after that she became his third wife. She gave him six children, but only two survived: Adolf and the younger sister Paula. When her brother became successful, she managed one of his households. Occasional business trips of the Imperial Royal Customs Officer Alois Hitler to Vienna resulted mostly in illegitimate children of his - in those days a very liberal city.

In 1936, in Switzerland, Hitler's biographer Konrad Heiden revealed about this Austrian part of the forest that one of Fuehrer's ancestors on his mother's side was Johann Salomon, and that it "has been proven that many Jewish Hitlers lived there," and that the "Rosalie Mueller, maiden name Huettler, is written on a tombstone in a Jewish cemetery in Polna." After annexation of Austria into Germany, one of the first moves Hitler made was to make all the villages and cemeteries with the names of his ancestors disappear, and in their place were established military training grounds.

Hitler's mother, who often called her husband "Uncle Alois" was quiet and modest. She went along with everything, even with the move to Linzstrasse in Braunau soon after the baby was born. She knew the routine: before the wall paper in one apartment dried out, her Alois was ready to move to another. The new apartments were mostly darker and moister, but for him the main reason for change was to move on and on. This time they moved to the border town of Passau, where the Austrian Customs Office had its branch on the Imperial-German soil. They did not anticipate to stay there for long and therefore moved their boy Adolf, not yet of a school age speaking Bavarian slang (Inset: High German dialect close to "yidish daytsh", i.e., Yiddish), to the city of Linz which he loved all his life very much.

When Alois retired, he bought a house on a farmland in Hafel at the River Traun, and at this quiet spot with a creek, between Linz and Salzburg, he raised bees and was a good neighbor. When all the furniture had been put in place, he sold the property and moved to the nearby town of Lambach. First into the house No.58. Later he rented a space in a smith mill which belonged to the miller Zoebl. Soon his son became of school age and was taken in by the closest one-grade village school in Fischlham. He was very good in drawing. Besides he sang loudly and expressively. In this way the Lambach Seminary acquired a new choir student.

Lambach Seminary was a mighty, long stretched baroque building dominating over the entire village. In Lambach's Trinity Church, also a magnificent baroque building, he was promoted to a mass server and was proud of his colorful gown.

For centuries the abbots of the Lambach's Benedictine Monastery were and still are carrying the swastika on their Coat-of-Arms. Here the boy for the first time heard about the Jews as God's murderers, who had the Master and Redeemer tortured and nailed to the cross.

6

The Austrian Seminary Lambach where the Missalboy Adolf Hitler for the first time heard about Jews who "murdered the God". For centuries the monks of this Benedictian Monastery bear the swastika on their Coat-of-Arms.

Das österreichische Stift Lambach, in dem der Messjunge Adolf Hitler zum erstenmal von Juden, den «Gottesmördern», hörte. Seit Jahrhunderten führen die Mönche dieses Benediktiner-Klosters das Hakenkreuz im Wappen.

Carpenter Joseph Ranzmeier in whose arms Hitler's father died one morning in the Inn Wiesinger of Leonding. "When I was about ten or twelve year old lad, I always had to go to the stinky bars," Hitler reported later to his lawyer Dr. Hans Frank about relationship with his hated half-Jewish father. "It was the most disgusting shame I ever had to experience."

Zimmerermeister Joseph Ranzmeier, in dessen Armen der Vater Hitlers im Gasthaus Wiesinger zu Leonding an einem Vormittag starb. «Da musst ich dann als zehn- bis zwölfjähriger Bub immer spat abends in diese stinkende, rauchige Kneipe gehen», berichtete Hitler später seinem Anwalt Dr. Hans Frank über sein Verhältnis zum verhassten, halbjüdischen Vater. «Es war die grässlichste Scham, die ich je empfunden habe.»

At this Catholic Church its radiance overwhelmed him. It was an experience which never occurred in his home. This caused his deep admiration towards the church lasting throughout his life. Often and quite successfully he did not pay any taxes, but not to the church to which he paid ardently, even in 1945. Lambach's Monastery educated him to its full ability and his sixty year old father added his own discipline to the student. But despite the rigid up- bringing, to a dismay of his teacher the student smoked cigarettes for which he was extensively beaten. Many times he ran for protection to his mother, to whom he was very attached. When his father commanded him to become a government servant, he rebelled and intentionally lowered his school grades. Simply like that: Adolf Hitler decided to live accordingly to his inclinations and to despise ordinary work.

From there the family moved to Leonding, closer to Linz where his father forced him to enter the Linz Imperial Royal State School, from which in the first year of attendance he flunked out. The boy was lazy and read only Karl May stories during class hours. The retired Imperial Royal Customs Officer did not witness any further Adolf's failures for while visiting the Wiesinger Bar in January 1903 he had a stroke and died there in the arms of Joseph Ranzmeier, a carpenter, also a frequent attendant of said bar.

Then the widow put her son into the boarding school in Linz. One of the Catholic governess there was from the same forest as Hitler. And because it was difficult to train the boy, they called him a "Jewish Rascal." Two years later his mother moved into a small apartment in Linz. But Adolf had to go on: after he repeated an exam, the Linz's Real School transferred him to the fourth grade under a condition that he goes to another school.

From those Linz's times he remembered well only a history teacher, Dr.Poetsch, a native of the Southern border country. He was a fighter for the Nationhood and held an opinion that the State of Habsburg was un-German. In the District Council he represented a German-National Parliamentary Group. After annexation of Austria in 1938, Hitler saw the aging Poetsch again. He spent one hour with him and told the people waiting outside the door, that "you have no idea how much I owe to this old man."

Adolf Hitler had to leave Linz and went to the State High School in the South part of Steyr. There, in the house of Ignaz Kammerhofer at the Greenmarket Plaza, people had mercy on him.

His first school report from the Steyr's Institute was so unusually bad, that he sneaked off with other "suffering comrades" to a far away bar. And when they got drunk, their mouths opened up. They called teachers "bureaucratic bums" and at that bar an already insignificant report lost it face value. Since then he could only -please excuse the expression - wipe with his bottom with it. Someone found this document and in February 1905 it landed on the desk of Institute Director. In it a remark was still readable that within a six-month period he missed 30 school days without any explanation. The situation got worse. After a conversation with the Institute's Director Lebeda, student Adolf Hitler solemnly swore never to drink again.

Since then Hitler's health condition worsened and everyone (but mostly he himself) was happy that this sixteen year old boy had ended his academic efforts. This was a new opportunity to drive with his mother back home, deep into the forest land to visit his aunt. There he drank lots of milk, ate well and quickly recovered.

The following spring saw him in museums and operas of Vienna. Later came Linz "filled" with his drawings, paintings and poems. He lived there in a furnished room provided by his mother in her residence. He also took piano lessons, and for two years "in the shallowness of easy life" he felt very comfortable.

Once came to his attention a blondish, well built girl named Stefanie. At five o'clock every afternoon he waited for her in shiny clothes at the corner of Smithgate. There this beautiful girl usually strolled with her mother. Her every smile made him happy. He never talked to Stefanie. In his letters he referred to her via a disguised name of "Benkieser" ("Candykid" in Hebrew-daytsh) after his Jewish classmate.

An upholstery businessman named Kubizek, who was just as excited about operas as Hitler, was his only friend and because of that Hitler was treated by him as a front runner. During long walks Kubizek listened patiently to his oratories, for Stefanie shall get a huge brand new house in renaissance style with a music room, which acoustics should be very important. "But where the piano should be placed?" financially broken student asked his friend Kubizek for an advice, daring to mention money. "But what is money?" asked the confident man being convinced that such "washrags" are easy to get with or without a decent occupation. When Stefanie did not laugh anymore like before - because some young lieutenants, those "vain hollow heads" courted her - Adolf Hitler decided to jump off the bridge into Danube and, of course, Stefanie should jump with him [10]. But neither one jumped, so this story, as well as the history of the world went on undisturbed.

In the fall of 1907, the young man decided to drive to Vienna, where according to his inclinations he wanted to be a painter, "a really graduate painter". When a suitcase filled with books, mainly about German heros, was ready to be taken away, his mother entered the room and on the arm of her son lying in bed she put her hand. A few months earlier this careworn woman had undergone a surgery for breast cancer, and so at this moment she muttered: "Listen, your father..." and faltered. Then she sat up straight and cramped her hands together. "Today I will tell you everything" she started quietly. "Maybe you will need this address in Vienna. Your father's mother became pregnant when she was over forty years old. She was working in Graz for Mr.Frankenberger, a Jew who came from Hungary and later on moved to Vienna. A son was born out of this affair who is your father. The Frankenberger family paid child support for Alois until he was fourteen years old. Then he learned to be a shoemaker. The Frankenbergers always wrote letters and often sent presents. They are noble people. Here, take the Frankenberger's address in Vienna. He is your uncle. Maybe...- " and here she stopped.

The terminally ill woman put a piece of paper under the pillow, kissed her son's forehead and left closing the door quietly. That night he stayed awake for a very long time and in the morning his friend Kubizek carried the heavy suitcase to a train station.

Three months later the Vienna vagabond returned to Linz. He was pale, scrawny, and hollow-eyed. "Incurable," said the family doctor Dr.Bloch, a Jew. To this remark the young man reacted furiously: "What does this mean? The sickness is not curable? Or is it so for doctors do not want to cure it!" Then the depressed son rolled up his sleeves and scrubbed his mother's home. Heated it and cooked her favorite meals. In 1907, three days before Christmas, the forty seven year old woman passed away, and two days later the funeral procession moved through the foggy streets near the Danube. The eighteen year old lad, dressed in a long black winter coat, carrying a cylinder hat in one hand, followed the procession. In the second hand he held Paula, his eleven year old sister. The Jewish Doctor Bloch, in his career of forty years, has never seen such a brokenhearted and a sorrowful young man.

During this long, silent and Holy Night, this lonely man walked through the streets of Linz until the twilight came.

A BUM IN VIENNA

Adolf Hitler, shortly before he took over the care of his terminally ill mother, had failed the exam in the General Painters School in Vienna. This rejection hit him "like a thunderbolt out of the clear sky." Broken and desperate he left the magnificent building at the Schillerplatz. In the province he was by far the best artist in his class, but this was Vienna, population of two million. Flunked - it was a well known word from the Real-School. Big hopes had died. For days he fought with himself and with the piece of paper his mother had stuck under his pillow when she said good-bye. Now it is the same with him: he is also a Jew, in a great need, and from this side the help should come.

He wandered through the Jewish cemetery of Vienna in search of a grave, and found several tombstones with the name Frankenberger and others with the name Hitler. Then he bought a postcard of the Vienna synagogue and spent a whole day painting it in aquarelle successfully. Next morning he got a caftan and in the afternoon proceeded nicely dressed through the well maintained garden at the Villa of Frankenberger in Hietzing. A girl opened the door and led him into a parlor. In the corner across from the large carpet stood an armchair. On top of it he put the package with his drawings - an aquarelle of the synagogue. Then he looked closely at the paintings of Frankenberger's ancestors hanging on the wall. They had the same, a little bit too big curved nose, which he has, too, and which his half-brother Alois and his half-sister Angela also have although they were born from a different mother. Then Mr.Frankenberger entered, a man in his sixties, well-kept and nourished. As young Hitler noticed, he had the same family mark - a big nose. Adolf, having been encouraged, started to introduce himself. He spoke fluently and said what he wished: "Your Family, your Honorable Father, your Grandfather, they did so much good for my Old Master (Father), let God bless Him forever. His son, who is now completely alone in this world needs your help. I do not ask for money. Help me to get into the Academy. You are so powerful." - The old Frankenberger put down his cigar and plodded across the parlor. "Listen, young friend," he started, "our side has paid for your father, that is true. But no one can say that the begetter came from our side. I am talking about my father. And who said that he was? About your grandmother, let us talk no more." He moved his hand through the air as the young Hitler stood there with his mouth open. "Listen," Frankenberger said again, "I am not a patron of art. I do not know anything about it. Wait" - he recalled something, "here in Vienna we have a kitchen for our old people. Do you want to do something there?" At this moment Hitler took his folder, bowed and left without a word. He ran out to the street, paused, took the synagogue-aquarelle, tore it apart, and threw the pieces over the fence. He continued running, stopped again, ripped the black caftan off his body, turned back, and threw the garment to where the pieces of the aquarelle laid. It got caught by a bush of withering red roses. "I will send all of you back to the desert," he threatened in his Bavarian jargon and rose his fist up. "Go back to where you came from. I will send you all to the desert. All of you!" Two passing people hearing this stopped in wonder. The lad ran further with his coattail flapping in the wind. He will make it without any help. He will work for himself until the next autumn and be an independent man. And so Adolf Hitler started looking for support again. It came from a Lady, a homeowner in Linz. Her mother knew Professor Alfred Roller at the Vienna Art Academy who knew the sculptor Panholzer. The sculptor agreed to prepare the young, downfallen talent for an exam in 1908.

Hitler wanted to have his friend Kubizek in Vienna. Why didn't this guy study music? Should this talented man shrivel in Linz? For the first time at Kubizek's father upholstery business Hitler put his talent of speech and his power of persuasion to a serious test. Kubizek wanted to pass the tiredly built business to his only son. The musical vocation, a great career as a conductor, a dusty lung's illness, and an early death as an upholsterer, all these contentions Hitler took into account, and in February 1908 he wasn't alone anymore in Vienna. He thought this as he lead his just arrived friend through the train station, across the Mariahilferstrasse, through side streets to the Stumpergasse No. 29, and to the backyard where he would share his meager room in the home of widow Zakreys (a woman from Boehmen) with his Linz's companion, who was supposed to study music in Vienna. The room and the house smelled like petroleum.

The next morning, when Hitler was sleeping, Kubizek went to the Conservatory, took an exam and passed it. When he returned and awoke Hitler, it was already noon. Kubizek was studying efficiently and successfully, and soon he earned money. As a tutor he gave music lessons to daughters of higher society.

At the same time Hitler studied under the sculptor Panholzer, but less and less enthusiastically. There was something that bothered him. Who was his grandfather? How did his grandmother live? Being over forty years old, did she really give herself to a nineteen year old son of Masters, that Frankenberger? What a terrible disgrace it was - this "seduction of hundreds of thousands of girls by bow-legged, disgusting Jewish bastards!"

The Opera was luring him in and he still had enough money to stay in place. After he read, what Wagner once confessed to Nietzsche, the philosopher, that "he really was a biological son of his stepfather, the Jewish actor Ludwig Geyer," he didn't miss any of his performances. [11]

So, Wagner too, the maker of the Nordic Myths was a Jew! Hitler like Wagner, also had to FIGHT TO OVERCOME THE JEWISHNESS IN HIM. Thus the Wagner's grave and Bayreuth became to Hitler, who grew up to be a man, the sites of pilgrimage. And his, later to be chief ideologist, Rosenberg, who also descended from a Jewish immigrant to Sweden [12], and became a member of aristocracy there, shouted with joy: "Bayreuth is the completion of the Aristocratic Myth. The essence of the whole art of the Occident has been revealed through Richard Wagner - the 'Northern Beauty', the 'Deepest Feeling of Nature', the 'Heroical Honor', and an 'Expression of Sincerity'."

So, in this direction was going an always hungry and defeated young Hitler. From now on he too wanted to "move into Walhalla (Hall of the Slain) after a heroic life," and above his bed he hung a saying painted by him artistically:

"We look freely and openly, we look steadfastly, we look joyfully over

to the German Fatherland! Heil!"

Since then he preferred the study of the Jewish question over the study of art. During many nights Kubizek, the student of music, had fallen asleep over his friend's expositions. At such moments Hitler woke him up and shouted: "Are you my friend or aren't you?" getting Kubizek to nod. "So, listen on!"

For days Hitler lived on milk and bread only. Once Kubizek invited him to a cafeteria and for a couple of marks bought him a pudding, his favorite dessert. "Does it taste good?" asked worried Kubizek. His grumpy answer was: "I don't understand how can you enjoy such a food next to those people." "Those people" were Jewish music students and Hitler withdrew to a corner and turned his back on them.

"But you like to listen to the two Jews, Gustav Mahler and Mendelssohn-Bartholdy" argued seeking the truth Kubizek. "Come with me" was the answer, and the obeying Kubizek went alongside Hitler, thus saving money on expensive cable cars. Their way led to the Brigittenau and from there to a synagogue. Hitler knew his way from earlier visits there. "Keep your hat on!" he grumbled and they both took part in a Jewish wedding.

The musically inclined Kubizek was hoping to divert his friend's attention from the matter he was stubbornly attaching himself to. But despite his efforts came out a declaration: "Today I have joined an Antisemite Group and I enrolled you, too."

A few days earlier Hitler gave the Police a deposition with this content: "In the Mariahilferstrasse, in front of Gerngross department store, a 'merchant' is begging. He is an Eastern Jew dressed in boots and a coat. He offers shoe laces and buttons." Begging was prohibited and Hitler claimed that he solicited. Other people claimed the same, and they took the intimidated Jew to a Guard's Station where a policeman pulled three thousand crowns from his caftan's pocket. To Hitler it was a fortune.[13]

At the same time the would be painter, who had to prepare himself for an entrance exam, was writing a poem. At the Conservatory Kubizek made acquaintance with a journalist from the "Wiener Tagblatt" ("Vienna Daily"). One day he said that he will be able to deliver to him a novel. At a later date Kubizek, together with Hitler, brought the novel to his journalist friend at Langgasse-strasse. It bore a title "The Next Morning". Hitler glanced at the journalist, immediately turned his back and yelled at the good deeding friend: "You idiot, don't you see that he is a Jew?"

In the fall of 1908, at the new exam, Hitler failed again. He wasn't admitted to the test-drawing. At that time Kubizek served two months in the military, even though Hitler advised him not to enlist, for in the life of a young musician "it will leave a blank space." When he returned to Vienna, his old friend Adolf was gone. He disappeared and could not be found again. "He left nothing behind? Not even a bid of farewell?" asked astonished Kubizek while the old woman Zakreys only shook her head with regret.

In Schoenbrunner Park stood a bench, where Hitler hungry for air and sun usually withdrew to. It just happened that a man named Grill walked by, and glancing there at the bench saw lying around anti-Semitic fliers, mainly "Ostara" magazines. After a short hesitation he sat down on a clear spot and pulled out of his coat a reproduced writing saying: "Here, take this. It is a gift from me." Hitler took a look at him and then at the writing entitled: "Against the Church's Official Machinery." It turned out that Grill, with the help of his writings, was trying to promote among people a religion of real and pure love. When Hitler started talking about the Jews as "people's parasites", who always are against good intentions, they met themselves at the subject. In this way the two zealots found each other. At last someone appeared who followed Hitler and who could be challenged in a political discussion, and who would not submissively nod like Kubizek. Grill came to this spot and promoted his teaching about true love almost every day. Hitler agreed with him with one exception that the Jews should be left out. Grill was a drop-out priest, who had spent his youth in a Catholic Monastery, and his point of view on this matter was different from Hitler's. One day, when their discussion reached a zenith, Grill suddenly confessed: "I was born a Jew! My father was a Rabbi." Since then Hitler's bonds with these people became stronger and lasted for years. Finally Hitler moved to a cabin in the Men's Hostel at the Meldemannstrasse where Grill made a living by addressing envelopes. From this traitor of Jewishness and of Catholic Church, Hitler could learn a lot. During long walks through the parks they exchanged opinions with each other. Grill taught his new friend Yiddish, too. They also walked for hours through the inner city and districts North of the Danube Channel, where Jews were numerous and easy to observe. Among almost two million residents of Vienna, about 200,000 were Jews, that is, ten percent. They spent many evenings and nights with Grill's friends - the Jewish Rabbis, and talked with them until their heads got hot.

Hitler wanted to learn from their dialectics and got acquainted with this precept: "First you must take into account the lack of wisdom of your adversary. If it is useless, look for a way out and pretend that you are a dummy. If this doesn't work either, then switch to a different subject and claim that everything is self understandable" - thus he learned a lot.

To Grill all people were alike, all good. "There are rabbits with blue eyes and rabbits with red eyes. They are all good." "No," Hitler counter argued: "Rabbits with red eyes belong to a bad race. And Jews are of a bad race."

Then Hitler want to visit the Holy Cross of the Cistercian Monastery in Wienerwald to get the address of Mr.Lanz, the publisher of "Ostara" magazines, i.e. to the Messenger of a New Racial Order. In 1899, out of this Monastery came Adolf Josef Lanz, also known as Brother Joerg. He united with a Jewess Liebenfels and since then called himself Dr.Georg Lanz von Liebenfels. Later on he rose his father Lanz, an upright Vienna teacher, to the nobility title of a Baron.

About his mother, born Hopfenreich (whose father was a Jew), he kept a conspicuous silence. Since 1905 he distributed "Ostara" magazines, which sometimes reached a circulation of 100,000. The "Ostara" dealt with Mary (Madonna) who was the "progenitor of the royal, blond, Aryan heroic race." Jesus was promoted to the Nordic "Fraua" ("Freyr" - God of Plenty) and since then Hitler constantly wondered whether the natural Father of the Savior was a travelling Greek artist, or a Germanic soldier. Lanz saw a difference between light blond heroic sons and ape-people (he did not consider women). Later Hitler summarized his religious madness in his best-seller book, as follows: " People's State must begin by rising marriage from the level of continuous defilement of the race, and give consecration owed this institution which was established for creation of images of the Lord and not monstrosities halfway between man and ape."

The "Ostara" magazine printed on its front covers: "Are you blond? Are you male? If you do not know then read 'Ostara's' library about blond and legitimate males!" An ordinary anti-Semite doesn't like a Jew out of envy or vanity, or just because he was raised like that. He has nothing against Arabs. The real anti-Semite knows, that next to the Jews, there are Arabs and Abyssinians, who are Semites too. So, through Lanz Hitler became a true anti-Semite.

In the Monastery of the Holy Cross the two young men found the Vienna address to this widely exposed sectarian, and in the beginning of 1909 the incoherent Hitler appeared before him in his City Office. Besides the missing issues of "Ostara" magazine, Lanz von Liebenfels also gave the visitors two kronen to drive home. Hitler accepted this gift eagerly. During certain conversation, in the Vienna Cafe "Under the Golden Bullet", Grill was firm and said: "This fellow is a nut!" - and from there on he stayed away from Hitler.

In the "Ostara" magazines of 1908 and 1909 were given instructions on how to measure body parts, and from them one could find out whether one has some Nordic traits, like the "length and strength of the big toe of a heroic person sticks out from all other toes", with accompanied pictures of buttocks shapes: "A" showed a lower, and "B" a higher race. This was a happy day in the poor life of young Hitler, for after thorough measurements he found in himself a predominantly Nordic blood line. Really, this Lanz was his man.

Because of Lanz's medical achievements, men important in public life visited him frequently. To them, for instance, belonged a Swedish author August Strindberg and an English Lord, in rank a British Fieldmarshall, nobleman Herbert Kitchener, who assured him that he will "Keep the stage racially clean, and will send the colored ruthlessly into the fire."

In Switzerland Lanz von Liebenfels met Lenin. Because Lanz thought differently, he dressed his opinion in fine irony: "Your ideas are right. But before they materialize, our counter-ideas will materialize first." That's how Lanz was a partner in conversation to the two men. The men, who shocked the first half of our century intensely. The most important statement of the Vienna "Reformer of the World" was: "We counter-revolutionaries give Jews the right to create their own State in Palestine."

Lanz von Liebenfels established a (Thule) Order (Society), and with the money coming from various sources created Order-Castles. In 1907, above the Castle Werfenstein he hoisted up a swastika flag. Hitler for upbringing of his Party elite created similar Castles (Inset: Fuehrer Hitler was a Member of the Thule Order - "Bevor Hitler Kam", page 246). Lanz also granted to the blond men a right to inseminate several women. Hitler was also happy because of the Villa Obersalzberg: "Here in the Berchtesgaden country I found a jumbled up population. Thanks to my bodyguards, from now in this area strong and healthy children will be running around." Lanz preached castration and sterilization of inferior races. It can't be said that Hitler missed any of Lanz's tenets.

Both had to repress, to cover up something in the line of their ancestry. And that's how these men found each other and while one gave up his ideas, the other took them in eagerly. This is what Lanz von Liebenfels wrote to his brother Aemilius on February 22, 1932, one year before Hitler came to power: "Do you know that Hitler is our best student? You will see that he and through him we, too, will succeed and will stir up a movement, which will make the whole world shiver. Heil you!"

A very special influence over the twenty year old Hitler had two outstanding Jewish adversaries, the Ritter (Knight) von Schoenerer and his follower, lawyer Dr.Lueger, who became Mayor of Vienna. Hitler devoured their writings and manifestations like he did with the "Ostara" magazines.

The difference between Schoenerer with his "All German Union", borrowed from Caesar, and the Vienna's elected Mayor, Dr.Lueger, with his "Christian-Social Party", was what Schoenerer asserted: "A Jew stays a Jew" to which Lueger counter-argued: "Christ is a baptized Jew." At that time Hitler was distributing flyers for Lueger.

There was no difference of opinion between these two leading Austrian Jewish antagonists as to selection of Jews or half-Jews for their closest cooperatives. For Schoenerer first in line was Galician author Karl Emil Franzos. For the latter would be a Social Democrat Viktor Adler, co-author of the Linz's "Great-German Program": "One People, One Empire!" Next was Heinrich Friedjung from Maehren, also a Jew. Lueger's representative was Vienna's Second Mayor, half-Jew Porzer. The famous saying: "I will determine who is a Jew" came from Dr.Lueger. From their work, years before establishment of the N.S.D.A.P. of Munich, originated the National Socialist German Worker's Party (N.S.D.A.P.) of Sudeten. Karl Wolff, previously a Parliamentarian for Schoenerer was the Party's establisher.

However, Schoenerer was thinking in terms of race but was not a socialist. Lueger was a socialist and therefore anti-Jewish, but not a racist. That's how the two men parted. From one man Hitler took the concept of race, from the other of socialism.

In Hitler's eyes Dr.Lueger was the "most powerful German Mayor of all times," and also in 1945 the newly emerged Socialists of Vienna associated this Jewish opponent with themselves: "Everything that was created at that time, bore Lueger's personal note; had originated out of his own initiative, or were decreed by him. Dr.Lueger became the man who paved the way for the Communal Socialism which, as an outcome of the productive strength of the Socialist Workers' Party of Vienna, was supposedly to fruit ten years after Lueger's death."

Young Hitler was not all right with the Socialist Workers' Party of Vienna.

The half sister Angela (middle) moved from the Jewish community kitchen in Vienna to the Hitler's household in Berchtesgaden as a housekeeper. The twelve volume "Jewish Encyclopedia" notes: "Even though the Jewish women seem to change their appearance, they show the racial Jewish features in a great clarity as once before."

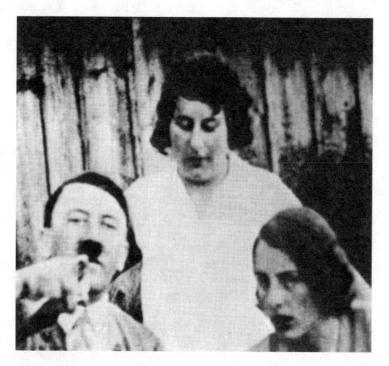

Die Halbschwester Angela (Mitte), die aus der jüdischen Gemeindeküche Wiens in den Berchtesgadener Haushalt Hitlers als Wirtschafterin überwechselte. Die «Jewish Encyclopaedia», das zwölfbändige jüdische Nachschlagewerk, behauptet: «Obwohl Jüdinnen in ihrem Aussehen wandelbarer erscheinen, so scheint es doch, als ob sie, wenn sie einmal ausgesprochen jüdisch aussehen, das Rassenbild in grösster Reinheit zeigen.»

Adolf Hitler als Neunzehnjähriger, als er bei der Böhmiakin Zakreys in Wien bescheidenes Unterkommen gefunden haste.

Adolf Hitler as a nineteen year adolescent at the time when he found shelter at the home of Bohemian widow Zakreys in Vienna.

Der unehelich geborene Halbbruder Alois, der wegen Bigamie und Diebstahls rechtskräftig verurteilt werden musste und dessen Augen-, Nasen- und Mundpartien auf den gemeinsamen Grossvater Frankenberger hinweisen.

Born out of wedlock half brother Alois, once sentenced for bigamy and theft. His eyes, nose and mouth are reminiscent of the mutual grandfather Frankenberger.

Shortly before Kubizek's return from the military, he had moved to the Felberstrasse in the Fifteenth District. When he didn't appear at the draft inspection, and therefore violated the Austrian military law, he moved into a hut at the Sechshauserstrasse and one month later he was a subtenant at the Simon-Denk-Gasse. That's how the money, which came from the low orphan-pension and from small inheritances disappeared. After several nights in coffee shops he ended up in the working District Meidling in a Homeless Shelter, which was built with Jewish means. He had to work at construction sites to prevent himself from starving.

At the lunch breaks, this temporary worker told elders about exploitation of people by Jewish homeowners who lived in Hietzing and by drunk Jewish employers in Grinzing. Because workers believed the Jewish press, which promised them jobs and bread, they threatened to push the young orator off the scaffolding. So he gave up and treated this experience of "work for bread" as a lesson which he never forgot.

The snow was falling and with snow shuffling the careworn failure made it through the winter. In the Monastery at Gumpendorferstrasse a soup for poor people was given out in the mornings. At noon the warm room of the Jewish Baron Koenigswarter offered shelter from the cold and a warm meal. In the evenings at the Homeless Shelter there was enough to eat, a piece of horse sausage and a crust of bread. And then came a long night on a hard wired plank-bed with shoes and few belongings stuck under the head, while a thin blanket and a jacket kept the body warm.

On the other plank-bed laid Reinhold Hanisch, a commercial artist of Sudetenland and a property owner, who had to disappear within the walls of Vienna under the cover name of Fritz Walter. Hanisch noticed Hitler's talent for painting and got an idea: "You will paint cards and I will sell them. Christmas is coming and we will earn some cash." Hitler painted well and with care. Hanisch distributed the hand painted postcards among various coffee houses and bars and the trade was booming. By Christmas they both were out of the worst and joined Grill, living in the Men's Hostel at Meldemannstrasse in the Twentieth District. For half a crown they could rent a room for one day and one night. Failures, dismissed officers, impoverished earls, bankrupt merchants, and semi-painters rented there for days, weeks, or months. In such a "School of Life" Hitler celebrated his birthday four times.

From postcards Hitler switched to picture paintings, mostly aquarelles, and Hanisch found thankful buyers among furniture merchants and carpenters. They requested little pictures that could be put on back of sofas. So Hanisch pushed the painter, for the earnings were dependent on his efficiency. The stuff was easy to sell, but Hitler painted only when he needed the money for rent, milk and rice. Most of the time he was sitting upstairs in the reading room of the Men's Hostel, read newspapers or gave political speeches. The subject was always the same but listeners changed. In the evenings the homecoming Hanisch always interrupted with thunder: "Finally go to work!" and the others exclaimed ironically: "To work, Hitler, to work, your boss is coming!" Hitler's objections that an artist is not a ballpoint pen but needs inspiration, didn't matter to Hanisch: "Artist! Artist through hunger at most!" he laughed.

The artist had commenced falsification of his art. He brown-roasted old-Vienna pictures in his married older sister's oven in Vienna, and stored them for a while in her moist basement. Usually a little bit too long and because of that nobody wanted to purchase such moldy stuff.[14]

Hitler, when wearing a dark caftan (looking like a frock coat, which a Hungarian Jew Neumann, a cabin neighbor once gave him), and because of a fluffy beard around his chin, and weaving hair on his neck, was mistaken by some newcomers for an Eastern Jew. Even Hanisch mocked at him: "At one time your father must not have been at home. Look at your shoes! They are of the 'Wilderness Wanderer' brand." But at that time the young artist didn't care about his appearance.

Once, after almost one year of working together, Hanisch did not claim the money for a picture he had sold. Hitler, after giving some thought to his evasion of a military duty, reported to the Police Commisionaire of Brigittenau what Hanisch had done. Thus Hanisch was prosecuted and in effect had to move to another location.

Then Neumann, a Jew from Hungary, who was more able to bargain, became Hitler's new paintings' salesman. It was the same Jew who gave him the frock coat. Purchasers of paintings were mostly Jewish, as for example the Hungarian-Jew Retschay, a main engineer; the Vienna lawyer Dr.Josef Feingold, and the picture frame merchant Morgenstern.

Another cabin neighbor, who stayed in the Hostel even longer, was Greiner, a young man who a short time before his ordination broke with Priesthood and now made a living from his paintings. He also was Grill's friend who was still living in the Men's Hostel. Many times the three men together cooked their milk with rice, even taking turns in stirring. A girl named Gretl was Greiner's model, and Hitler also claimed - yes - to have known her very well. When the mother of the blooming beauty discovered scratch wounds and bite marks on her body (caused by Hitler), the modelling was finished. To balance this out, Gretl was suddenly engaged to a baptized Eastern Jew. In response, that man received a letter from Hitler: "A German girl who fraternizes with the villains of the shameful filthy money mongers and who offers herself to a stinky, bristly, black and wild pig Jew, is a disgrace. The only thing that is morally right for a Jew is to marry a Jewish Rebekka, or to fry that obese goose-Jewess. Only then will she wonder about miraculous German heroism."[15]

Hitler, stranded in the Man's Hostel, to satisfy human or male needs, in the evenings ran occasionally through the streets of the Leopold City where girls were waiting and willing to help. And who was behind all of this? The "icy-cool and likewise shameless and efficient conductor in this business, a Jew."

In the coffee shops of Vienna the young Hitler was known as an efficient specialist, who unnoticeably could place fishes' air sacks filled with red ink under the seats of plump Jewish girls. When the sacks ruptured, the ensuing embarrassment was enormous.

All of his life Hitler knew very well how to discern between the highly educated tall Western Jews, and the Eastern, constantly streaming in, trading and jabbering, those Caftan-Jews. This big difference and many centuries old enmity between both groups was fully clear to him. When the First World War was lost, Polish Jews populated Berlin in masses. It was Rathenau, the Jewish Foreign Minister of the Weimar (Soviet) Republic, who talked about "Asian hordes on Brandenburger's Maerkisch sands." So he conspicuously agreed with Hitler and wrote: "One must walk the way, the Nature is walking, i.e. the way of 'Nordification'. A new romance will come - romance of the race! It will glorify the pure Northern blood and will create new concepts of virtue and of vice. The main appearance of our time is the mixing of races, and with this, degradation of character."[16]

After a dozen years of his experience with those poor trouser's dealers in Vienna, this "Phaeacia City" ("City of Parasites"), the embodiment of disgrace and incest, Hitler pointed out: "Of course, they do not look like these in Linz. Throughout centuries their appearances there became European and human." In Linz, he was well disposed towards Jews. In Vienna, he became their enemy and an anti-Semite.

The rising Zionism enhanced Hitler's curiosity. This movement "came to the fore-front for confirmation of the Jewish character." Doubts came over as to what will happen to the Palestine as a "Jewish State, a place of refuge for these rags, or a 'Center of Education' for would be scoundrels and crooks."

The aim of the battle against the Jews was clear to him, but the solution to the problem he could not yet define. Therefore it is not true, what he declared one decade later: "To that which I have once created I must add a little. I need not change an iota."

Grill, the Jewish Monastery student was lost, so nobody heard about a new religion which could have come from Vienna. Kubizek changed himself after the First World War. He became municipal office clerk, a father, and in 1942, when the Second World War was about to be lost, he was a fellow member of the Party although not quite convinced. Hanisch, after his time in prison, spread many lies around the world in which numerous publicists believed. In 1938 Gestapo got a hold of him, and shortly thereafter his jail guard found him hung in the cell. Hitler's friend Greiner was jailed in 1922 with an already very well known Party leader (Hitler) in the Bohemian quarter of Munich, called "Stinging Nettle". There Hitler urged him not to "give to anybody, not even to the closest members of the Party, any information about his younger days." Later Greiner, the engineer, as an important manufacturer, met several times with Mussolini. In 1938 Heydrich's police promised him an "induction into a concentration camp in case he were to break his oath of silence." In 1947 Americans collected Greiner's memory book and destroyed all the available copies. Lanz von Liebenfels received a letter from Rosenberg prohibiting him from drivelling with blond women of a penitentiary under an excuse that "The Nature gave us women as slaves." And, although a bell has not rung yet on the biggest clock, before anything else his task was to promote Hitler's aim of founding a Jewish State in

Palestine. In 1954 Lanz also considered himself a victim of the Nazi regime when he left this grateful world with the last sacrament of the Catholic Church.

In this "Hard School of Life", by association with Eastern Jews, with people of mixed Jewish blood, with religious sectarians, petty dealers, and loafers of backyards and filthy kitchens, coffee shops and Men's Hostel in Vienna, Adolf Hitler prepared ground for the materialization of a goal of his entire life: to get rid of Jews by any possible means - first from Germany and then from Europe.

Lanz von Liebenfels, Sohn der Jüdin Hopfenreich, Herausgeber der antijüdischen «Ostara»-Hefte, war in Wien der «Mann, der Hitler die Ideen gab.» Sein Kernsatz lautete: «Wir Gegenrevolutionäre gestehen den Juden das Recht eigener Staatengründung in Palästina zu.»

Lanz von Liebensfield, son of a Jewess Hopfenreich, publisher of the anti-Jewish magazine "Ostara". He was in Vienna "the man who passed his ideas to Hitler." His motto was: "We counterrevolutionaries confess to the Jews full rights to their own State in Palestine."

Guido von List
Das Geheimnis
der Runen

Titelblatt eines «Ostara»-Heftes des jüdischblütigen Lanz, der sich mit einer Jüdin Liebenfels verband und seitdem Lanz von Liebenfels nannte.

Cover sheet of the "Ostara" magazine, published by the Jew Lanz who associated himself with the Jewess Liebenfels and since then called himself "Noble Lanz-Liebenfels".

CONSCIENTIOUS OBJECTOR AND A WAR VOLUNTEER

In May 1913, Adolf Hitler, a twenty four year old painter, and an Austrian conscientious objector out of persuasion and not out of inclination, came to the art town of Munich, known also as Athens of the River Isar. He left Vienna because the ground there finally became too hot for him. At the sudden departure, a friend of his mother, the Jewish Lady Dr.Loewy, living in Vienna's Schottenring (Elite's Circle) gave him the money for his journey.[17] At the Registrar Bureau in Munich he introduced himself as stateless person. He found a room for rent on Schleissheimerstrasse with a family of a tailor named Popp. The first evening the family got information from him about what was going on in the Austria-Hungary: "Just take a look at the Colonel Redl, Chief of the General Staff, a homosexual, a slut and spy for the Russians. When I left Vienna, this noble man, because of those crimes shot himself with a bullet into his empty brain. All people at the top of the magnificent Imperial Royal Army are Jews, like Redl." The master of tailors, Josef Popp, himself being a member of a converted Jewish family, once was working in elegant studios of Paris.[18] "Il s'est brulé le cerveau, he has fried his brain instantly" he nodded. "You are right, Mr.Hitler, not to serve such a gang of rabble." "Look" - Hitler continued, "how long do you think this rotten State can exist? Austria, that mummy, since long ago has ceased to be a German State. She is rotting German culture and its way of life. She commenced actions of destruction, and the socialists and the Jews are the guilty, and they are the Doers in that Vienna (once a German Capital), together with the Emperor Franz-Joseph, who is old and dumb."

One evening in the basement of a brewery, with white sausage and beer, people gathered for rounds of tireless speeches of an Austrian writer Lindmann, but Hitler was more oratory: "Let us consider the unholy treaty of the German Reich with the doomed Austria-Hungary. What do you think, Gentlemen, what this treaty will do to the German Reich? It will drag you in, Gentlemen. Anyone, I tell you, should separate oneself from such an alliance for what is destined to fall, should be pushed down." Every time Hitler gleaned Nietzsche.

In the evenings Hitler walked around well-kept and immaculate. He lived prosperously. Painting for him was the only way of living. He sold a lot of paintings to a respected art dealer at Maximiliansplatz at a price worth their value. Among the three thousand painters in the city, Hitler was not the worst. But to questions, raised by his companions at the brewery's cellar about his professional goals, Hitler always responded shortly: "A goal of my career? There will be war, my friends."

In the afternoon of January 18, 1914, when the day of establishment of the German State was celebrated, Hitler painted the Brandeburger Gate in water-colors. The detective Herle climbed up the stairs almost losing his breath. Knocking abruptly at the door of his room with a separate entrance, he surprised Hitler with the unpleasant news: The fugitive must appear within two days in Linz. In case of default, he will receive an official warning. As a precautionary measure two police officers in uniform climbed the stairs, also, and took the painter away from his easel to the Austrian consulate in Munich. There he had an opportunity to show what he had learned during those three years of living in the Vienna Men's Hostel, i.e. his cunning ability and skill of deception. He stated there that by no means he is a fugitive but only a little bit careless as any young artist in training, without any political clout, poor and very sick. As he said that, the eyes of fellow Austrian countrymen moistened, so in effect they reported back to Austria: "According to the statement made by him, as it is presented on the enclosed Affidavit of Justification, and to this Office's own impression, all of this is true and therefore we resigned from carrying out his extradition."[19] He was granted a two week extension, and because Hitler was a pauper, he was allowed to travel for free to the closest military installation to get a medical examination. Thus out of his "Trick Box", the knowledgeable conscientious objector had pulled quite a lot with the results as he wanted: "He is unfit for the military and auxiliary services. He is too weak and unable to bear weapons." That night the brewery basement saw a happily drinking throng of freshly looking men and among them the great artist leading a conversation.

Barely half a year later, the First World War broke out and a completely healthy Hitler in front of the Hall of Field Masters swung his hat at the war proclamation onto which thousands of others signed their readiness for a voluntary registration. Hitler instead sent immediately a request to the Bavarian King for permission to serve in a Bavarian regiment, for his "jubilation and thankfulness do not know an end." Next day he was accepted into the service. Thus conscripting to the Austrian Army, called by Germans "The Comradeship of Shoe Lace", spared him.

During the war Austria-Hungary fell apart as Hitler predicted. Hitler was sure that after the war and after repudiation of foreigners, the Germanic Austria will unite with the victorious German State, and that the Jews and socialists, treated by him as twins, will disappear from the stage. Hitler applauded the war seeing it as the means of this purpose: The influence of Judaism upon people of Germany and Austria, (i.e. of the two Emporiums) shall cease. He favored such a sequence of events, so his happiness grew by an hour: "The pack of Jewish leaders became abandoned, lonely and forsaken. The time has come to take action against the Jewish contaminators trying to install deceitfully a 'Society of Comradeship' ('Communal Society'). Now someone has to do a quick job on them without the slightest consideration for their cries and complaints. The jabber of the international solidarity shall instantly disappear from the heads of the German working class," Hitler talked to himself with more and more excitement, while bundling up his laundry and tying it up with white ribbons at the residence of the Popp family. "The leaders of that whole movement shall be put behind bars right away. Someone should finish them shortly thereafter. All means of power should be used for the extermination of this pestilence."

After a few weeks of training with the 2nd Bavarian Infantry Regiment, called the "TRICK", Hitler with such notions in repertoire, and singing patriotic songs in the rain, was tramping across wet turnip fields and hedges, and "attacked" Flanders. After a few days the well prepared for war regiment was melted down to one half its strength and after a few more days to one quarter. "Maybe the volunteers of the TRICK regiment never learned to fight the right way. They only knew how to die like the old soldiers." At the first stand-still opportunity, the Soldier Hitler was promoted to a Lance-Corporal and honored with the Iron Cross Second Class. The war was only a few months old.

That is how the war continued. The dispatch rider Hitler soon became an "Old Hare" at the regimental headquarters. Officers of the TRICK knew Hitler by name. To the non-commissioned officers and comrades his relentless reading was dubious. In written speeches he laid down the reasons which caused the war. The Jews of the Austria-Hungarian Government were the guilty ones. "The sooner the Jewish covenant will be broken, the better it will be for the German nation with Austria's people combined. Surrendering of the Habsburger Monarchy is not at all a sacrifice, when, through it, the Germany reaches a confinement limitation of its opponent. We have not put the steel helmets on our heads for preservation of the abominable dynasty, but for the rescue of the German Nation from these Jewish international APOSTLES OF EQUALITY." Often comrades contradicted him out of defiance, but often only to excite him. "What do you want?" he then yelled back: "The War has to be run, otherwise the world will become a big storehouse which will belong to the Jews in which Germans at best would be bookkeepers only."

The former commander of the TRICK, Colonel Spatny, issued this judgement: "The constantly restless and sharp front line in the Northern France and Belgium, along which the regiment acted, in regards to self-sacrifice and personal courage has put great demands upon its every member. In this respect Hitler to his comraderie was an ideal example. His exemplary, model like behavior, in all tactical situations has made a powerful effect on the regiment. On account of this and in connection with his nature, and his admirable personal modesty, he enjoyed a great attention of his superiors as well as of those equal in rank."[20]

When nobody wanted to run anymore with the reports through the heavy fire to those in front persevered companions, Hitler always volunteered. It was a rule that with important reports two men had to go for only one might make it. Before Hitler came to power, his one time assignee lance-corporal Brandmayer, nicknamed by him a "Partner", recalled: "I just sat down next to Hitler, there was a direct hit in the middle of a hallway. The ceiling dashed and tore into thousand pieces. The splinters splattered everywhere into a distance. Paralyzed by the shock I still wasn't aware what terrible thing just had happened. And when I came to myself again, I saw how Hitler salvaged seven injured and four dead bodies. And that's how it was with these reports which had to get to the front: We jumped from one shell crater to another. Pieces of exploded material and dirt mercilessly showered down on us. My nerves failed. I wanted to stay there where I was laying. Then Hitler talked to me kindly and gave me words of encouragement, saying that one day our heroism will be rewarded thousand fold by our Fatherland."[21]

The shortage of the non-commissioned officers was felt stronger from year to year. Hitler never became non-commissioned officer in the six year time of civil service. Later some officer had stated: "Hitler doesn't have any leader qualifications," and surely this was not right. The war didn't bring what Hitler had hoped for - the elimination of Judaism in Germany. In the beginning of 1915 he wrote to his friend assessor Hepp in Munich: "I think about Munich many times. Each one of us has had only one wish, that soon it would come to the final reckoning with this gang. Should the gang perish, it won't cost anything. Those of us who will be lucky to pass through and see their homeland again, will find it cleaner, cleaned up more from the foreign exotic. Through the daily sacrifices and sufferings, which hundred-thousands of us endure; through the daily stream of blood, which flows here daily against the worldwide enemies, and not only of Germany, they will be smashed. But with them will also be broken those within, the forces of the International Communism. That would be worth more than the victory of our entire country. With Austria this will come to as I have always said."[22]

In 1916 Hitler was badly wounded in the thigh by an enemy fire as he volunteered to deliver a report to the front line through heavy shooting. In a military hospital in Beelitz near Berlin, he discovered some changes in the country being tired of the war. In no way would the heroism of the front soldiers be rewarded thousand fold, as he had promised to his "Partner". The wounded Hitler, as he later said, was thinking about the "whole trick of fate, that kept me at the front in a situation, in which one accidental trigger pull by a Negro could kill me, although I did serve my Fatherland at many different locations, and with various kind of services." By giving speeches he shook up and excited masses for he was capable of doing that. And his special sort of a service was his imagination. But among eight million soldiers he was an unknown man. "Over all it was better to keep a mouth shut and do a duty at any post as best as one could."

During his time of recovery Hitler relied mostly on advice of the Jewish physician Dr.Stettiner, especially when he looked for a confirmation of the soldier's hand-book from which he taught himself the military art in any regiment battle position. Once, the physician came to Hitler's bed and amazingly pronounced: "I thought you were more reasonable." Thanks to this helper of the suffering creatures, Hitler found a confirmation of his point of view about "decomposing strength of all Jews." In reality the pacifistic Dr.Stettiner divided human beings only into two groups: those who cause wounds and those who have to heal them. According to Hitler's memoirs "the offices of the hospital were also occupied by the Jews. Almost every scriber was a Jew and every Jew was a scriber." "The disgust crept up his throat," and that's why he asked for a permission to return hardly healed to his regiment on the front line.

A typical Jew, lieutenant Hugo Gutmann, there was the one who handed Hitler the Iron Cross First Class. About Gutmann, Hitler's "Partner" Brandmayer had this to say: "As an adjutant of the regiment's lieutenant Eichelsdoerfer, I was also functioning many times as a substitute for Hugo Gutmann, the lieutenant of the Country Defense, an officer with a Jewish affectation and mannerism. He didn't have a very good reputation with the group of messengers. In time to come this fearful semi-Officer to me was a dislikeable superior."[23] So it was that Hitler placed his IC First Class into a pocket. It would be of use to him later because he was "very serious about performing as an orator after the war."

Then it came to a strike by the munition workers in the Homeland. For Hitler it meant that: "The International Capital will be introduced to Germany and an internal goal of the Marxist deception of masses will be accomplished. And the authors of this low scoundrels' trick, are the candidates to highest positions in the revolutionary State."

In November 1918, after being afflicted at the front with mustard gas, Hitler afraid of losing sight, awkwardly walked around the Prussian Reserve Military Hospital in Pasewalk of Pommern (as it is in the "Mein Kampf") when "suddenly and unexpectedly there came sailors on trucks and incited to a revolution. Among them were a few Jewish boys as 'leaders' in fight for 'freedom, beauty, and dignity' and for the well being of our (German) people. None of them took part in the war campaign. At that stage of their round-about way, those three Orientals went back to the Homeland from the so called 'Gonorrhoea Military Hospital' and now are hoisting up the red rag within".

"BUT I DECIDED TO BECOME A POLITICIAN"

An often cited phrase of the "Mein Kampf" exactly reads like this: "With Jews there is no agreement, but only a firm yes or no. But I decided to become a politician." Politics and the battle against Judaism for Hitler were the two sides of the same coin. In general, what is right now and will later follow, from the Hitler's heap of rubble an observer must pick out something.

For instance: During the war France was a "Hereditary Foe", but after the seizure of power, the German speaking Alsace-Lorraine in his speeches was "renounced forever". At an earliest opportunity Hitler would like to acquire colonies, but again he stopped the long lasting drive toward the South: "At last we ended the colonial and trade politics of the prewar time."

Or the Soviet Union: For over a decade it was regarded as the "deadliest enemy", but at the conclusion of the 1939 Pact made in Moscow, Hitler felt like being "more or less among old fellow members of the Party."

Mixed Soviet-SS-Commission in a beautiful harmony sketched out hundred year settlements of farmers on the Eastern soil, which two or three years later Norwegians, Swedes and South Tyrolers would intensely "Germanize". The Polish prey was brotherly divided, and Stalin to Hitler, even during the war was "an ingenious guy, who doesn't let the Jews 'get the art'." An endless string of pleasant speeches about the "wedding of the 'Nationalism' with the 'Social Sense of Justice'" had praised this first economic partner, who was of greater importance than the USA, for it was not tormented by scruples as is today the largest syndicate in the world, I.T.T., which feelings about socialist states need not any explanation. Through the years praised by Hitler the "right of the people to be free and independent", was meant as rightful liberation of the Sudeten Germans (Inset: Germans in the South i.e. of North-Western Czechoslovakia) and it was a message to "the guy Chamberlain, who had spoiled my entry into Prague." Half a year later, after the liberation, the foreign language speaking Czechoslovakia vanished.

Hitler only about a single point wasn't shaky and stubborn, like a Roman, who at any opportunity swung his "Ceterum censeo" (meaning: "Karthagene must be destroyed") in the face of a competitive Semitic Karthagenan, that "the European Judaism in Europe is at a wrong place."

Everybody once in life has to start from scratch, and that's where a career of the ready-to-serve corporal Hitler as a professional politician began in Munich, with counting of excess laundry at the 2nd Bavarian Infantry Regiment. For Hitler this genesis began again at the end of 1918 in Pasewalk. The war comrade Schmidt was helping him too. One night, when the corporal groaned into a pillow: "Back into the desert, all back into the desert," Schmidt shook him up and uttered: "What are you talking about, Adolf?" At that moment the corporal turned over and kept on dreaming and talking.

Bavaria, as the first German State, had become a Republic, and an Eastern Jew Eisner, whose true name was Kosmanowski, nominated himself as a Prime Minister with "eighteen marks in a pocket." The leaders of the Communist Soviet

Republic of Bavaria were Russian Jews, Lewien, Leviné-Niessen, and Tobias Axelrod. Their Ruling Comrade Landauer had declared: "Everybody works as they want. All subordination will be lifted, and the legal way of thinking about this will too." The Secretary of the Foreign Affairs of the Republic wired to Moscow: "Proletarians of North Bavaria are joyfully united. We want peace as always." The telegram was intertwined with citations from Immanuel Kant's "Vom ewigen Frieden" ("About Eternal Peace") 1795, Thesis 2-5 - for the quotations carried an important message, that his predecessor "took with him the key of no return to the Ministry (resigned)".[24] A "Red Army" was formed, which was joined by the released Russian prisoners of war. Later a Democratic Minister Mueller-Meining made this comment: "With soldiers coming home, scams, women, and children moved along screaming and crying. Men without any quality of martyrs were at large: robbers and murderers, among them the killer of women, Christof." As it was ordered, Hitler stayed in the barracks with a red band on his arm, grinding his teeth, his hands tied and with a feeling of "sickness due to the whole situation."

Prime Minister Eisner, an Eastern Jew, in the street was shot to death by Count Arco, a student of Western Jewish origin. Eisner's bands stemmed from a racial "Thule-Orden" (Inset: a secret Society devoted to violent anti-Semitism. "Thule" means a mythical home of a German race), and were financed by Western Jews, Logen brothers and several others, among them Professor Dr.Berger, also a Jew. Headquarters of the Munich's National Forces were located in a work room of the Thule Club in the famous hotel "Vier Jahreszeiten" ("Four Seasons".) The chairman, a Saxon named Adam Glauer, who called himself Freiherr (Freeman) Baron von Sebottendorf, claimed: "The Thule people were the first to die for the swastika."

In Berlin at the same time Bernardowitsch Sobelson from Galicia, who called himself Radek, tried to incite people to a Spartanic (leftist) revolt. But it was suffocated in the Jewish blood of Karl Liebknecht and Rosa Luxemburg.

In May of 1919 the Soviet Republic of Bavaria, with the help of an outside military force under General von Oven was driven away. The force consisted of a "White Guard" under Army General von Oven, Volunteer Corps under Epp and Oberland, and the Navy Brigade under Erhardt.

Munich's battalion, to which Hitler belonged, was mobilized but undecided. There too, until then still an unknown corporal of the First World War jumped onto a chair and threw himself into politics: "Comrades, we are not revolutionary guards of the vagabond Jews. Sergeant Schuessler is very right when he suggests to stay neutral." It was not necessary to say anything more, so the battalion stood-by. When the "White Guard" moved into Munich, an investigative commission with corporal Hitler was formed. It tracked down all those, who were on the wrong side during the Soviet's time. "His determined indictments removed the unspeakable infamy caused by the military treasons during the Jewish-Soviet Dictatorship" - so people praised him.

Hitler was taken over by Captain Karl May, a leader of the News Services. As it is understood today, at this post Hitler became an agent of the Counter-

Espionage Services, for short MAD (Militaerisch Abschirm Dienst). The training took place at the University of Munich. Professor Karl Alexander von Mueller recalled this event: "A very fascinated small group gathered around a man, who impetuously and with growing passion was persuading them with a rare guttural voice. I saw a pale face of an un-soldier with a hanging string of hair, a mustache cut short and striking big, light blue, fanatically cold shiny eyes." Mueller asked Captain May, what did he know about this "oratory talent." May knew a lot and sent his best man to the "Sternecker Inn", where in the evening of September 12, 1919, in the Leiber (Lover's) Room, one of many political splinter-groups, the "German Working Party", had a meeting with 46 participants. Hitler listened to a long lasting and boring (in his opinion) lecture on economics, but when Professor Baumann demanded separation of Bavaria from the State to Austria, Hitler woke up, as he recalls: "Then I couldn't help myself and had to tell this erudite Lord my opinion." An expression of his opinion lasted fifteen minutes and the Sectarian fled in the middle of the lecture. Then the German Workers Party leader and tool maker Anton Drexler whispered to the recording secretary, a locomotive driver, sitting next to him: "Man, he has a gob and we should make use of it."

Hitler could make use of this exhausted club with seven marks and fifty pfennigs to their register, even though it was "a mixture of the worst kind," he thought, "a ridiculous little creation." However it was possible to shape this club into a right format. "Its contents, the goals, and its way could still be determined, which is impossible to do with already existing large parties." This was the reason why corporal Hitler joined the club of Anton Drexler. It extensively assembled colleagues from Munich's main workshop of the arterial motor-way. As a profession Hitler stated a painter. Within a few days, thanks to his "large gob", he became a chairman of the Party's Advertising Section. In the barracks sergeant Schuessler, later First Manager of the NSDAP, took care of his correspondence.

Here in Munich, in a short time an anti-Jewish battle team was installed and it grew because at the River Isar the Soviet Government of Russian Jews was very active. This in effect put an entire middle class into fear and shock. At that time in no other city of the German Reich (State) could Hitler win the masses without any financial support.

At the meetings he punctuated his speeches with Yiddish for he knew how to jabber. Thus with the cheer he succeeded, too. "This is the international language of the Jewish stock-exchange dictatorship. These people are united under the same origin, the same religion, and the same language - and in 'one hand' they have all of them."[25] Hitler could also be serious.

In a very civil Democratic Union of Munich, after presentation by the Mayor Peterson of Hamburg, someone, who was known as a "screamer", announced his wish to speak. Then that "someone" climbed up to the rostrum, put his hands in the pockets and waited for a keyword. "Hands out of your pockets!", from below came as anticipated to the speaker's joy. So he started: "Gentlemen, I don't belong to the people who talk with their hands!" Present Jewish businessmen

Der Gefreite Adolf Hitler (Mitte) während des ersten Weltkrieges in Flandern. «Fur die Rettung der deutschen Nation vor diesen internationalen Gleichheitsaposteln des Judentums haben wir uns den Stahlhelm aufgebunden,» versuchte er seine Kameraden zu überzeugen.

Corporal Adolf Hitler in Flanders (middle) during the First World War. He was always persuading his comrades about a need to: "put the Steel Helmet on in order to rescue the German Nation from the Jewish International Apostles of Equality."

The leaders of Munich's Soviet Republic in 1919, Jews Kurt Eisner alias Kosmanowski (above) and Eugen Levine (below). Without their preceding activities, the later successes of the thirty year old agitator Hitler could not be possible in Munich.

Die Häupter der Münchener Räterepublik des Jahres 1919, die Juden Kurt Eisner alias Kosmanowski (oben) und Eugen Levine (unten). Ohne ihr voraufgegangenes Wirken sind die anschliessenden Erfolge des dreissigjährigen Agitators Hitler in München nicht denkbar.

kept silent and with bewilderment and thoughtfulness listened to the calm demonstration which affected them very much.

"I am able to talk," Hitler happily realized. The excitement of the audience was his achievement and by this token it gave him the voice. He knew how to do variations, with which this young excited Alps' student yodeled: "I urge you, take a look at our health resorts. Today you will find two categories of people out there: the Germans, who after a long wait go there, or maybe are there for the first time to get some fresh air and to recover, and the Jews who go there to lose their fat or to go outing in our mountains. Whom do you find there in a brand new magnificent yellow boots, with nice back packs in which there is nothing important to find? And for what! They are only going into a hotel up there, mostly to a point where the Alpine Railway ends. That's where they stop. That's where they are sitting around in a radius of one kilometer, like the blowflies around a carcass. Those people are truly not from our working class, neither from intellectual nor the physical one! Mostly you will find our people in the ragged suits climbing up from the ground, mainly because they don't want to be embarrassed by their clothes made 1913-1914 A.D. and in them to enter a perfumed atmosphere."

Captain May, who with time changed his orientation to a Democratic Socialism, and who died at the end of the Second World War in a concentration camp Buchenwald, was replaced by Captain Roehm. "My name is Ernst," introduced himself Roehm sipping beer and then offered to the corporal Hitler to call each other by "you". Thus Hitler entered a circle of officers and former leaders of the Volunteer Corps, who appreciated him even though at beers he didn't pay much attention to their past battle engagements in the Baltic States nor in the Oberschlesien, nor about German resistance against the 1923s French entry into the Ruhr's Industrial Valley (Basin) as they were supposed to do. Hitler, a combat veteran knew how to make up those late home-comers and he did it with exciting speeches for fifteen up to fifty marks per day. The Criminal Commissar Feil reported about such meetings to his superiors as follows: "According to my personal view and my feelings, Hitler, with those adventurers from the Oberschlesien, as it was the case with the Jewish "pogrom" there, if nothing else, would become a leader of the Second Red Army like the one we had in 1919, just to commit robbery, murder, and plunder against the Jews."[(26)]

The "Munich Post", under a title "Jewish Rush", reported about one of those meetings in this way: "There appeared anti-Semitic middle class people and young students accompanied by their parents or by other grown-ups. Mr.Adolf Hitler gave a speech and behaved more like a comedian. After every third sentence his couplet-like presentation refrained: 'Hebrews are guilty' .... One thing has to be recognized here: Mr.Hitler admitted that his speech was motivated by a racial hatred."

On February 24, 1920, the German Working Party became the National Socialist German Working Party which soon was known all over the world as the NSDAP. Hitler and Party founder Drexler advised each other: "Now comes a big jump into the general public" argued Drexler. "Yes, Toni, how do you want to achieve that?" asked Hitler. "By going to the banqueting hall of the Hofbrauhaus (Brewery Inn)," was the response.

Shortly thereafter red placards were put on display with the imprint: "To the Suffering People". With the admission to the hall for forty pfennigs it was filled up. About 2,000 people appeared. When Hitler, a second speaker, wanted to say a word, a brawl started. Finally the speaker was accepted but became timid, though the applause in the course of his speech was stormy. Hitler announced a program of the NSDAP consisting of 25 Sections. Thirteen of them were directed against the Jews. Here are some excerpts: "No Jew can be a citizen." "Because it is impossible to feed all the people of the German Nation, hence members of a foreign nation should be expelled." "All foreigners who migrated after August 2, 1914 into Germany, will be forced to leave immediately." "All war profits will be confiscated." Explaining the program Hitler said: "The workers always have been told to 'Migrate to Russia'. Wouldn't it make more sense if the Eastern Jews were to stay there, for there is plenty of work to do?" "When it is necessary to take a couple of eggs away from a little hamster then the government shows an astonishing energy. But it will not use it if that hamster's name is Hummelsberger but Isidor Bach." "First the guilty ones, Jews, must go out, then we will clean up ourselves. Next should go criminals, for instance black marketeers, racketeers or usurers, for fining them is of no value." Then at a conclusion of the meeting a resolution was issued refusing the Israeli cultural community of Munich a special assignment of wheat flour for matzos in the amount of 40,000 quintals "because there is an insufficiency of bread for the 10,000 seriously sick people on the street." The resolution was accepted unanimously. In a report about this first mass meeting of the just created NSDAP, Hitler concluded: "A fire was lit from the heat of which one day a sword will come and will give back freedom to the Germanic Siegfried (German Hero) and life to the German Nation. Next will also come elevation of the Goddess of Pitiless Revenge because of the perjured act of November 9, 1918." Then the hall had slowly emptied. In such a way the movement has begun its course !

With a swastika, which for the first time a little choir boy encountered in the Lambach's Seminary, the artistically inclined Hitler designed Party's Flag and Insignia. It found its place in the middle of the Party's Emblem. The wife of the dentist Krohn sewed the first flag, and in May 1920, at the installation of NSDAP's Town Group of Starnberg, she decorated the rostrum. In a circular Hitler demanded: "The Party flags are to be put up high at all public meetings, hall entrances etc., and taken along during demonstrations. Party members everywhere and at all times, are to wear the Party insignia. Jews, who will offend them will be arrested."

Within the Party Hitler created "Storm Troopers", in short called SA (Sturm Abteilung). Their task was to protect the assembly room during meetings. Leftovers of the Army Union, the Volunteer Corps, and of the Residential Militia - which were established during the Soviet time - rolled into SA. Here is a police report about its first operation: "An assembly room was full. A man, who called Mr.Hitler a monkey, was taken out in calmness." Roehm, who, like Hitler, turned his back on the Army, later on became a very important leader of the SA, and was actively engaged in the politics. In Court Hitler justified formation of the SA in this way: "As of 1920 bombings of meetings and attacks on speakers have taken place. In response to this terror, and for the sake of meetings and protection of speakers, as well as leaders, the Security Department was created from young Party members. They call themselves "Storm Troopers".

At that time a chairman of the Bavarian Union, Ballerstedt, rendered separatistic speeches and glorified France before the heaven. Once he did this in Hitler's presence, who "would rather be hanged in a Bolshevik Germany than be happy in a French Germany." So, he jumped in front of his SA's comrades and hit the man's face with a dog whip. For having done this Hitler was imprisoned for one month in the Munich jail Stadelheim. This occurrence naturally raised his prestige in the SA. As far as his way of living in prison was concerned, it was not any worse than in the Men's Home of the Compassionate Brother (Monk) at the Lothstrasse, where he once rented a sleeping spot. In order to be busy in the evening leisure time, the Storm Troopers put up posters with this restriction: "No access to the Jews!" and tore down existing posters of their enemies. In addition they painted swastikas on the walls or over the enemy's slogans as they reciprocated with a mutual respect. The specialty there was a physical "testing" of people who looked like Jews. In effect, a Diplomat from South America was hurt unpleasantly when on a staircase they discovered that he was circumcised. Having finished such successful operations the activity thirsty young men went home with a joyful song on their lips:

> *"Throw them out, the entire Jewish gang,*
> *Throw them out of our country!*
> *Send them back to Jerusalem,*
> *There they will be among themselves, with the tribe of Sem!"*
> *("Schmeisst sie raus, die ganze Judenbande,*
> *Schmeisst sie raus aus unserem Lande!*
> *Schickt sie wieder nach Jerusalem,*
> *da sind sie wieder unter sich bei ihrem Stamme Sem!")*

At the meetings Hitler gave them the following orders, which in the eyes of SA fighters seemed to be unnecessary: "We should not converse with the Jews, because they are strangers, therefore they have no right to interfere with our affairs just as wouldn't a German meddle with the politics of a Jewish State of Palestine." And this last phrase was a beautiful dream which came true shortly after Hitler's death.

An emphasis put on partial Jewish origin of the agitator (Hitler) by the opposing news media had lost its strength. Even the socialists' "Munich Post" - called by Hitler without any respect as a "Ratsch-Kathel" ("Spit Bowl") - stopped its offensive remarks about Hitler's "previous engagement to a daughter of an Eastern Jew who migrated from Galicia (Austrian Poland)."

However, because of that, there was fighting in a Sterneckerbrau's office of the NSDAP (into which one could get through a long dark hallway), at that time still moderate as far as a battle with Judaism was concerned. In Northern Germany sprouted the German Socialist Party. Some of the Munich's Party members strived for a merger with those people. Others demanded that the Northern Germans dissolve their Party and join the NSDAP unconditionally in groups or as one. Those in Munich, who stuck to a democratic leadership of the Party (which existed until summer 1921), saw themselves opposing others who wanted to see Hitler as a leader with dictatorial powers.

The best horse of NSDAP's stable and the successful inspirer of masses took to travel. He stayed in Berlin for a few weeks where he lived mostly in salons. When he returned to Munich he found an opposing faction. In effect, on July 11, 1921, Hitler gave an explanation for his resignation from the NSDAP: "It is watered down and isn't able anymore to lead a battle for destruction of the Jewish international forces in our country." The situation got serious and the Party became afraid that without its "drought-horse" and the best speaker, it will perish into nothing. Hitler demanded in writing an acceptance of his position as the "First Chairman with dictatorial authority". Party leadership agreed as follows: "In recognition of your extraordinary sacrifices in the interest of the movement, with only honorary rewards for your accomplishments, for your unique oratory talent we are giving you dictatorial powers and welcome this cheerfully if after returning to the Party you will take over the position of its First Chairman."[27] So, Hitler's plan fruited and on that day the National Socialist movement, with its good intentions, became Hitler's movement against the Jews. The main goal of destruction of capitalistic economic exploitation was from now on overshadowed by the goal of Jewish expulsion, and in charge of this was the Fuehrer himself. Some people resigned from the Party. Among them was a former sergeant in the "Trick" regiment, Rudolf Schuessler. He immediately moved from the Party's office in the Sterneckerbrau into the Jewish Aufhauser Bank, where six years after Hitler's capture of power he was still active.

The new leader traveled a lot and made contacts with National Socialists in Austria and Sudetenland while collecting money in Switzerland from just about anyone, including Jews. The latter were afraid of the Bolshevik dispossession.

Party's publicity leaflets also reached Swiss' industrialists. The fliers carried hints of communist danger which impressed them terribly. Especially was affected Colonel Pirchler, founder of the Swiss Fatherland's Union. He invited Hitler to the Zurich's hotel "Sankt Gotthard", close to the villa "Wesendonck", where Hitler presented his program in front of forty renown people. Large sums of money were given to him by industrialist Oehler and by sugar manufacturer Frankenthal.

Hitler also went to his birth place Braunau. Then he visited Linz, the city of his love on the River Danube. At the same time he elucidated his fellow countrymen in Innsbruck, Salzburg, Hallstein, Vienna and St. Poelten about the Jewish question. Even there he used a right tone: "In an endless love, as a Christian and as a human being, I have learned in many places how our Lord finally took charge and raised the whip to chase profiteers, a breed of vipers, out of the temple! But His immense fight against the Jewish venom for benefit of this world, that I am aware of with my deepest feelings, after elapse of two thousand years is still in fact tremendous, and because of that our Lord had to bleed to death on the cross."

The movement took over the Southern region of the country. In the North it was not developed yet. Then a man came to help, about whom will be said more in the next chapter. In October 1922 Julius Streicher won over a Nuremberg group of the German Socialist Party and shortly there after the rest of the Party followed. At a meeting in Austrian Salzburg, the North German Socialist Party was dissolved and at the turn of 1922-23 most of its members joined the NSDAP. To Northern Germany went a pharmacist of Landshut, SA Leader, Gregor Strasser with his brother Otto. Naturally, it was thought, that by gaining strength through such a tactic, a revolt against Berlin would break out and the Party would take over the whole State. After a bloody down fall of Munich's Soviet Government, the Bavarian People's Party created a conservative government, whose leaders on one side were a little bit pro-monarchy - i.e., as it can be said - servants to the Rome, and on the other side hostile toward communists and Jews. With all the restrictions and their program, they were torn between these two and other forces seeking unity of the State, that is, communists and National Socialists. When the State socialist government in Berlin demanded disarming of the Bavarian Resident Militants, Munich's government answered: "Weapons need to be taken away from those who want them." State Counsel Meyer thought differently: "The State's government is a disguised Soviet-government." And these men advised the Jews: "This question would be more at ease if certain circles of the religious community would hold back a little, especially by not showing publicly, that they take for granted an enjoyable life while others are in need." This conservative Party demanded that "inciting of the general public by politically minded Jews from abroad should finally come to an end because their actions are detested, also by their occasionally respectable Bavarian believers." They did not even spare Hitler by putting him in jail, but because of an "insufficient evidence" they would let him go the next day to speak again. The most powerful personality in that government, Munich's Police President Poehner, made a distinction between immigrant Eastern Jews and local Western Jews, and because of his strong actions - according to various opinions - he was loved or feared, even far beyond the country's borders.

After seizure of power, Hitler took a trip with the District Commander Wagner around Munich. They passed Prince's Karl Palace, which was called vernacularly "Hero's Palace" after the previous President of the Bavarian People's Party. Then Hitler asked him what is a pension of the Hero, and at the response he fell into rage: "A former President of Bavaria can't live on 600 marks (it was a salary of a local school principal). Make sure, Wagner, that his pension is doubled."[28] In November 1923, everything was as usual: The pact was made. The Bavarian government and Hitler's National Socialists agreed, à la Mussolini, to march on Berlin in order to "chase November's criminals, who in November 1918 from their armchairs stabbed the German Army with a dagger in the back."

Soon enough it became clear to Hitler, that an alliance of the State Commissar General Kahr with the Bavarian government has in fact created only a revolt and is not about to lead to a march on Berlin. Hitler, out of this realization came to a conclusion: "If Bolshevism continues to march West, this means that Christian culture is in danger and must be saved, and a common interest between Bavaria and France should exist. But with radicalization of the North it can come to a separation of Bavaria. Not because a separatist tendency grows here, but because there is no other way out."

A Bavarian "Revolution of the Federalists" was planned for November 12, 1923, but Hitler forestalled it and threw them into his own pocket. In the evening of November 8, Hitler put on his long black coat and pinned to it a shiny silvery Iron Cross First Class. In the Citizens' Brewery Cellar the State Commissar General Kahr spoke in front of several thousands people. They were not an ordinary people, but invited "members of government, parliamentarians, executives of various authorities, military personnel of the old Bavarian Army, as well as representatives of the German Armed Forces, of a University, of the press and of artistic circles, if not to mention persons from the financial and economical elite."[29] After a while festively dressed and unnoticeable Hitler squeezed into the assembly hall and under the pretext of a security measure ordered an on-duty police officer, who recognized him, to clean up hall's entrance and the street. With this TRICK the police cleared the way for Hitler's SA, which armed with machine guns, immediately marched in and took position. Due to this action the police commander had a second thought and by telephone helplessly asked his Chief Commander Dr.Frick for orders. And he got them: "Keep the street in order." Therefore within the Third Reich he became the Secretary of the Interior with preference for keeping streets in order.

At this time the gentleman in a dark frock coat jumped onto a chair, fired a shot into the ceiling, stormed through the silent majority to a rostrum and yelled, still with a revolver in his hand: "National revolution has broken out. The assembly room is occupied by six hundred heavily armed men. If right now you will not be quiet, I will set a machine gun on top of the gallery. State Army and the Country Police are already approaching under the swastika flag."

Then Hitler pushed the three astonished dictators of Bavaria, gentlemen Kahr, von Lossow and Seisser into a side room. Famous First World War pilot Goering, with his Pour-le-Mérite around his neck, stepped up to the rostrum and made it clear that in the adjacent room the State Government will be formed. "And, actually," he commented, "you should be happy, for you can have your beer here!"

General Ludendorff, Commander-in-Chief during the First World War, for a long time on Hitler's and Goering's side, was brought in. At that time a national and social revolution was his wish. Therefore during the war he rejected a nobility title offered to him by the Emperor.

Hitler assigned positions and introduced to the gathering names of persons, even those who were not present: "Governing the State - Hitler; National Army

- Ludendorff; Police Chief - Seisser. The authority of the Provisional German National Government is the sole power of this Land and herein conscripts the power of all German regions, which from this very moment can start a march on the 'Hotbed of Vice' - Berlin. This morning the people will either find a German National Government or all of us are dead!" Everyone rejoiced over this good prospect, which these four men in the side room of the Assembly had taken up on their shoulders and all with their hands were betting on the deal with Hitler.

Next morning, at the Field Army Hall, someone permitted to shoot at the people who in obedience to Hitler's orders overnight trickled into Munich in thousands on foot or in trucks. On the house walls following notes were glued on: "These statements which at gun point were forced on us - General von Lossow, Colonel Seisser and me, are null and void." The notes were subscribed by General von Kahr, a Commissar of the State.

In the vanguard Hitler and Ludendorff were marching. Hitler with a gun in his hand. A man rushed to in front shouting: "Don't shoot! His Excellency Ludendorff is coming!" But shots commenced thundering at the Field Army Hall. Fourteen National Socialists died at the Odeons Place. Two more fell on Roehm's side while he was surrounded in a neighborhood by the Country Police. Numerous were wounded, among them Goering with a shot to his abdomen, and Hitler, who with a dislocated arm ran for safety. The rioters were shot by the fellow-men who on the previous days swore an allegiance to them. Goering escaped abroad. Hitler found a shelter in a villa by Uffing at the Staffel Lake. But police found him nevertheless while Mrs. Hanfstaengl, born Heine in the USA, a Western Jewess, was taking care of the wounded man.

Ten years after seizing power the NSDAP announced: "All of you did not die for nothing!" And some truth lies in this: "Through this rebellious deed a unity of the Reich (State) was guaranteed, for within the next few days a planned strike by the Bavarian sectarians was prevented. Reich's Youth Leader Baldur von Schirach, half-American, who learned to speak German at the age of eleven, today on retirement wrote:

> *"Was sie auch Dome schufen,*
> *uns sind Altar die Stufen -*
> *der Feldherrnhalle."*
> *("They also built some Cathedrals,*
> *but for us the altars are terraces -*
> *made of the Field Army Hall.")*

In the beginning of 1924, Hitler and his rebels were sentenced to a confinement, but no earlier than Christmas he became a free man again. Such a tremendous strength was thwarted, at a moment, when it wanted to send the unloved government with help of machine guns to the Devil or to the Orient - for the times were like this.

"THE JEWS ARE OUR BAD LUCK"

This saying came from the great historian Treitschke, and Hitler pounded it into people's heads until the last stable boy in a poorest corner of a forest knew, who is to be blamed for his bad luck. But he did not reveal all that Treitschke recommended: "They should become Germans - regardless of their beliefs and holiest reminders of their ancient times which are venerable to us all."

In the "Bat Bar" of Munich (this happened in the twenties), behind a table sat together with a slim Hitler recently dismissed from the army a stocky gentleman speaking a Viennisch jargon. After a sip of beer, lost in thoughts, the man was glancing at the waitresses' ankles with his little black eyes. He was a Hungarian Jew, son of a rich silk merchant, and a very close friend of the poet Dietrich Eckart, who published a small anti-Jewish paper "For a Good German". Eckart mastered very well a German style of speaking cultivated by Eastern Jews, which he learned in Berlin thanks to his association with best social circles. Through him Hitler met this peculiar man now paying for the beer, who disguised himself under a fictitious name (Ignaz) Trebitsch-Lincoln: first as a Hebrew student of theology and shortly thereafter as a sectarian preacher of the Gospel in New York; later as a pastor in England; as a director of an oil company; as a representative of liberals in the British Lower Chamber of Parliament and then as a spy for Germany. All of these functions he did almost simultaneously. Britons still assume that Trebitsch-Lincoln was the "only foreign agent who has ever become a member of the Lower Chamber."[30] If they only knew.

The conversation was about Jews and Jewish global endeavors. "There you are right, Mr.Hitler," exercised Trebitsch. "Exaggerations about Jewish people have been their own fault for they always have fought among themselves. Think about Karl Marx, his exact name is Mordochai, whether you agree to this or not, and what he said: "What is the worldly Jewish culture? Schacher (Thievery). Who is their worldly God? Money. And remember what said Weininger, our great Vienna philosopher, also a Jew: 'The Jew does not know what love means. He only knows the body. He wants to defile it!'"

"Now tell me, please, Mr.Trebitsch," Hitler asked, "what do you think about Palestine as a solution to the whole caboodle?"

"Two beers," Trebitsch-Lincoln exclaimed and mused. After a moment and another sip he beamed with his beautiful Vienna charm loudly and gaily: "I've got it - THE NATIONAL SOCIALISTS AND NATIONAL ZIONISTS UNITE!!! Your wish has God's ear." To this Hitler responded solemnly: "It is the same aim, but the means are different. The Lord be with us." And he took a deep sip, too. Trebitsch-Lincoln began talking enthusiastically about a declaration of the Anglo-Jewish Foreign Minister Balfour: "Well, the whole declaration is only a letter from Balfour to his lovely Lord Rothschild, who was in his seventies. But the case presented in this letter is very simple: the Britons should give us their land and we will bring our people there. However, some minor pressure might be necessary. We want to build a house which will take in all the Jews, and they, as well as all the other nations will rest in peace." Then he plowed eagerly through

Next to Adolf Hitler (who already became the "Fuehrer" in the twenties) stands half - Jewish Julius Streicher. Streicher's main job was to fight the Jews. Behind him stands a man with beard, the full Jew Moses Pinkeles alias Trebitsch-Lincoln who financed the "People's Observer" and Hitler's Party as well.

Neben dem bereits zum «Führer» aufgestiegenen Adolf Hitler (links) Anfang der zwanziger Jahre der teiljüdische hauptberufliche Judenbekämpfer Julius Streicher (Mitte) an der Seite des volljüdischen Moses Pinkeles alias Trebitsch-Lincoln (rechts mit Vollbart), der den «Völkischen Beobachter» und Hitlers Partei finanzierte.

Moses Pinkeles alias Trebitsch-Lincoln died in 1943 shortly before his try to reach Tibet from China. The chief ideologist of the NSDAP, half-Jew Minister Alfred Rosenberg on page one of the "People's Observer" published for him an extraordinary obituary.

Moses Pinkeles alias Trebitsch-Lincoln 1943 kurz vor seinem Tod, als er versuchte, von China aus Tibet zu erreichen. Der Chefideologe der NSDAP, der teiljüdische Minister Alfred Rosenberg, verfasste den ausserordentlich ehrenden Nachruf auf Seite eins des «Völkischen Beobachter».

A close friend of Hitler, Dr. Ernst Hanfstsengl, son of Jewess Heine from New York, until 1937 was the Chief of Foreign Press Department in the NSDAP. During the Second World War he became Roosevelt's advisor.

Dr. Ernst Hanfstaengl, Sohn der New-Yorker Jüdin Heine, bis 1937 Auslands-Pressechef der NSDAP und enger Freund Hitlers, der im zweiten Weltkriege zum Berater Roosevelts wurde.

Hanfstaengl, im Freundeskreis und von Hitler «Putzi» geheissen, beim Anlegen des Fallschirms auf dem Flugplatz Staaken im Februar 1937. Es war ein rauher Scherz, als man dem etwas ängstlichen Intellektuellen erklärte, man werde ihn im Auftrage des Führers über rotspanischem Gebiet zu einem Sondereinsatz abwerfen.

Among his friends Hanfstsengl, as well as by Hitler, was called "Putzi". Here he is putting on a parachute at Staaken Airport in February 1937. It was a practical joke when it was explained to the somewhat frightened man that following Fuehrer's order he will be thrown out of the airplane into the Spanish territory seized by communists.

the existing differences between Western and Eastern Jews: "Who built up the economy? The ships owner of Hamburg Mr.Ballin; or the top secret Councilman Simson, and other people like them. And who helped the Princesses to get out of mud when their safes emptied? Bleichroeder was the main banker to the Emperor Wilhelm, that is who. And Strauss with the Vienna waltz, was a gift to the people from heaven," he shook himself slowly. And suddenly in rage he continued: "And how about the Eastern Jews? Who will smash the Warsaw ghetto. This hiding place of the underworld deserves..." "What now?" inquired the curious thirty year old Party speaker. "I will tell you what" - Trebitsch intimately put his fleshy hand on Hitler's lower arm, "I know who you are: Frankenberger. Tell me, what do we, the Western Jews of the Reich, of Austria, of Hungary, have to do with those bug ridden Jews in caftans over there?" Hitler briskly pulled out his arm from under Trebitsch's hand and with his eyes flashing said: "Never say Frankenberg. Or I will yell loudly about you: Moses Pinkeles! Moses Pinkeles from Hungary!" Pinkeles alias Trebitsch-Lincoln was a silent personality. He ordered another beer and retorted concretely: "How much do you need?" "One hundred thousand" was the response. Trebitsch pulled three bundles out of a side pocket and threw them on the table. "Count it!" and Hitler did: "Thirty thousand. Within one month the 'Voelkischer Beobachter' ('People's Observer') will be mine!"[31] Trebitsch got up and took his coat. "You should know," he pointed his finger at the still seating Hitler "that the anti-Semitism can be of value only if the Jews take it into their own hands!" "From yours?" Hitler looked up. "No, from the painter Liebermann, a Jew like me." Hitler stared into his empty mug. "How right he is! Just like an artist," he mumbled and got up, too.

To the revolutionary editor of the Party newspaper was introduced Rosenberg's old friend, a Hungarian Jew Holoszi, also called Hollsch from Holland, son of a rabbi [32].

On December 17, 1920, Hitler became owner of the "People's Observer" and an administrative duty was assigned to Dietrich Eckart. After a while the newspaper was shut down for a month and later for a week because of its "Jew-baiting" themes. This raised its circulation in the following years to over one hundred thousand. When the prohibition affected Hitler's right to speak then he printed his speeches. To create subversion in the Reich's Army - as was meant by Hitler - soldiers received special issues. On November 16, 1921, Hitler recorded in Munich's "Court Register" that he is in possession of all shares of the "People's Observer", which before were manipulated by the THULE SOCIETY. Since that day Hitler was not a pauper anymore. Trebitsch-Lincoln served as one of the best anti-Jewish secretaries of the "Observer". Later this "Eater of Eastern Jews" praised the former Chief of Police Ernst Poehner as follows: "Once Chief Poehner with his loyal advisor, District Magistrate Frick on his side, was the only high ranking government dignitary with a courage to be first a German and then an Official."

When Pinkeles (a full Jew alias Trebitsh-Lincoln), after his unsuccessful attempt to make the British Empire insecure as far as Tibet died suddenly, on the front page of the "People's Observer" was placed an obituary, honoring him extraordinarily and signed by the Editor-in-Chief Alfred Rosenberg.

This memorial article started with the "Kapp Rebellion" (of March 13, 1920, in Berlin) and extolled Trebitsch-Lincoln as a press consultant to the East Prussia District Director Wolfgang Kapp. At that time corporal Hitler, still a member of the military news services in civil clothes, together with Dietrich Eckart flew to Berlin. Their pilot was Ritter (Knight) von Greim, later General Field Marshal in Hitler's Air Force. When they appeared at the main entrance to the Parliament, there stood a nimble, small Moses Pinkeles, known here too as Trebitsch-Lincoln, and warned: "Scram to Munich. Everything is off and Knapp fled..."

Eckart and Hitler, however, were not in a hurry to flee, for they had shelter with a Lady of the Highest Elite, wife of the Jewish piano manufacturer, Bechstein. Eckart knew her very well from his Berlin days, so Hitler became her good friend too, and there he was always welcome. To him she was a good asset due to her many connections. For her, Hitler also was such an asset in a field of various provisions. Later when he was imprisoned in Fortress Landsberg for his troublesome and rebellious endeavors, the police received a statement from Mrs. Helene Bechstein about him, to wit: "Two or three times my husband supported Hitler in publishing the "People's Observer" in Munich. I have helped him too, but not with money. Rather I gave him many pieces of art and a notice that he may do whatever he wants with them. These pieces of art were of the highest value."

Mr.Frank (also of Jewish origin), Berlin's coffee producer under the brand name "Kornfrank", through Mrs. Bechstein and Eckart was acquainted with Hitler. He entered into a contract with Hitler and loaned him over "60,000 Swiss franks. As a security for the loan Mr.Adolf Hitler transferred to Mr.Richard Frank an emerald platinum pendant with cut diamonds, a ruby platinum ring with cut diamonds, a sapphire platinum ring with cut diamonds, a ring with 14 carat cut diamond, a Venetian relief sculpture, and a red silk Spanish case with an elytron decorated with golden stitchery. This loan was to be paid off by August 20, 1926, at the latest."

The very lovely Hanfstaengl's Villa in Munich, as Hitler described it, stood wide open for the successful "DRUMMER" (he liked to be called as such). The director of the Fine Art Publishers, known by her maiden name as Mrs. Heine from New York, since a shocking experience during the Soviet dictatorship changed her pacifistic attitude into the opposite one, and her half-Jewish son Ernst became an inspired and enthusiastic Hitler's fan. Called by his friends "Putzi" (a "Fop") this Harvard graduate was a heir of this well established business, and he was glad to help anyone with foreign money during inflation - at one time he gave one thousand dollars, a fortune in those crazy days. Back then in Berchtesgaden, where Hitler liked to retire with male and female companions, Ernst Hanfstaengl was a welcome visitor and as a joker made them laugh imitating manners of his former teacher, father of Heinrich Himmler, who had raised him and a few princeses.

Later on, Goering and his men scared this somewhat frightened friend of art, who often expressed his point of view not too very firmly. Mostly he spoke of his sufferings during the First World War, in New York, when his shop windows were smashed by rouges, which to him was much worse than any soldiers' war experience at a front line. In February 1937, at the Airport Staaken they put on "Putzi" and his shaken bones a parachute (he was then a Chief of Foreign Press of the NSDAP) and flew him at "Fuehrer's" command on an allegedly secret mission to the Spanish war arena. The airplane was filled with hand grenades hanging everywhere. The seats were made of bare metal. During the flight blood starved companions passed around pictures of mutilated corpses of Spanish women. The whole event was filmed. At a certain moment pilot set the plane to shake and its engine to grumble. It was just a funny undertaking which ended at the airport in Klein Polenz, close to Leipzig. This wonderful film was played before the Leader Hitler and received an appropriate applause. So, Dr.Ernst Hanfstaengl was led to believe that his life was in danger; that his contribution to the German society was finished and under such dictum the Chief of Foreign Press disappeared. Even Goering's letter of March 1937, could not entice him to return home to the Reich from Switzerland: "I assure you that this whole affair was supposed to be only a harmless joke. I expect you to believe my words," but this was not convincing enough.

Many bad stories were heard about Ernst Hanfstaengl, but about Hitler the worst. His sister Erna, obviously, was also not immune, but whenever Hitler made obeisance to his wife by placing hands on his chest, he always deeply recalled her husband. During the war Dr.Hanfstaengl, a refugee from under the swastika flag, became an advisor to President Roosevelt whom he knew from his Harvard student days. According to his own research into the matter of origin, Hitler and Roosevelt were of the common Jewish stock. This thought stuck fast through all these years and decades in the mind of this vagabond of the two worlds, as the Jewish journalist Rudolf Kommer on the day of Rathenau assassination in 1922 told him: "Also in the opinion of Rathenau, the condemned march of 'Asiatic Hordes' on the Brandenburg Maerkische sands, is a hopeless scramble to make themselves into a likeness of the Balder's blonds (Norse's god of blonds). God have mercy upon us Jews and you Germans, when one day the mental poison of the Jewish SELF-HATRED, or in the world's view a split insanity of mentally and morally defect mongrels, will attach itself to the brainless brutal instincts of the 'beastly blond' trimmed gangsters."[33] Probably never before things were said more explicitly about Hitler and Heydrich.

Gottfried Feder, the leading Party theorist on economic questions, didn't have any scruples about taking money from the Jews. This educated and traveling extensively man, made multitude of contacts with businesses, banks, and industries and for the NSDAP disposal mediated funds from the Jewish banks.

These funds of several thousands of marks or franks, which came from the Jews grew to millions. To millions also grew highly desired US dollars. About those monies, flowing from Mendelsohn & Co., from von Kuhn, Loeb & Co. from Warburg, and from Samuel & Samuel, will be reported on in another part of this research. Likewise, about fulsomely praised English newspaper magnate Rothermere who, when looking at him in the spot light, will be seen as a German

Jew by the name of Stern.

The man, who by deliverance of "German Socialists" of Nuremberg, crucially eased Hitler's way into the Northern Germany, was Mr.Streicher. It would be worthwhile to pay a closer attention to this greatest anti-Jewish agitator of the Nazi movement. After the First World War this professional elementary school teacher was the first who joined "Independent Social Democrats", to which belonged Eisner of the Munich's Soviet. The Eastern Jews didn't trust him, so he left and founded the "German Socialist Party" in Nuremberg. At the 1920 conference in Salzburg it came to an agreement between pretty well competitive anti-Jewish parties GSP and NSDAP: to the North of the River Main the GSP should be active, and to the South Hitler's National Socialists. One exception to this game was Julius Streicher. He did not go along with Hitler and remained Leader of the South GSP with headquarters in Nuremberg. In a due course Streicher fought Hitler by using virulent invectives, verbal or printed in a widely circulating weekly magazine the "German Socialist". Streicher went even further and tried to ruin Hitler with the help of NSDAP's founder Drexler on his side. This situation lasted for two years. Then a former Military News Services employee obtained evidence proving that Streicher was not a pure Aryan.

Hitler asked Streicher to come from Nuremberg to Munich. They met in the Schwabinger's "Osteria Bavaria" and by a cup of coffee Hitler put the evidence under his nose. Only a few days passed by when Streicher with his Nuremberg comrades in arms put himself under command of the Munichians. In this way a gate to the North was pushed wide open. After only a few weeks out of the limited Bavarian National Socialist Party rose Hitler's movement of the whole Germany.

"Whoever wanted to get close to him, only could come close through a manly deed," said later Streicher who in the meantime foppished himself with a mustache a la Hitler. He was that person who on November 9, 1923, at the Field Army Hall in Munich jumped in front of gun barrels shouting: "Don't shoot, His Excellency Ludendorff is coming!"

With a low life style, he (Ludendorff) bade to a foreground his best. In response to all the complaints about this partly Semitic anti-Semite, Hitler had only one answer: "Maybe you don't like the nose of that fellow Party member Streicher, but remember that when he was lying next to me on the pavement at the Field Army Hall I promised myself never to leave him, as long as he doesn't leave me."

When Streicher, at the beginning of war the Leader of Franconia, crossed the line and was thrown out from the NSDAP by the highest Party court, Hitler changed his mind. He wasn't kept in the Party as a Regional Leader but as a publisher of the Party's magazine "Stuermer" ("A Storm Man").

This anti-Jewish gutter magazine founded in 1923 lasted for the next two decades full of stories about Jewish ritual murders and sexual crimes. In the Third Reich it was the only permitted pornography magazine far ahead of its time. Publishing Chief of the "People's Observer", Mr.Amann, put it straight from a hip, that it is a "filthy swine paper, which I will not touch." Even more than the gutter articles, this disgrace magazine stirred up sensations under the forest's canopy with drawings which were beneath dignity, and from which sensitive souls had bad dreams. The designer of those drawings was a Jew Jonas Wolk alias Fritz Brandt.

In 1919, after leaving the communist Independent Socialist Party, Streicher was afraid of Jewish revenge. Fellow Party members in Hamburg smiled pitifully at him when upon arrival he insisted on preparing coffee himself - as if the waiter in a dining caboose of the train wanted to poison him. And he could swear to this.

The revenge came later and it caught up with him in Nuremberg, where war criminals were hanged, but he was strangled (1946). Standing in front of thirteen steps to the gallows, he yelled loudly: "Heil Hitler!" When he was questioned about his name, he answered brusquely: "You know it." The priest accompanied him up the stairs, and when on the top he shrieked: "PURIM FESTIVAL 1946 - now it is time to go to God." ("PURIM" is the Festival of Joy after a slaughter of Gentiles).

In the surrounding dead silence, after a fall of his body through the trap door, a long groan was heard. The German observers called this execution the "scariest of the night". Two German employees of the crematorium who helped in unloading of dead bodies, pledged to keep this event secret. The box into which they put Streicher's body had the inscription: "Abraham Goldberg" for he was him, indeed.[34]

When analyzing close relationships between Hitler's movement and Western Judaism, it is necessary to take a closer look at the later would be political "Successors of the Fuehrer".

Rudolf Hess was born in Egypt to a mother with a British passport. This First World War pilot went to the University of Munich as a Science Assistant to Professor Haushofer, a Catholic of Jewish origin, who specialized in a subject of National Economy, and was married to a Jewish lady. Hess and Haushofer treated themselves as brothers of the THULE SOCIETY. Back then, Hess was the author of substantial precepts of the Party. Section one said: "The Party is anti-Jewish." Haushofer belonged to a group of "Truth Seekers," led by a Levantine - Jewish hybrid, George Ivanovitsh Gurdjew who operated in Georgien, France, and in the USA managed various sects and religious denominations. This specialist, who knew "everybody and everything", made Haushofer and Hess studying occulistic doctrines of Tibet his friends. Already in 1903, Haushofer, together with Gurdjew, travelled through Himalayas, and later this Levantic sectarian moved for years to Tibet to educate Dalai-Lama. When Himmler, the Reich's Leader of the SS, found out that Hitler's physician Professor Morell gave the Fuehrer siringes from Tibet, and that Morell knew both Haushofer and Gurdjew very well, he sent out an expedition there into the impassable high mountains. They returned unexpectedly soon, but with a present from Dalai-Lama to his colleague Hitler (Inset: in one of the monasteries in Tibet a swastika is venerated to this day).

It was Haushofer who coined the slogans "Lebensraum" ("Space for Life") and the "Kontinentaldoktrin" ("The Continental Doctrine") both of which incited

Hitler to battles in the Middle East and Eastern Europe.

In 1933, son of Haushofer, also a Professor of National Economy, was assigned by the Fuehrer to Rudolf Hess as his Staff Member. Most important missions around the world were entrusted to him. The senior Haushofer at that time received Presidential Post at the German Academy in Munich, and later was considered as the Father of Hitler's Pact with Japan. The Japanese never planned to attack Siberia. So almost none of Haushofer's teachings and predictions held ground. Just after the war was lost, he and his wife committed suicide.

Among the Jewish ranks, Western Jews known as Sephardim stand higher above the others, the Aschkenasim. The emphasized word "even" says it clearly enough, as a Merchandise Stores founder Tietz said it in the book "Jews in the German Economy" by Zielenziger Jew, Berlin, 1930: "The clan originally stems from Holland, probably "even" from the Southern France."

After migration to the United States of North America the Sephardim lodged a complaint about the "Rabble", which threatens to flood the US' coasts. Thus slandered Eastern Jews complained that because of their immigration they would be treated by the "Aristocratic Jews like criminals."

Professor Dr.Hans Guenther, specializing in Racial Sciences accounted ninety percent of all the Jews in the world to the Eastern Jews, and in his "Information on Race" of 1923 he came to this conclusion: "Based on observation it is apparent that the dispersion of Jews among non-Jewish people causes endless commotion which in effect escalates to hatred. Understanding of this phenomenon should be undertaken courageously by the Zionism itself. The Zionism should see it clearly that only the removal of Jews from the cohabitation with non-Jews will create dignified relations. Establishment of an up-standing and appropriately secured Homeland for the Jewish people in Palestine seems to be politically possible."[35]

Hitler kept himself preoccupied with this man, with his writings and doctrines. In 1935 at the National Party Day, "Nuremberg Laws" were proclaimed which among other things prohibited marriages between Aryans and Jews, as such marriages might result in a "Disgrace of Race" and so they should be punished by death. On this National Party Day Hitler presented an award to this highly educated Professor Guenther, and from that moment on, in the III Reich, he was the highest authority on the racial questions.

Despite the importance of the promoted by him idea of an "HONORARY ARYAN", for Hitler it was not difficult to chose between the two concepts: "Adaptation", as propagated by Treitschke, or the "Palestine Solution", as propagated by Guenther.

"MY STRUGGLE",
A PIECE OF ART FROM LANDSBERG ON THE RIVER LECH

Considering the awful consequences of a decision to become a politician, many would put such an occupation on a hanger. But not Hitler, who a few days after a failed excursion was caught at the Field Marshall Hall and apprehended in the Hanfstaengl's Villa. At that very moment he asked for a pen and paper and wrote down: "To everybody! Do not fall into despair! Be united! Follow the temporary leaders truthfully and obeyingly and serve your Fatherland but not its corruptors. Written and signed by Adolf Hitler."

It was already night, one hour by car from Munich, when the police delivered their prisoner to the Fortress Landsberg on the River Lech. "Accommodate him well" said a policeman and left. The guards shook and woke up the well sheltered nobleman Arco, who four years earlier on an open street shot to death the communist Premier Eisner-Kosmanowski. "Come on, get up, the Fuehrer is coming!" The nobleman rubbed his eyes and recognizing Hitler stretched his hand out joyfully. But Hitler did not reciprocate as everybody knew that Arco was of Jewish origin and the newcomer wanted to be a politician, and from now on a legal one.

The physician on duty, Dr.Brinsteiner, confirmed a "head fracture of the humerus" and diagnosed that a partial stiffness of Hitler's left shoulder would remain, but despite of this he would be able to stand trial. For leadership over the trial fought the Social Democratic Government in Berlin, as well as the Catholic Conservative Central Government in Munich, but in the end the Bavarians succeeded. At the beginning of 1924 the trial took place in a former dining hall of Munich's War School at Blutenburgstrasse. The failed rebel using his "big gob" dominated over the trial perfectly. He often needed hours to answer a question and the audience listened and noticed each word. Representatives of French, English and American newspapers were present too. "This Hitler, indeed, is a colossal guy" applauded one gentleman from the Court of Justice. A dispute was about the "criminal gang of Berlin". Everything went smoothly and after three weeks the "Gentleman Defendant" finished his discursive. Throughout the trial nobody even mentioned previous involvement of such Gentlemen as Kahr, von Lossow, and Seisser. All of them were acquitted. For Hitler the judgement was lenient - with a prospect of probation. Ludendorff, who as the new Commander-in-Chief had already issued a few commands, also was exonerated and this irritated him: "I accept this acquittal with shame, which my uniform and my medals do not deserve."

In Landsberg a man can serve time, in the prison language called "Sitting on the Arse". Guards and prisoners received the same provisions. Hitler had a living room, a bed room and an orderly to keep them clean. Also the new arrivals, condemned for rebellion, got their best with refreshments such as "Enzian" or "Steinhaeger". Hitler received books and entertained visitors. Among them were very active friends and fans with whom he sometimes conversed for hours without any intervention by the assisting guard who "at the end of each visitation had a problem with stopping Hitler's performances."

When Rudolf Hess was sentenced in a separate trial, they moved this Leader of the National Socialist Students Union into a quietly situated wing of the fortress where Hitler also lived. It was branded "Field Marshall's Wing". Once or twice a week Professor Haushofer, a Western Jew and a specialist in the field of national-geopolitics, appeared there. Haushofer was Hess' friend and full of ideas. When he brought in a typewriter the work began. Thus the Private Secretary Hess typed what the "Big Leader" dictated and two or three imprisoned partners attentively listened. At evening parties he spoke in front of many other comrades and it was an escape from a daily boredom caused by playing ball in the courtyard or cards behind tables. On such occasions the Security Guards also gathered outside the stairway hall and listened. Their mouths never released any disturbing sounds. In such a way the "MEIN KAMPF" was created.

The speeches cannot be measured by an impression they make on the university professors, Hitler believed, but by the effect they make on the ordinary people. The Hitler's "Work of Art", an important tool in achieving a final victory, consisted of anti-Jewish lectures recited by the imprisoned Party Leader at the State expense in this "High School of Education".

In the index of "Mein Kampf" the term "Judaism" appears a hundred times, but such as France or Russia only a dozen. And even there the Jew is responsible: "Contamination by the Negro blood at Rhein, in the heart of Europe, corresponds to the sadistic perverted passion for vengeance by this sworn chauvinistic enemy of our people, as much as does the ice-cold thinking of a Jew, through whom began bastardization of the central European continent and deprivation of the white race of the foundation of self glorifying existence through its infection with the inferior humans. What France, led accordingly by the Jewish plans, stimulated by her own passion for revenge, is doing today in Europe, is a sin against existence of white humans, and some day will provoke all vengeance spirits of a race which recognized racial pollution as the original mankind's sin." And furthermore: "The most terrible example offers Russia where THIRTY MILLION people, in a truly fanatic savagery or an inhuman torture were killed or starved by the Jews, only to secure the Jewish literate men and the Stock Exchange bandits who want to gain power over masses." Hitler, the Reich's Chancellor and Leader, later on admitted to his Foreign Minister that his "biggest mistake" was the contemplation about foreign politics which found space in the Landsberg's "Work of Art."

It seems wrong to be talking about "Mein Kampf" as a far reaching "Schedule of a World Conqueror". Hitler wanted room in the East of Europe: "The duty of our National Socialist Mission is to bring German people to a political understanding, that this mission's goal is not an intoxicated vision of a new Alexander the Great whose dreams are to be fulfilled. But that it is a more efficient work of the German plough which can be changed only into the sword." And with this he finished: "Germany in the future Europe will only have two allies: England and Italy. Today we don't fight for the status of a world power but for the existence of our Fatherland, for the unity of our nation, and for the daily bread of our children. Today Germany is not a world power. Even if a temporary impotence of our Army would be overcome, we will have no pretense to such a title."

However the "Schedule" provided Eastern Europe to the Germans after expulsion of Jews from the areas of their influence: "The Destiny it seems points us into a certain direction. By placing Russia into Bolshevik hands a robbery was committed on the Russian Nation and is intelligentsia, which until then brought about and guaranteed its existence. To Germans and by Germans related England, the Destiny provides an extended Empire without mercy for the colonized people." Furthermore: "Hopes for a rebellion in Egypt are exactly miserable. The 'Holy War' to our German 'Block-Head' players can only give eery feelings and nothing else. As a pure German, who evaluates humanity on racial grounds, I am not allowed to link the Destiny of my own people with the destiny of, as they are called - the 'oppressed nations'." Hitler did not understand until his last days that the led by him Germany could not go into a ring with the "Germanish Brothers" of England. Some other time he asked a Swede: "Mr.Dahlerus, please explain to me why I could not get into an agreement with the English government? Because you seem to know England well, maybe you can solve this puzzle for me?" When a few days later in September 1939 the Great Britain declared war on the German Reich, Hitler sat behind his desk motionlessly and stared far beyond. He didn't fall into a rage yet. He was just sitting totally still and after a while, which seemed to him to be eternal, he asked: "Now what?"[36]

Back in 1924 to the comrades imprisoned in Landsberg everything looked very simple: Germany will acquire Eastern Europe and the Germanic England the whole World. The allied Italy will change the Mediterranean Sea into her "Mare Nostrum". America is far away and eventually will become a heaven for the godless people.

Most of his believers were strict Catholics, from whom he knew about the letters of Apostle Paul: "God does not love Jews for they are despised by everybody." Hence the Landsberg's orator could easily play a game against the Jews under an excuse of continuing the "GOD'S WORK".

The hatred of his real or presumed Jewish relatives, acquired by Hitler during his Vienna days, was enhanced by teachings of Schoenerer, Lueger, and Lanz von Liebenfels. Landsberg's lectures on theories of racial exponents like Darwin, Mendel, Boelsche, Gobeneau, and Guenther were complemented by periodic visits of Haushofer and Rosenberg with their LAND EXPROPRIATIVE tendencies borrowed from the Jewish (Inset: KIBBUTZIM'S) People's Commissars who ruled the Soviet Russia and tore it down to pieces. Haushofer, supported by his assistant Rudolf Hess, the "Egyptian", reached out very far and from all sides had grasped strongly with his pliers an already huge Reich. And Rosenberg, born in Estonia, according to his passport only for several months a German citizen, knew a lot about the seizure of power by the Jews in Russia. He fled with White Russians to Paris and pretty soon found refuge in Munich, where he wrote about what was going on in the Soviet Union: "The Russo-Jewish

Revolution", "The Jew Question", "The Protocols of the Learned Elders of Zion and the Jewish World Politics" were the best-sellers.

Rosenberg through the Jew Pinkeles, and as a manager of the "People's Observer" had access to finances, and knew what Hitler presumed about his distant Jewish origin, which was obvious due to his name. However, after he described to his Fuehrer - with "Meyers Dictionary" at his hand - how in 1492 Torquemada, a converted Jew as the Spanish Grand Inquisitor, rid Spain of almost all Jews, baptized ones notwithstanding, then it was certain that during Hitler's imprisonment nothing would stay in Rosenberg's way to a career as a Representative of the Leader. He was a very freely expressive ideologist who could show to others the Fuehrer's written bequest: "My beloved Rosenberg, from now on you will lead the movement!"

It would be too cumbersome to list all acts which, according to "Mein Kampf", the Jews have committed or would commit in the future. Hitler pleasantly characterized them as a "tuberculosis bacteria" or as "pests". Because so many things in Hitler's "Work" are described in detail, as well as they are widely known and correct, in 1945 the Conquerors prohibited Germans from reading it and the prohibition became the "Law of the Land". The ensuing generations (Inset: up to 1974), for this reason, cannot form any opinion on the subject matter, though they should.

For the purpose of general education it is proper to point out, that hardly any people of this world have the self-preservation drive so strongly developed as the so called "chosen ones". The best evidence for this is the existence of these people throughout the millennia.

To make a distinction between good things and bad, it should be added that if the Jews with the help of their Marxist beliefs win over the people of this world, then their crown will be a death wreath for the humanity, and this planet will be pulled through Ether with no one present, like million years ago.

It cannot be doubted that Hitler promised the Jews banishment, and in case of war their destruction, and that he relied on wars just like any other realistic politician. "If twelve or fifteen thousand Hebrew criminals were gassed at the beginning of 1914 and during the war, like the hundred thousand of our best German workers were on the battle fields, the sacrifice of millions would not be have been wasted," he said.

Hitler's idea that he was sent by the Almighty, who by the prolongation of the Second World War was guilty of millions of victims, was already expressed in the "Mein Kampf": "I do believe that I am acting in the interest of the Creator. By fighting against the Jews I am doing this at the Will of God."

Hitler's "Work of Art" is divided into two volumes. Excuses by his opponents or by his fans that they did not read it are fishy. Politicians on both sides picked from it whatever they needed. Radio stations broadcasted its content vehemently. Schools' evening meetings with the Hitler Youth, the SA, or the SS in attendance, were impossible without citations of the "Mein Kampf". Since 1933 District Attorneys and Judges followed the guidelines of "Mein Kampf" without any reservations whatsoever, and trivially interpreted such terms as "a

Citizen versus a Subject". Even the little ones started their readings about the Hitler's movement through the fable books which the parents received at their wedding from the Marriage Register's Office. A favorite saying, which on Monday mornings was put on display and tendered in Halls of each Faculty by the local Party Leaders taught: "Every man has his best advisors standing by, but a decision is made by one."

The second volume could not be finished in Landsberg due to a premature release of the prisoner home. This release created damage which was soon removed by the prohibition of Hitler's speeches after his first performance in freedom. The prohibition lasted two years. During that time an accounting sergeant and a business leader of the Party, Max Amann, was typing everything what his "employer" in his Villa on the Obersalzberg had dictated. For both it was the work of their lives. It was the "Mine Struggle", which in Germany was printed in ten million copies and translated into many languages of the world, including Russian and Chinese, and brought to the author a flat fifteen million marks, from which, until his violent death, he had used up half.[37]

HIS STRUGGLE, AN AMERICAN SUCCESS STORY

Whoever wants to do research on the cause of the outbreak of the Second World War, is advised to consider a fortune telling caricature printed at the conclusion of the Versailles Peace Treaty in the "Daily Herald". It shows two main perpetrators, U.S. President Wilson and French Premier Clemenceau leaving a marble building, and behind one of its columns an European baby standing naked and crying. Above the child's head is seen the inscription: "1940 CLASS" ("1940 A CALL TO ARMS"). President of the Federal Republic of Germany, Theodore Heuss, must had had similar feelings when in 1932 he wrote: "The birth place of the National Socialist movement was not Munich, but Versailles."

Hitler was in the fortress of Landsberg. The leadership of the Party was not sized by the theorist Rosenberg, the "Coffee Aunt" alias "Gossiper of the Party", but by the militant Ludendorff. His main theme was the "Slanderous Dictate of Versailles", and in May 1924, for his National Socialist Freedom Movement candidates, during the election to Parliament in May 1924, voted about two million Germans. Encouraged and stimulated by his wife, a neurology physician, Ludendorff switched to another theme, which he did not leave until the end of his days. It was: "The Rome and its struggle against coal and steel extremism". And all of that happened in Bavaria. Everything was rotting.

In the beginning of January 1925, the first significant move Hitler made after his discharge from the Landsberg's fortress, was a courtesy visit to the Bavarian Prime Minister, Held. This Catholic politician was glad to hear: "Your Excellency, the act of November 9 was my mistake. From now on I will help to strengthen the authority of the State. We are united in the fight against Marxism. And how about Ludendorff's struggle against the Church? I will put it straight: I have nothing to do with Ludendorff! No more!" With this Held was overjoyed: "The beast has been tamed."

The second significant move was the following visit to Ludendorff and its outcome: "What are your North German gentlemen talking about?" Hitler wanted to know. "Is the danger of extreme mining greater than the Jewish danger? Who are these ignorants in the North, these Messrs Wulle and von Graefe? To build up my movement I need Catholics of Bavaria as well as Protestants of Prussia." At this dictum Ludendorff tried to contra-argue, but got a reprieve: "Don't hit me with the cassocks of women and priests," retorted Hitler without clicking his heels. And that is how the two "Marchers of November 9th" parted.

Two weeks after this clarification Hitler called his most trusted men to the starting point of the November's riot, the Citizen's Brewery Cellar. Four thousand men came and in an overfilled Assembly Hall listened to him: "I will lead the movement myself," he declared. "No one will dictate to me!" During the two hours of Fuehrer's argumentation people climbed on tables, hugged each other and screamed until they were hoarse. The son of the people believing that he has been lost, has returned.

After the renewal of the Party, the "tamed beast" struck the prohibition of his speech in Bavaria, and soon the same followed in most of the other German regions. In 1928, the last region which lifted the prohibition, was Prussia.

Because the German economy has improved, it was not good for Hitler. Out of three million unemployed in 1923, thanks to foreign credits, two and half million people had jobs. However, Hitler didn't get confused. His instinct guided him correctly and he shared this with his cadres:

"My Dear Party Members, this is a short lived prosperity. Exploitation of Germans by a flood of Eastern Jews into our country is caused by the Versailles Treaty and its levying contributions which without any doubt will plunge all circles of our society into an economic misery. But through that we will get the power. Just wait!"

After that Hitler took a creative leave of absence and spent four years in Berchtesgaden. In 1929 the expected misery came almost overnight and it was started by the "Black Friday" on the Wall Street of New York. Then in a breathtaking advances, during the next four years, Hitler conquered first the State Chancery with the Parliament, and soon thereafter the Presidential Chair and the Armed Forces, and thus an unlimited power over the whole State, the German Reich.

The orator of masses, who once was sentenced to silence, assigned the Party work in Northern Germany to the land custodian (former Jesuit student and druggist) Gregor Strasser, for he had a lot to do with organizing the Party. Pretty soon he founded a Party within the Party - "Working Division of the North-Western German District Governor of the NSDAP." Especially in the Ruhr Basin (Valley) the people gathered under the swastika flag. There the people awoke politically because, in 1923, France entered the Basin under a pretext of providing telegraph poles, which were missing during the delivery. The loudest one in the Basin was Strasser's secretary Dr.Joseph Goebbels. As a Party member, this young man urged Hitler, living comfortably in Southern Germany, to render more peaceful actions: "I demand exclusion of the petty bourgeois, Adolf Hitler, from the NSDAP", and Strasser was happy. Hitler handled this storm in a glass of water with an easy hand. He called a Party conference to Bamberg. But most of the Northern Germans had neither the time nor the money for a long journey, so they didn't attend. Hitler explained everything to his people and thus convinced them. Almost all of the Southern Germans who came supported him. Defeated Goebbels noted in his diary as follows: "Oh, Lord, how little we have in common with those pigs down there. My inner stability has been shaken hard. I am only half a person."

Two weeks later, after Hitler guided kindly the unstable man Jupp Goebbels around Munich, he was a full person again and his scrupulously kept diary showed this: "I love him. I bow to this greatest one. To this political genius! We go out to eat and drink with enthusiasm."

Gregor Strasser could never forget the chameleonic posture of this man from Rhein. But Hitler applying the Roman rule "divide and govern", sent them both to Berlin where they could quarrel conclusively. This move commenced a racial struggle within the NSDAP.

48

It is obvious that this anti-Jewish spokesman of Germany, with his nativity odium, surrounded himself with men, who could show just as little as he could about the favorable evidence of their Aryan shining cleanliness. The Chief was not bothered with this by his followers and had the needed peace, particularly from the Jewish managed news media, which could not touch this sensitive subject in fear of getting its own throat cut, at least for a while. He thought that Jewish half-breeds are more intelligent and more willing to cooperate. But Goebbels started a battle and the Jewish grandmother of Heinrich Himmler, who was an Italian fruit-stand merchant, was drawn into it. In this way the competitive enterprise of the Storm Troopers SS (which Himmler was about to build up), was threatened with damage. Rosenberg - who appeared at that moment - intervened and stumbled upon Goebbels past, who in school was called a "Rabbi", and whose ancestors could be found among Holland's earlier Spanish Jews. The Party theorist from Estonia, Rosenberg, also made reference to Goebbels' Jewish Professor Gundolfinger, who graduated him from Heidelberg, and softly added: "The entire propaganda of Goebbels is, of course, Levantic. The question of racial origin makes Goebbels' position difficult, and I believe that we all should understand his situation." These high waves were levelled even more by another advisor of Hitler, a young lawyer from Munich, Hans Frank, at this time on an Arbitration Board, whose Jewish father was converted from Mosaism to Roman Catholicism in Bamberg. Ever since the end of the twenties, the Party discipline ruled in matters of origin, and an old Lueger's saying shined in its renewed form: "I will decide who is a Jew." Thus the term "Honorary Aryan" has been invented.

All this didn't point to an upward movement. At the Parliamentarian elections of 1928 the National Socialists received less than one million of the forty million votes, i.e. not even half the amount they had gotten four years earlier under Ludendorff.

In the hot summer of 1929, all these quiet times, which created opportunities for all kinds of personal teasing (stemming from the ancestral entanglements) came to an end, mainly because of a plan by a certain Owen D. Young from the "Chosen by God" the United States of America. He contributed to the German youth a burdening 110 billion marks, which had to be repaid within the next 59 years. To Mr. Young, thinking in the category of US dollars, this amount seemed to be manageable. This brilliant economic scientist did not mind that German workers in those days brought home only eleven marks per week in unemployment benefits.

The young generation, which did not start the First World War, had to pay for it with hunger (eating only turnips) and thus flocked in great numbers into the SA. Nothing was more natural: they came because Hitler beat the drum loudest at the "Reich's Committee for the German Plebiscite", in unison with the "German National People's Party" of Alfred Hugenberg (combatting the "Young's Plan" for reparations payment). A "Draft of the Law" against slavery of the German people was issued and started with this logical explanation: "The Reich's Government, in a solemn form, has to let the foreign powers know that the enforcement of war reparations by the Versailles Treaty stands in contradiction with the historical truth."

While four million hard working and over burdened people were signing the "Draft", the New York Stock Market crashed on the famous "Black Friday" of October 1929. About that time a young broker on the Wall Street, Curtis B. Dall, Roosevelt's son-in-law, four decades later explained how this could have happened: "The crash resulted from a greed for money. This operation was performed with recklessness, without any talent and energy. The destruction was monstrous. Actually speculation of the "Drop in Prices" (Baisse/ Slump Speculation) is not wrong, provided no criminal tactic is being used. In my opinion Ben's tactics weren't far from it. Until then I did not know that the greatest and fastest profit flows to the powerful bankers and creditors, when they sell shortly before the crash they created."[38]

After a few days, the deeply indebted Germans felt what just had happened. The suicide rate increased sharply and all of a sudden the masses of unemployed people or part time workers stood idle on the streets. These four-and-a-half million people, who were willing to work, got together to discuss what is happening. Then they turned either left to the Communism or right to the National Socialism. The Social Democratic Government of the State (called by Hitler "Carrying Out Government") disappeared without a sound and then on the political stage appeared Bruening, a politician of the Catholic Center. He instantly started a game with "emergency-regulations" but got no applause.

The unemployed mused and meditated in their work places or in the Storm Troopers' meeting halls, by mistake entering a wrong bar, or by a bare choice joined this or that movement in the game of life or death. The Communists' and National Socialists' combat troops, counted over 100 dead and 10,000 injured in their ranks. Almost a Civil War swept the country with turmoil in the assembly halls. Rocks, cudgels, chairs, and beer mugs were the main weapons. Nothing counted except a political conviction. The author remembers as he assisted home a new friend from school. "What is your father doing out there?" asked him my worried mother. "He plays a Communist", the response came out proudly from his six year old chest.

People were hungry. The lines in front of the employment offices grew. Policemen on horses hit people's heads who yelled "Bread! Bread!"

When a man had to choose between freedom and bread, he chose bread, especially when he had a family or wanted to establish one. This is how Hitler won the crowd. The SA troops were made up of desperate teenagers mustered to obey orders, who wanted to be patriots and to find in bars or restaurants a bowl of soup and eventually a friendly climate to stay in.

In a due course the Storm Troopers constructed barrack-like housing for themselves. Goering returned home from Swedish exile. Roehm returned from Bolivia and took over the leadership of the SA, and after a while few hundred-thousand men followed his commands. "When Adolf orders to be at the Victory Gate at 6 o'clock tomorrow morning, then we will be there!" Roehm thundered. All of that cost money. And the money came "from people you would least expect", said the Reich's Chancellor Bruening.

Hitler in his struggle against the Eastern Jews was supported financially then, as in the following years, by the New York's Western Jews who, up to this day, don't permit a burial of Eastern Jews in their cemeteries, even if they lived in New York through three generations.

"I never talked about this in public," Bruening wrote his friend Dr.Pechel, "but in the interest of Germany it might be necessary to reveal how the same bankers in the fall of 1930 searched for ways to influence American Ambassador Sakett against my government in favor of the Nazi Party."[39] Bruening even much later never "talked about this publicly", although he was a professor at some U.S.' university.

Early enough in the twenties, Mr.Warburg, a banker of Hamburg, advised Reich's Premier Ebert to stop the migration of Jews from the East. When a Wall Street messenger, who was about to bring money to Hitler, asked Warburg for an opinion, he laughed at him: "Hitler is a strong man and Germany needs him. By Jews, Hitler means the Galizian Jews, who pollute Germany since the war began. Jews of pure German origin he acknowledges and treats as equals. These Eastern Jews influence the Social Democratic Party and the Communist Party. He will get rid of them for sure. Not because they are Jews, but because they are Communists and Social Democrats."

In 1932, the SA alone cost about 180 million marks. With the other expenses of Party employees, election campaigns and airplane travels, the amount came to 300 million marks. About one sixth of this sum came from dues and donations of the Party members. At the end of 1933, a very well known Dutch Publishing House after a study of documents, issued a report about the shabbiest rest a few hundred million marks spent throughout the years. The report disclosed many names and soon after its publication it was sold out. Nobody then complained, but during the occupation of Holland all documents were destroyed and the publisher Schoup found his death in the hands of GESTAPO (Secret Police of the Reich).

The report showed that at one time ten million dollars and another time fifteen million were transferred by the Bank House Mendelsohn & Co. in Amsterdam. With similar sums operated other Houses: Kuhn, Loeb & Co.; J. Morgan & Co.; and Samuel & Samuel, which were not restricted by a fixed playing field.[40] The Swissman, René Sonderegger (Severin Reinhard) in his book "Spanish Summer" published in Suisse, 1948, had disclosed the messenger who was delivering monies to Hitler: "The man, whom bankers sent to Germany to test the question of a German revolution, was the young Warburg. He was smart, educated, possessed good manners, and had mastered German language perfectly when he worked several years in the Bank House of his uncle in Hamburg. Warburg, equipped with the highest regards, found himself in Germany and soon met Hitler in Munich. Hitler was very pleased to have shaken hands with this rich American."

And then, H.R. Knickerbocker, world widely known American journalist, forecasted in his 1932 book "Deutschland So oder So?" ("Germany like this or like that"), exactly this: "The American investments in the European Continent are the best, but only on the battle fields."

Of special benefit was also Sir Henry Deterding of the Royal Dutsch Shell Co. whose money came through the Samuel & Samuel of London. Even after Hitler's seizure of power this oilman continued to spend money on Hitler. A hint of this may be found in the "Hamburger Fremdenblatt" ("Foreign Newspaper of Hamburg") of February 15, 1939: "In 1937 ten million guldens were transferred over". A few days before this info appeared, Sir Henry expired in St. Moritz and was buried ceremonially in Dobbin/ Mecklenburg. Country Bishop Schultz, a Party Member from Schwerin, honored him with this passage: "With the boldness of Napoleon, with the spiritual power of Cromwell, he had fought against the spirit of destruction and degradation of all human rights by the deeds of the World's Bolshevism. For him the prosperity of Germany was a prerequisite to saving the world from Communism."

The founder of Shell, Marcus Samuel, a Jew, was a supporter of Sir Henry Deterding. Once he collected shells in East Asia and in London he turned them into money, hence he gave his company a "Shell" logo and brand name. During the oil boom of the First World War from Samuel's company emerged a nobleman, Bearsted, whose "Shell of Baku" in 1918 was expropriated by the Soviets without any compensation. In Hitler's Third Reich the rights of the Russian oil companies were revoked, so the Samuel's Shell raced to fill in the gap.

Heinrich Mann, a writer and a brother of Thomas Mann, shortly before the end of the Second World War was urged to say a word to Berliners: "Now you can know how it really was. Violence was the main obstacle to your revolution. Several Trust Magnates held your social movement back by using it against the nations. Their Commander Hitler was un-German, just like them."[41] Heinrich Mann came in to speak right from New York.

The "Neue Zuricher Zeitung" ("New Zurich's Newspaper") No.758 of May 2, 1946, wrote: "When Schacht during the Nuremberg Trial talked about the attitude of foreign powers toward the Nazi Government, and the help they conferred upon it, the court decided that these things had nothing to do with the trial matter and therefore were inadmissible."

Either one, Hitler or Gregor Strasser, Leader of the Organization of the Reich's Office, accepted revenues from the large Jewish banks. The Chief of the News Services of the Reich's Army, General von Bredow, knew about this very well. On June 30, 1934, during the "Night of the Long Knives", von Bredow and Gregor lost their lives, too. Knowledge is not only power, but it can also be dangerous.

Dr.Abegg, Chief of the Prussian Police from 1926 until 1932, fled to Switzerland with documents pertaining Hitler's foreign financing and in Zurich built the famous "Abegg Archives". He informed the public about Hitler's documents carrier: "Documents, concerning the secret funds, were located in a furniture truck. In between 1929-1932 the truck constantly rolled back and forth between Berlin and Munich. This way the truck could neither be taken by the Prussian nor by the Bavarian police."

During the 1930 Parliamentary (Reichstag) election, the National Socialists won six million four hundred one thousand two hundred ten (6,401,210) votes. The 107 political representatives of this Party (instead of the usual twelve) moved into the Reichstag, all of them, of course, in brown shirts. Authorities in power agitated people to vote efficiently, for as democrats, they wanted to know what was going on. Finally they got it: in July 1932 almost 14 million Germans voted for Hitler, and his Party by far was the biggest. To the presidency over the Reichstag (called by the National Socialists "Young's - Parliament") was raised Hermann Goering.

The restlessly walking preacher of the German Movement (who more than often switched from his fast Mercedes limousine to an even faster Party owned airplane), only twice in those years of successes experienced misfortunes. Both times they were personal ones - of course - with political overtones.

Alois, Hitler's older half brother, left home early and caused a lot of mischief. He was jailed for theft and bigamy. Among other things he "produced" a son in Ireland who, known as William Patrick Hitler, behaved as if he was struck by a lightning. To this sprout of kinship, the regular work was a contrary thing and so he rebelled: "Supposedly I should earn 125 marks, but on this starvation pay I can neither live nor die." For this reason in 1930 nothing seemed to be more natural to him than to blackmail his wealthy uncle, Adolf, using the Jewish origin of his grandfather as a tool. He was hinting that "in connection with some newspaper statement, there would be a great deal of interest in making certain facts public regarding history of our family."[42]

So, an attorney was needed and at hand was the cunning Hans Frank, who when called, sat across from the Fuehrer in his nine bedroom parlor suite at the Prinzregentenplatz in Munich, and in anticipation of something good listened: "It is a disgusting and blackmailing story," started Hitler. "Please, look, my Dear Frank, you know who is your Honorable Father, also a Jew but a German through many generations, and not one of those Galizia's caftan wearers. Do you know how it is, when one can't see clearly anymore? Who is my grandfather, father of my father? There are the Frankenbergers, enormously rich Jews, who paid for his up-bringing for fourteen years, when no one else wanted to do so. They are a nice pack. Take this story and get this blackmailer off my back." Hitler sat up straight and continued: "My Dear Comrade Frank, the matter of your origins someone may bring-up, too. I promise you, I do have means and I will help you with this, alike I helped my friend Hoffmann." Then he jumped out of the chair and opened a drawer. "Here, take this", and handed the young attorney a bundle of money. "Go on travelling right away, and tell me when you will need more. I have to get this matter off my back!"

Thus, in 1930, Hans Frank became a searcher of Hitler's ancestors, spending more time in Austria than in the Old Country. Vienna, Graz and the memorable forest were his favorable destinations. The fact that on each visit the Austrian authorities treated the archives searcher as an unwanted foreigner, bothered Frank very little. Finally he clarified everything just the way it should be. During the war, places of Hitler's deep roaming in the forest land, gave way to important military training grounds. This permitted Hitler to breathe more easily.

On the same occasion many documents disappeared pertaining the origin of Frank. About this, in face of death in his Nuremberg cell, he had written: "There was also a correspondence between Frankenbergers and Hitler's grandmother, which lasted for years. The general tendency of all concerned parties was to silence the very public opinion that Schicklgruber's illegitimate child was under care of Frankenberger's alimony obligations. I have to say that it cannot be excluded that Hitler's father was a half Jew, born from Schicklsgruber's close relationship with a Jew of Graz. According to this, Hitler was a quarter-Jew. This explains his hatred towards Jews, which stems from the blood related anti-kinsmen psychosis." Since these shady deals became publicly known all over Austria, in the Austrian Supreme Court (within the Reich's Court after annexation), a position was established with Frank as the Attorney of State. This position permitted him to take care of Child Support Applications by Aryans who gave birth to illegitimate children. In order to receive child support, it was sufficient for a mother to state that she only assumes that the fathering was done by a Jew.

The other misfortune in those years was of a similar kind: In Linz, when Hitler on a cloudy December day 1907 accompanied his mother to her grave, his older half sister Angela followed in a horse buggy. She was in her last days of pregnancy. The happy event of birth took place within the first few days of New Year, and afterwards her lovely girl developed well to the excitement of all. She was named Angela, for short, Geli. Her mother, a young widow, was an upright person and in Vienna made a living as a cook in a Jewish community kitchen. After her brother made money through his book "Mein Kampf", he hired her as a housekeeper in his "Haus Wachenfeld" ("Home of Weapons Field") on the Obersalzberg in Berchtesgaden. The pretty college graduate, Geli, who wanted to study music, moved into uncle's Adolf big apartment at Prinzregentenplatz in Munich. Things went along quite naturally until late Summer 1931, when Geli found herself pregnant. For that she was very happy. But uncle Adolf suggested abortion. This caused among them a big quarrel. One beautiful September morning, just as the housekeeper went out to buy bread, some thoughts overwhelmed Geli: "You have learned too much about Mendel. About hereditary laws and about hereditary sciences. You are scared that your Jewish blood will be at work and a bowlegged child with curly hair will be born. This is rubbish, I say, a rubbish thought, I say" ... and a shot was heard - Geli died from a bullet to her heart.

Hitler received the gruesome message by a phone call from Hess' secretary in a bar while on a car trip to Nuremberg with his close friend Hoffman, a photographer, and this was unbelievable to him.

About noon he was back in Munich completely broken and announced that he will commit a suicide, but the attending Hess took the pistol away from his hand. Hitler threatened to abandon everything, but the Party members who were weeping with him, advised not to do so and encouraged him not to give in to the cruel fate. Dr.Guertner, the powerful Bavarian Justice, took upon himself the task of finding the murderer, but concluded that it was a suicide. The same Dr.Guertner became the Secretary of Justice of the III Reich. Hitler also had his own Confession Pastor, Father Stempfle, who was an enemy of the Jews. On June 30, 1934, during the "Night of Long Knives", he was liquidated with Hitler crying: "They murdered my poor Father Stempfle!" Shortly after that two perpetrators were rewarded with promotions. The Catholic Church does not bury suicide victims in the holy soil. But the Priest, who buried Geli in the Vienna cemetery did, thus letting a doubtful Otto Strasser know that: "Out of this single fact, that I gave her a Christian burial, you should draw a proper conclusion."[43] The Hitler researcher, Konrad Heiden, in introduction to 1936 Hitler's biography wrote: "The statement has to be changed only at one point for the death of Angela Raubal to me doesn't seem to be a suicide anymore" (and in 1944, on page 388 he added: "Father Stempfle knew that Geli's unborn child was fathered by her uncle.") In 1969, about this point commented suspiciously short another Hitler's biographer, Allan Bullock: "It is best to keep the case of Geli Raubal a secret."

These types of contradictions in Fuehrer's life did not hinder American money from streaming in. For one million marks the Party was able to purchase its "Brown House" in Munich. Only two of over forty parties in the German Reich won considerable number of members and votes: the NSDAP and the Communist Party of Germany, the latter financed by the East.

No capitalist likes to lose an effortlessly snatched money, but the Wall Street by investing billions of dollars into Germany was acting logically, for it put millions as a security against the communist expropriations. The long lasting antagonism between Western and Eastern Jews did not play a decisive role here. The calculation was simple: if Hitler goes to war, which is not improbable, certainly the Wall Street will not become poorer.

Hitler proclaimed many times and openly that: "The American capital investments in Germany will be more secure under a National Socialist Government than under any other government." Why then Bruening, the Chancellor of the Reich was doubtful?

The Party Leader flew by plane and delivered speeches; rode in motorized colonnades across the country and also delivered speeches: "Don't lose your faith in the future of our people, of our Great Fatherland, in our victory in the struggle for our just cause which serves them both. As long as I live, I belong to you and you belong to me!"

This TACTIC worked everywhere and the British Military Attaché, Thorne, wrote to his Ambassador in Berlin: "All their Cadres combined feel, that the Nazi Movement is the best available ONE for keeping the youth of this country in discipline. This will also keep them off the road to communism."

The slogan "JEWS ARE OUR BAD LUCK" dominated all the speeches rendered before industrialists, Party leaders on the right and on the left, in market places and in halls, in many variations everywhere, dependent on the audience. Sometimes thousands of people were waiting in the rain, still at three o'clock in the morning for the late arrival of the Fuehrer's airplane, which was late due to bad weather conditions, but at last he came. And they saw him, and listened to

Adolf Hitler thanks his first propagandist Dr. Joseph Goebbels who significantly contributed to Hitler's success in seizing power and later he prolonged the war. He was born to Spanish-Dutch Jews and in school was called "Rabbi". His Jewish mother-in-law Friedlander lived in his household until the end of the war.

Adolf Hitler dankt seinem ersten Propagandisten Dr. Joseph Goebbels, der zunächst entscheidend zur Machtübernahme und später ebenso entscheidend zur Verlängerung des Krieges beitrug. Von spanisch- holländischen Juden abstammend, in der Schule «Rabbi» gerufen, lebte in seinem Haushalt bis Kriegsende seine jüdische Schwiegermutter Friedlander.

Dr. Hans Frank, Hitler's Attorney at Law, son of Jewish lawyer from Bamberg. During the Second World War of what was left of Poland, he made it "free of Jews". At the Nuremberg Reich's Party Day in 1933 he announced: "The Jewish question can only be solved by establishing a Jewish State."

Dr. Hans Frank, der Rechtsanwalt Hitlers, Sohn eines jüdischen Bamberger Anwalts, machte während des zweiten Weltkrieges das restliche Polen «judenfrei». Auf dem Nürnberger Reichsparteitag von 1933 verkündete dieser Jurist: «Die Judenfrage ist rechtlich nur dadurch zu lösen, class man an die Frage eines jüdischen Staates herangeht.»

Father of Reinhard Heydrich, the "Man of the Final Solution", was a Jewish musician. In Riemann's Music Dictionary he is listed as "Heydrich, Bruno, actually Suess." Another son of this Bruno-Heydrich was not accepted by a student body, which was concerned with Aryan origin of its members, but not his "Jewish Ponims" ("Jewish Pantomime" - a Jewish gesture).

Der Vater von Hitlers «Endlöser» Reinhard Heydrich, ein jüdischer Musiker, der in Riemanns Musiklexikon als «Heydrich, Bruno, eigentlich Süss» erscheint. Ein anderer Sohn dieses Bruno Heydrich wurde von einer studentischen Verbindung, die den Arier-Paragraphen hochhielt, seines «jüdischen Ponims» wegen nicht aufgenommen.

their idol who was rescuing them from their humiliation and poverty.

And the Jews made all of this easy for the "Speaker of Masses". They also talked about the terrible things, including gassing: "Let the gas sneak into the playroom of their children, so that they can slowly expire along with their dolls. We wish that the wives of Church Committee men and of Chief Editors, the mothers of Sculptors and sisters of Bankers, all them together find a bitter and agonizing death. Whoever leaves this 'Fatherland' in the lurch, will be blessed." (44)

Fighting all of this with no holds barren, but mostly through the magazine "Die Weltbuehne" ("Worldstage"), was an Eastern Jew, Tucholsky, under aliases Ignaz Wrobel, Kaspar Hauser, Theobald Tiger, and Peter Panter.

Before 1933, the Jewish population in Germany was about one percent. Over 50 percent of the news media, movie industry and banking operations were in Jewish hands. In Berlin 55 percent of lawyers and 52 percent of physicians were Jewish. 15 Jews controlled 718 positions on the Boards of Directors.

Foreigners who visited Berlin and experienced life only at the Kudamm (Road Corner - popular tourist street in Berlin), or other nightly excitements, with delight talked or wrote about the "golden twenties", for they could not find there the unemployed, the hungry or part time workers.

In 1930, a Western Jew, Stern, who was best known as the Lord Rothermere, a British newspaper magnate, and a brother of another newspaper magnate Lord Northcliffe, judged the situation in this way: "When we will take a closer look at the transition of the political power to National Socialists, we will find, that it has many advantages. First of all it erects a strong barrier against Bolshevism. In Germany it eliminates the serious danger of Soviets' advances against European civilization and their win of an invincible position in the strategic center of Europe."

In his book, published in 1939, Stern-Rothermere stated: "Hitler suffered due to the incompetence of his ruling men. He found it offensive that members of a foreign race could conduct business in Germany or Austria excellently, while his own countrymen starved in poverty."

Emigres in their "Paris' Daily Paper" reported that the German Jews bargained with the "Brown House" in Munich, about setting up special Jewish formations within the SA - for nothing is more popular than success.

SOCIALISTS LEAVE THE N.S.D.A.P.

Individuals and the entire social groups, obviously, are expecting too much from the uneasy coupling of Nationalism with Socialism.

Furthermore, Hitler, before the Economists in Hamburg, in Ruhr Basin or the unemployed people in the Sport's Palace in Berlin; or before the indebted farmers of Mecklenburg, spoke not about the promises but about the future plans of development.

The confusion created by Hitler's statements regarding Socialism and the so called "agreements" with the Jewish financiers, was evident everywhere.

Section 17th of the Party's Program provides for 'non-pecuniary expropriation of land.' Hitler explained before the doubting peasants that: "Because the roots of NSDAP stem in the private ownership of land, from which NSDAP developed itself, the phrase 'none pecuniary expropriation' only has an application to cases where the land was not legally acquired, or in people's view is improperly managed. Then, if a need be, it should be expropriated. First and foremost this was directed towards the Jewish land speculators."

When someone requested Mr.Goebbels to explain what the Socialism means, he responded tangibly, but with a Levantic philosophy: "The National Socialism is not yet fully defined, but in the stage of creation. It is still modified and for this reason it can not be totally embraced. The National Socialism has simplified the German thinking." Corresponding to this were the conjectures of foes within the socialist camp: "In the beginning the inflexible Adolf Hitler was acting decently. Today, he is only a creature of the big industry. Does anybody really think that the iron and coal magnates would give away their mighty pecunia to the Union whose goal is to expropriate them and later on to honor Teutonic God by hanging them on the nearest street lamp?"

Also Mr.Tucholsky, who wrote under many pseudonyms, seemed to be in a great despair: "So, this is internal politics? No, it is not what you think. A couple of prisons, a dose of brutality against the Jews, against a handful of Republicans, a curtailment of the State Banner, a prohibition of the German Communist Party - it is nothing else."

Just recently immigrated to the U.S., Albert Einstein, saw the whole thing and the Wall Street's financial support not particularly bad: "In the National Socialist movement I see only a temporary consequence of the currently critical situation as an illness of a new born Republic (Inset: Soviet Weimer Republic). Solidarity of the Jews is always appropriate, but a specific reaction regarding the election results is unnecessary."[45]

The former Justice Minister of the State, Otto Landsberg and a member of the German Socialist Party, calmed himself and others about what is to be expected: "You are still an unexperienced colleagues who overestimate the danger which comes from those Jewish baiters. Personally, I saw such anti-Semitic sentiments flowing in and out. In the eighties, in my home city of Ostrowo (Russia's Poland), those sentiments were strong, and my brother in a College suffered there a lot. When a few years later I visited the same College, these sentiments weren't there any more. It would be wrong to treat such baiters seriously."

And the Prussian Premier Braun, also from the G.S.P., described the overall confusion, which everyone ascribed to Hitler, as follows: "This prototype of a political adventurism, which through the filthy golden well of the rotten demagogic agitation of all the desperados and hope-losers, as well as of the familiar circles of the capitalistic profiteers, of a reactionists conviction lacking judgement about today's 'State of the People', with the enemy's deadly opposition - on how to ruin it, despite of all that it has created, is a nebulous Third Reich which must be won, as Hitler promised to all citizens on everything that they wish, and at any cost of its various components."

In May 1930, the younger brother of Dr.Gregor Strasser, Otto, in consideration of the substantially unsupportive capital, wanted to know what really was the position of socialists in the NSDAP. The well known pact between Hitler and the mighty Economic and Industrial powers had bothered him, as well as Gregor and many others. By then he published the "Letters of National Socialism" which made his position in the Party strong, and his decisive discussion with Hitler in presence of his brother Gregor in Berlin's "Hotel Sanssouci" made it even stronger. Regardless of this, Dr.Strasser's worries did not diminish, hence he recalled the discussion not too enthusiastically.

Hitler's opinion about the tenets of socialism was clear: "Look, dear Party Comrade Strasser, an owner of a factory depends on the production means and his employees' eagerness to work. When they go on strike then his so called 'property', becomes completely worthless. Besides, on what grounds are these workers demanding to take over the property or its management?" And then Hitler continued furiously: "Look, most of the workers want nothing more than bread and entertainment as they have no interest in great ideals, so for this reason we cannot really count on winning them over in considerable numbers. We need to select the new 'GENTLEMENSHIFT' which will be driven not by somebody's compassionate morass, but specifically by mustering up superb racial basis. Such a rule without any conditions attached thereto, will be preserved and secured by a massive support."

After this dictum Strasser, a former member of the German Socialist Party, said to his boss with all the courage: "Honorable Hitler, if you will uphold the capitalistic system, then you cannot talk about socialism! Then our Party's adherents will be socialist in the first place and then they will act accordingly with the Party's program which particularly promotes socialization of the corporate businesses." To this the recalcitrant Strasser got a reply: "Your interpretation of socialism is wrong for it does not mean that these businesses must be socialized nor that they can be socialized, specifically if it were to be done not for a benefit of the Nation. So far this has not been done, otherwise a crime would have been committed and the economy disarrayed. In reality, for the sound economy, there is only one solution: a responsibility lifted up and an authority elevated down."

After this explanation Hitler hastily produced a note and passed it to the Governor of Berlin Joseph Goebbels with an order: "Otto Strasser and his associates must be thrown out from the Party in a disgrace. As long as I will govern the NSDAP, it will not be a disputant club of literates without roots or of chaotic Salon-Bolsheviks. It was not created in order to doctrinate political fools or the wandering birds."[46]

Strasser, who did not find socialism in the NSDAP, went under a different banner. Its proclamation read: "Socialists, leave the NSDAP!" and he released his rage over the "Oriental Sultanate of Hitler" freely: "We find ourselves in opposition to the 25 Sections of the National Socialist Party Program, which are a part of our washed out socialist formulas and their weakest aberrations which they took from the socialistic precepts, in the process offending the spirit of the National Socialist Program. Thus now, with relentless consequences, came to light the betrayal by the NSDAP of its basic principles!"

To the socialist opposition, together with Otto Strasser, went several editors and half of the Party's newspapers, various leaders of the Hitler's Youth movement, a couple of Party functionaires and finally some provincial and state officials, all of which later were called the "Black Front". But the majority of Party comrades stayed faithful to the Fuehrer and brother Gregor during the next two years.

Hitler, now with big money, stormed forward from one success to another. Otto Strasser with the "people of the left on his right", in his further political life was homeless and unlucky: after Hitler's seizure of power, his closest Jewish friend Mahr, in exile in Prague, who was drafting and smuggling leaflets to the Reich, disappointed him once again. Mahr, a skilled cooperative, was active at the first front line with Himmler's SS and was guided by soon to be promoted Heydrich (the three quarter Jew) of the racist Elitary Order (Society), but finally was arrested by the Czechoslovak police and put behind bars for one year. The same fate met another Jewish agent of the SS by the name of Pollak, who was "sniffing" among the immigrants. In a due time it also came to a hunt for the Ex-Nationalist Strasser from one country to another, and as far as Canada, where during the war he found asylum. In the middle fifties, ten years after the war, this straight forward fighter for Hitler was once again disappointed, because his supporters of the Federal Republic of Germany did not allow him to enter his "Fatherland" where after subduing many obstacles on his way home, he was rebuked and got into some trouble. When Strasser "whistled", then all the Judges of the Republic's Court in Karslruhe, mostly former Party Comrades, pointed their fingers at him as the one for whose head Hitler designated a one million mark reward: "His support of then just created NSDAP was more significant than his later opposition to it"[47] - so turns the World.

Into the "Help Prisoners" office of the SA, bursted in a "Pig Snout", a very well known pillar of brawls, and with his hanging lips and articulate and limited words, he reported to a noble Miss Jolande von Pescatore sitting behind a typewriter: "Blondi, Blondi, we are sunk in the bucket. Fuehrer bought a Mercedes for 40 million, so the SA has a crackling in the soup." The SA rebelled and the connection with Otto Strasser was broken, as with his speeches and news articles unmistakably, too.

The highest Commander of the SA Pfeffer von Salomon and the Chief of Berlin's SA Stennes, previously a Commandant of the Police, hit the Party's table, dialed on the telephone Munich central, and called the "Big Shot" again. And then from the other side came a proper grid of sounds: "This is Dr.Goebbels' Guard. The Governorship of Berlin was taken from Himmler's SS by attacking SA-men, that is what must be noted. The furniture was thrown to a bog. And the SS-men had blood on their bottoms - what is learned is learned."

Stennes quickly decided to deprive his Fuehrer, Hitler, of power completely, and the cry: "Adolf betrayed us Proletarians!" came out of all Berlin's SA fighters lips. With their flattering Swastika Jacks, the SA groups on both sides of the River Elbe converged on Stennes, for everyone knew that he was the Head of Conspiracy.

In Mark Brandeburg, Mecklenburg, Pommern and Schlesien, the Party's "Help Troops for Hitler" did not go through the fire. No one in these ranks sang the marching song, as it was during the days when city dwellers were lured to their windows by:

> "Hitler is our Fuehrer,
> Him not tempts the Golden Calf,
> That from the Jewish thrones
> To his feet rolls:
> That from the Jewish thro-hones
> To his Fuefeet rolls."
> ("Hitler ist unser Fuehrer,
> ihn lockt nich goldener Sold,
> der von den juedischen Thronen
> vor seine Fuesse rollt:
> der von den juedischen Throhonen
> vor seine Fuehuesse rollt.")

A popular melody to this debatable text was taken from the communists.

At that time safes of the SA were empty. And it just happened that on a short notice Hitler came from Munich in a fury. He went from bar to bar, promised money, posts, Parliamentary seats and a quick victory.

The SA finally stopped yelling and got rid of its golden blessings with a manly composure behind it. With Pfeffer von Salomon and Stennes, the main components of the socialist thought were removed and put to rest in the Gestapo's detention camp (Pfeffer), and in a far away China (where Stennes found a safe haven as an advisor).

At last came gold and Roehm, with "free gonorrhea which Nature provided for him as a punishment for his life" and who, since he was wounded in his face, felt like a man. Any way - lauded Hitler - the SA is "not a moralistic institution for an education of highly born daughters."

In 1932, on his brother's and on the Stennes' path trudged also Gregor Strasser, up to this date a Leader of the State's Builders, and a true Leader of the Party in Northern Germany, second in importance to the movement. "This course", wrote the man who through constant frictions and stresses became a diabetic, "I can not opinion well and I am not responsible for."

The would be Nobel Prize Laureate Carl von Osietzky in his magazine "Die Weltbuehne" ("World Stage") on January 1933, page one, cheerfuly printed: "At the beginning of 1932, the Nazi dictature stood in front of the door. At year's end Hitler's Party would be jolted by a violent crisis if the long knives (next year) were put in sheaths and only Fuehrer's ears were visible."

In Berlin's "Emperor's House" Hitler read Strasser's heavy letter and roared - as usually - suicidally: "If the Party disintegrates I will put an end to my life within 3 minutes."

While the entire world was calling and looking for him, Gregor Strasser took a back seat and peacefully with a Berliner's mannerism drank a little "Graecum" one after another without any politicking peers in sight. One evening, in order to relax, he got on the express train to Munich and the next morning drove with his family by car to the Southern Tirol, then occupied by Italy (which against strong opposition, Hitler left alone). Thanks to many Party Comrades the Gregor Strasser's "anti-capitalistic nostalgia" had returned. It also returned to Strasser's intimate enemy Dr.Goebbels, later Minister of the State Propaganda. His long lasting personal referee von Oven, who in Goebbels' Schwanenwerder Villa due to urgent nightly reports lived next to his bedroom, in 1944 at a reception got a reprimand from the Saxonian Governor Mutschmann: "Even though you have not gotten a medal yet, My Dear, at an opportunity like today's, at least you have to wear your Party's insignia." "I cannot do that Your Honor", Wilfred von Oven responded - "In May 1932, I resigned from the NSDAP."[48]

REVOLUTIONLESS ASSUMPTION OF POWER WITH TORCHES

To the surprise of all, the National Socialists during the Imperial Elections of November 1932, lost more than two million votes. The Communists gained three quarter of a million votes. The raising awareness of Hitler's alliance with the big powers, as it was explained by Strasser and Stennes, had born fruit. The NSDAP was falling apart. People were leaving the Party everywhere. In Berlin the SA -men, brought-up to an esteem, stood arm in arm with communists during the strike of Transportation Workers. They worked well with each other. Together they begged passerbys even for small donations in order to establish "A Fund for the Striking National Socialist Factory Opposing Cells" or for the "Opposing Revolutionary Labor Union." Chief of Staff Roehm wrote: "Lovely Petty Bourgeois, powerlessness is now gone. I do claim that Communists' Red Frontline Combat Bands are very good soldiers."

Hitler paced back and forth with long steps for several days within the Halls of Berlin's "Kaiserhof" ("Court of the Emperor") and around. He moved on to travel from region to region demanding endurance, loyalty and wasn't stingy with promises. The following month, despite of all these efforts, he lost almost half of the votes in the Thuering's election. An end of the NSDAP was in sight and the District Leader Goebbels noted: "The worry about money makes it impossible to work with a clear mind towards the goal. One feels so bad inside, that is longing for nothing less than abandonment of this entire operation for a couple of weeks."

Chancellor Bruening was replaced by the Politician von Papen, but he also failed. Then the Army General Schleicher took the lead but literally nobody wanted to obey this man, not even the Army, which half a year later didn't react when the SS-men shot him behind his desk.

Hitler's Party neither paid its employees nor its debts. The SA -men banged with collecting cans on the streets of large cities like Berlin, Cologne, Duesseldorf or Essen. They were happy for every penny they could get. The insulted big factory-owners of Rhein or of the Ruhr's Basin looked out of their office windows and saw how their hopes were disappearing, alike Hitler's. "Mayday! Mayday!" phones of the economic leaders ringed everywhere as they were seeking advice. In the evening of January 3, 1933, Gregor Strasser came back to Berlin from his Tirol's vacation in a healthy condition and with a determination of taking over the helm of the Party masses and of the impoverished NSDAP. In this state of affairs Hitler took a night express-train going West. In Bonn, his driver Schreck was waiting for him with a Mercedes and at the crack of dawn and through a rising fog they drove to a country side. Shortly thereafter they ate breakfast at a house of the War Comrade Dressen in Bad Godesberg. Next they drove to Duesseldorf, turned to Koeln and arrived there before noon. This was a historic late mid-morning of January 4, 1933, when they stopped in front of a luxurious Villa at the outskirts of Koeln. The owner of the Villa, Baron von Schroeder (the "le riche financier d'origine israélite" as Otto Strasser wrote in Paris), was waiting at the stairs.[49] He was ennobled in 1868 by the Prussian King and was a co-owner of big banks in Germany, as well as in the World of Anglo-Saxons. His family pursued money business for generations. This banker, who was known to have connections with the American Concern I.T.T., asked the Honorable Guest Hitler to leave his companions Himmler and Hess in a side room, and then guided him to a second floor. There, the former Chancellor of the Reich was waiting, currently the most trusted man of the President von Hindenburg, who in the opinion of many was in a stage of senility.

Von Papen, being festively dressed, got up and in with firm steps approached the future Fuehrer of the German Reich. And before the time came to have lunch, these Gentlemen agreed in unison that Hitler will be Reich's Chancellor; von Papen Vice-Chancellor and Hugenberg and other conservatives, who were sympathizing with the money-givers, were to take over ministerial positions. For similar positions from among the National Socialists, as a reward, Hitler chose his co-strugglers Goering and Frick.

The "Rich Financier of Israeli Origin," Baron von Schroeder, who pretty soon wore an uniform of the SS-General, after the War recalled before the International Military Court in Nuremberg: "When the NSDAP on November 6, 1932 suffered a set-back and passed its zenith, in the interest of economy and in fear of Bolshevism, its support was urgent and paramount."

This meeting could not remain secret despite of all the precautions. The newspapers from January 5th on, reported about it with a great glamour. So Goebbels stopped feeling "bad inside" and no longer wanted to abandon the entire operation. To the contrary he said: "Finances suddenly improved. If this act succeeds, we are not far from power."

Next, Hitler went to a small county called Lippe, where 90,000 citizens had to vote. Goebbels followed him and set foot in the Castle of Baron von Oeynhausen, converted for this occasion into headquarters. There they both competed with their speeches. They invited farmers to almost all the village bars. Money were not important anymore. Ten days later they won about twenty percent of the votes. Having gotten such a good result, they started again making a big noise which they branded as the "Signal Lippe" ("A lip signal").

Since that moment, exactly two weeks have elapsed: On an early Monday afternoon, January 30, 1933, a man, who had his Austrian Identification Documents returned to Austria, was announced to be legally the Chancellor of the German Nation. In effect, deep into the night, twelve lines of brown and field-gray colonnades were passing in front of the Chancery of the Reich with burning torches. On its balcony, the forty-three year old Chancellor with his glancing eyes looked onto the sea of lights. Next to him stood Hindenburg, resting on his cane. Goebbels, a cheerfully natured Rheinlander, situated opposite the "Kaiserhof", celebrated the event as if it was a "Carnival of Koeln".

Carl von Ossietzky, who soon died in a concentration camp, was very wrong when on page one of his "Weltbuehne" dated January 31, 1933, he stated: "Every German can be the Reich's Chancellor! So the heads of multi-children families do not miss your chance!" As the Germans, so the World would not be able to cope with such a perspective. Is it not that simple?

First everyone tried to make a good impression, except the SA, which was after facts. Hitler prayed over the radio: "Let the Will of the Almighty God guide our Work. Let Him shape our will. Let Him bless our farsighted understanding so that our people will trust us." More and more often the word "Amen" concluded his performances. Public warnings towards the SA made by the Chancellor of the Reich were clear: "I am ordering you the strongest and the blindest discipline. Whoever by a single action will try to disturb our way of business life, will be treated as one who is acting consciously against our National Government."

The Fuehrer's Representative, Hess, in a circular to all Party members, prohibited extravagances of any kind against Jewish Department Stores in Karstadt, in Tietz and so forth. The same order was applied to Jewish banks like Deutsche, Dresdner or Commerz Bank. The State Secret Police (GESTAPO), which previously was subordinate to the so called "Brother-in-Law" Goering, dissolved all the concentration camps under management of the SA. The second largest Criminal Court of Stettin had sentenced the manager of a camp to thirteen years of imprisonment for mistreatment of inmates. Thanks to a special patronage by Berlin's SA Leader, Count Helldorf, for a certain Herschel Steinschneider alias Eric Jan van Hamussen (an ardent Party member and a Jew from Vienna), has been established within the Party a position of "Clairvoyant". Due to his tricks, as if by an educated magician, and his propensities, fantasies and foreseeing, he became famous and many people were coming to him for an advice. The "Voelkische Beobachter" ("People's Observer") presented him to its readers with large photos.[50]

The former, now retired Premier of Prussia, Carl Severing, who many times prohibited the SA from wearing brown-shirts, had nothing else to do but take his dog out on daily walks under the blooming trees' canopy of Bielefeld, while his Social Democratic Party Chairman Loebe was declaring allegiance to the new order: "Stay united behind the Government of the Reich".

President of the Prussian Council of the State and Mayor of Cologne, Konrad Adenauer, and a future Chancellor of the Federal Republic of Germany, did not want to jeopardize "the successfully materialized National Revolution and the accepted Government for we appreciate the struggle against Marxism."

Also the future President of the F.R.G., Theodor Heuss (1949), who empowered Hitler's Government with two-thirds of the Parliamentary Delegates, proclaimed laws to make contracts and to change the Constitution without the vote of Parliament in accordance with the maxim: "Do as you like."

Then it had to happen. A Dutch communist set the "Chatter Shack" (Reich's Parliament) on fire. Just after work, as Hitler and Goebbels were sitting and listening to Wagner's recordings, the "Bude" went up in flames. It excited them both so they said: "This is the sign. It's the signal of the light. It begins." But nothing began. Only leading Communists and Jews from the leftist Parties, at night, were taken out of their beds and the morning brought an ad hoc issued "Ordinance for Protection of the People and State", which posthumously gave prisoners the right to seek Justice.

When the seizure of power had taken place, the German Jews did their best to reciprocate: "We members of the National German-Jewish Union, established in 1921, who in time of war and peace put the welfare of the German people and of our common Fatherland first before our own, are strongly attached to both. That's why we have welcomed the change of power in January 1933, regardless of how hard it is on us. For we see, that, it is the only way to redress the damages have been done by the un-German elements during the tragic past fourteen years."[51]

Jews all over the world were mockering these well-meant people and referred to the Sacred Scrolls (Torah): "Heil Hitler, get rid of us!" When on March 24 in the "Daily Express" they declared WAR against the Reich's Government in the field of "economy and finance", and called for a "courageous unity in a Holy War against Hitler's people", the NSDAP (in comparison to what has happened later) replied with restraint, and for the oncoming Saturday called a "very calm and orderly boycott of Jewish businesses, so that at exactly 10 o'clock A.M. the Judaism will learn against whom it declared war."[52] On Monday the signs "Germans, don't buy from Jews" were removed and people continued their purchases where ever they were the cheapest.

The battle song "When the Jewish blood squirts off the knife, then things will be even better" was prohibited. But the march-song "Patience, betrayed brothers, Judas' throne is already shaking" was allowed. The words to another song with a nice melody "Today Germany belongs to us, tomorrow the World" under a threat of punishment were changed to: "Today Germany listens to us, tomorrow the World."

In "Mein Kampf" the rugged or boisterous phrases were declared by Hitler invalid, but he did let the "Paris Midi" ("Short Skirt Girls of Paris") newspaper know: "My book announces a combat, but because it was written in prison it is filled with insults and curses. I wrote it with the indignation of a pursued Apostle. However, there is a substantial difference between the political program of this book and the Chancellor of the German Reich. I am not a writer but a Statesman. In the Book of History I am the corrector of 'Mein Kampf'."

Hitler also wanted some restrains in German relations with the Soviet Union, where Trotzki-Bronstein, a Jew, was removed from power, and shortly thereafter the Jewish avantgarde of the People's Commissars. He said: "In contrast to the Soviet Government, the Reich's Government is willing to nourish a kind and fruitful relationship for both parties. The Government of the National Revolution sees itself as capable of rendering a positive policy towards the Soviet Russia. The struggle with Communism in Germany is our own internal affair and we will never permit any outside intervention. The Reich's political alliances with other powers, were developed over mutual interests and will not be broken."

In February 1933, the Reich's Chancellor talked very often about visiting Stalin. A "Peace Manifesto" was prepared for introduction to the whole World with this intention: "We will give Europe a present of peace for one hundred years." But Stalin declined to meet with Hitler, apparently due to the German Red Comrades, who having no interest in staying in Hitler's concentration camps just arrived in the Soviet Union.

Roehm, in his entire life never thought about a surprise attack on the Soviet Union. Based on all the SA encroachments on their opponents, he was a man of "Life to let Live" as both Strassers, Gregor and Otto combined professed to a refugee and a former SA Leader Walter Stennes. Contrary to the Hitler's ascetic inclinations, they all knew how to appreciate a nice wine and a delicious meal. For themselves and for "their" people they wanted peace. Enjoyable drinking with former adversaries, like the Englishmen, or with a French Military Attache, made this First World War Officer Roehm very serious.

To him Hitler's racial approach was a "trash" due to the following conviction: "Who can guarantee to me that in the Church books everything is written correctly?" Without much thinking, Roehm appointed a former Major, Franz von Stephani of Jewish descent and an ardent Zionist, to the rank of General, i.e. the SA Groups' Commander. The SA Chief Roehm had his own approach to the "Jewish Question", which basically did not differ much from the Party's Program, but underway was forgotten: "All German Jews are to remain in Germany as citizens, provided they shall have a permission to hold posts of university professors, public prosecutors, judges, bankers etc. Careers of Jewish First World War participants are not limited, but the Eastern Jews, who migrated to Germany after the War, will be deported."

The commissioned Army had to become a People's Army via a merger with the SA. In this way a Motorized Defense Army trained as Infantry was created. This concept was not applauded by many despite Hitler's insistence: "The German Army of the future must be a motorized one!"

The Reich's military men were on Hitler's side. The future Commander-in-Chief of the Air Force, Hermann Goering, was promoted by the President of the State and Field Marshall, Hindenburg, from the rank of Retiree Captain to the rank of General. At the same time "The Reich's Union of German Officers" threw out of the "Union" the Retiree Captain Ernst Roehm. The SA was discontent and wanted to limit the influence of current Groups' Commanders and openly called for a "Second Revolution", that is - for serious social changes, which actually they were fighting for. Hitler's deprivation of power was not considered. So the Roehm's rebellion never took place.

Nevertheless, some documents of Roehm's planned removal of Hitler have surfaced. They were counterfeited by a man, who was considered to be the worst figure of the regime. With Roehm's destruction he had finished his own journey-man's (Jewish) dole. When Reinhard Tristan Eugen Heydrich, a Jew, who, according to Himmler "overcame the Jewishness within himself", took under his command the Jewish baiters (and later the murderers of the Einsatz Commandos), and in 1942 was killed by Czech partisans, the Chief of Hitler's SS Body Guards, civil warrior Sepp Dietrich was overjoyed: "At last that pig kicked the bucket."[53]

The entrance of this politically authoritative person and mass murderer, Heydrich, into the National Socialist movement, was a mistake made by the "Last War Cadet Officer of the Year", Himmler, who could not see a difference between an Officer of the Radio News Service and an Officer of the Secret Service News. In 1931, Himmler, possessing such a faculty appointed Heydrich to a duty of a Chief of the Security Police, later known as the Sicherheitsdienst (SD).

Heydrich, a telegraphist and a sexual pervert, served in the Navy but after having insulted a girl who was impregnated by him, was discharged under allegation of "disgracing the soldier's honor". Reinhard Heydrich was convinced that some almighty force eliminated his predominantly Jewish traits. According to the name specialist Mr.Kessler, many Jews with the name Goldman had changed it to their favorite " Reinhard" (meaning "Pure to the Full Extent")[54]

That Heydrich was a Jew, came from a man who knew about this, a quarter Jew himself, Rudolf Jordan, Commander of Halle-Merseburgs. Quite soon in the Riemann's Music Dictionary no one could find an entry with a name of the father of the SS Secret Service Chief Reinhard, "Heydrich Bruno, actually Suess", but only of "Heydrich Bruno". The photographs of this musician with a dark curly hair, who looked as if he was about to jump off the screen of a successful movie entitled "The Jew Suess", and whose son due to the "Aryan Laws" could not be admitted to a "Duel Club" regardless of its pantomime's character, had ironically been bought out at a great cost.

Reinhard Heydrich was the son of this Jewish musician and of a half-Jewish actress.

At the time when Heydrich, as an apprentice to the post of Chief of the Security Services discovered that Hitler's and Himmler's grandparents were Jewish, and as yet did not destroy or change his own Identification Documents, nor remove cemetery tombstones, especially of his grandmother Sarah, the two Superiors, Hitler and Himmler, advised him what to do, and agreed to keep him at the post as planned. They also ordered Heydrich to change Himmler's Jewish-Italian grandmother into an Aryan by forging her I.D.

This trio also decided to kill the truly devoted bombastic speaker Roehm, who as a Commander of four million SA -men, was always insisting on the observance of the Party's Program. The killing task was assigned to Reinhard.

In a due course a falsified document was delivered to the Chief of the Army, Blomberg, who right away informed Hitler that he received the following Roehm's order: "According to the order of the Chief of Staff Roehm, every large Group of SA should protect its headquarters with a Company of heavy machine guns." Then Heydrich's man appeared before Colonel Franz Halder in the City of Muenster. The man was dressed in the uniform of the SA High Group Leader in rank corresponding to the position of General, and reported to Halder that: "At this Army Corps area I will be your successor in the rank of Chief of Staff. Please sign me in." For a confirmation Halder drove to General von Fritsch in Berlin and was assured that: "Retaliatory Forces are ready for action." Next, one morning of June 1934, Chief of Defense of the Armed Forces found a "Confidential Order" from Roehm on his desk. Nobody knew who put it there. Its content was: "The time has come to resort to arms."

The Army Corps area Commander in Breslau, later General Field Marshall von Kleist, received similar orders and could not rid himself of a feeling that something was wrong out there, as he stated: "I am under an impression that the Reich's Army and the SA are agitated against each other by a third party." The Chief of the Armed Forces, General von Reichenau, listened to this and exclaimed: "This might be true. But now it is too late."[55]

It was too late. The Reich's Army supplied Heydrich's "Hunting Commandos" with weapons and casernes, where to they brought people who were put on a "Reich's List". Being in a hurry, they placed them against the wall and shot to death without blindfolds. Only in 1957 it was possible to identify the victims by name. One hundred ninety one where on this Heydrich's list. No one was a Jew. And almost no one had anything to do with the SA.

At dawn of that June 30, 1934, when all was over, Hitler rushed to a Country Inn, not far from Munich, and chased unsuspecting Chief of Staff, Ernst Roehm out of bed. Roehm, who did not expect such a visit, nevertheless had next to him a book in steel and leather, ready for a present, as a proof of SA's loyalty to Hitler. Anyway, Criminal Police took Roehm to the prison Stadelheim in Munich for Hitler hesitated to shoot his comrade on the spot, with whom throughout the past fifteen years he was so close and informal.

When Hitler returned to Berlin, the SD Chief Heydrich handed to him a document, which he himself dug up from the files of Mr. von Tresckow, the most prominent Representative of Berlin's Criminal Police at the turn of century. There it was written: "It is very rare that homosexuals have a strong and honest character. They don't have the willpower, and they prefer to use feminist weapons of intrigue, hypocrisy, and lie. They seem to be unfit to serve in responsible positions of any government. In the closest surrounding of a Monarch they are calamities."

The Commander of the Concentration Camp in Dachau, after receiving Heydrich's telegram from Berlin, entered Roehm's cell and emptied a full magazine from his revolver into Ernst's body. The bleeding man rattled: "My Fuehrer, My Fuehrer..." and died.

Roehm was the last Socialist to leave the highest post in the NSDAP. Soon afterwards Reich's aging President von Hindenburg died, and from there on at the "Switches of Power", in Berlin, STOOD NO ONE WITHOUT ANY MIXED JEWISH BLOOD IN HIS VEIN. Hitler promised to the Reich's Army support in the destruction of his combat comrades 'cause the Army shall remain the "Only Arms-Bearer of the Nation". But several days later he commenced formation of the "Waffen-SS" ("SS-Weapons"), and thus an almost unlimited power in the Reich was assigned to Heydrich. Himmler, the "frightened bourgeois" with a pinze-nez on his nose, became the Reich's Leader of the SS and a troublesome Heidrich's supervisor.

Under such circumstances, on a beautiful sunny day in the Obersalzberg's High Mountains the Fuehrer comforted the fifteen years younger Heydrich with this mirage: "There will come a time when you will be my successor," for he felt a close tie to this man through music and even wiped his eyes when he played a violin.

EVERYTHING RUNS SMOOTHLY

The basic trait of a dictatorship is, that it does today what it condemned yesterday, and won't do tomorrow, what it promised the day before yesterday. Only the profit counts. If chaos is of threat to a Democracy, then illusions and beliefs in a Messianism are of danger to all wise and arbitrary rulers. Till this day the people have not created a form of government which would last forever.

Hitler, after getting tutorial classes by the conservative journalist on economy, Mr.Funk (who soon became Economy Minister), still did not understand anything about political economy. So his success in governing to this day is incomprehensible. Probably this happened by his leaving the economy to the economists and by sending a great number of bureaucrats (who are known for impeding all progress) into retirement. Also by eliminating remnants of the cast system he allowed people to act selectively and in full authority as the Darwin's theory proclaims: "The fittest succeed". Socialization of companies or department stores, as the Party's Program provided, was not pursued.

A third of the Nation, which used to live on public support, had work long before the mobilization and compulsory military service was established. "To let billions of man-hours lay fallow, is an insanity and a crime," explained Hitler, when in March 1933, except for 94, he won 441 seats in the Parliament what gave him an unlimited power.

After Hitler first dug some dirt with a shovel, and ended this ceremony with a slogan: "Let's Begin", soon afterwards "Streets of the Fuehrer" and the "Reich's Superhighways" were weaving the German land. Volkswagen (People's Automobile) plants were constructed on lawns and in fields, to which workers contributed by buying bonds and saving thousands of marks for a car. Work Services became an obligation of both genders, and for any honest National Socialist a core of socialistic thinking. On drained lands villages were formed and on watered sandy soils rye was grown. If a German were to be asked then about the lands in the East, he or she would silently tap own forehead with a finger. People wanted work and bread, and in no way they were more nationalistic or chauvinistic than the French or Russians.

The most impressive shows were performed during the Reich's Party Days in Nuremberg. During one of them the Reich's Labor Service men were marching to the Zeppelinfield, with bare, tanned chests, and with shovels on their shoulders which blinked in the Sun a thousand fold. One of the men asked loudly: "Where are you from, comrades?" - "From the East Sea coast!". And again came answers to anew posed questions: "From the Mountains of Bavaria!", "From Ermsland!", "From the Black Forest!", and finally one united call of many voices thunderously rushed over the field: "From Germany!!" The questioner came forward again and the spectacle ensued: "What are you, Comrades?" And they answered: "Workers!", "Farmers!", "Artists!", "Technicians!", and then again thundered out of the thousands young men throats: "Germany!!" Those were the men, who a few years earlier saw the hungry people roaming idle at street corners or sitting on the park benches, and who a few years later were marching across

Europe after getting a message that the War was imposed upon them.

And Hitler said to them: "The German people desire nothing more than equality. If the World decides, that all weapons shall be put down to the last machine gun, we will acquiesce to such a convention. If the World decides that certain weapons shall be destroyed, then we will do it first."

But the World did not decide on anything like that and in the German Reich two years after such speeches were rendered, the compulsory military service was established as it already existed in the neighboring countries. Because in 1935, the military forces of the German Reich were still weaker than those of Belgium, public opposition to the rearmament prohibited by the Versailles Treaty was even weaker. It was just as weak as the twenty years later (in the fifties) an opposition to the rearmament of provincial States of the Federal Republic of Germany, prohibited by the Potsdam Conference (July 26, 1945).

In 1934, right at the beginning of the new Reich, a Pact of Non-Aggression was made between Hitler and the respected Polish Chief of State, Marshall Jozef Pilsudski. Also a Concordat was signed with the Catholic Church, which according to widely spread opinion in Germany, had given Vatican too many privileges. Three quarters of a year later, after military service in the summer of 1935 was established, a Naval Agreement between Great Britain and the Reich followed. It limited the German Navy to a level of 35 percent of the English fleet. This agreement with the "brotherly people" of the North was the "happiest day in Hitler's life", and whoever saw the tears of happiness in his eyes, had to believe it.

When the German troops several months later marched into the demilitarized Rheinland and declared its sovereignty, the European countries expressed only their deep understanding. Until 1938, the German Reich's spending on armaments was not higher than that of France, which since the end of the First World War, beside the maintenance of the Maginot Line, had mustered her Army in full battle preparedness.

During those years Hitler allowed elections to take place, so that 90 percent of the people could agree with his politics out of their deepest convictions. Also, around the whole World he enjoyed an almost complete admiration. By the same token, after death of the President Hindenburg, he was "The Fuehrer and The Chancellor of The German Reich."

In 1938, Churchill sent to Adolf Hitler this open letter: "If England would be pushed into a national misfortune, which could be compared to the misfortune of Germany in 1918, then I will ask God to send us a Man of your Willpower and Mind."[56]

Sir Neville Henderson, the British Ambassador to Berlin, added: "Any country should be happy to have such a Leader who, no matter how he started, has immensely freed a creative power of his Nation and left it to the people's advantage."

The English "Daily Mail" wrote: "Faith makes miracles come true. The Germans found themselves with an authentic belief in their deeds. A change of this kind is an essence of the people, and reflects their inner aptitude effectuating acceptance of the Nation's foreign policy. Yes, such a change of attitude of the people in the history of mankind has never occurred in such a short time."

And the former Prime Minister of England, Sir Lloyd George, through the "Daily Express" expressed his feelings in this way: "It is not the Germany of the first ten years after the war. It was broken down, depressed and bent down by worry and incompetence. Now Germany regained confidence in itself and is full of hope towards the future. It is overwhelmed with a determination to govern itself without any intervention or foreign influence. For the first time since the war ended, a common feeling of security has prevailed. The people are happier, and so is Germany."

In such a climate members of the "Veterans Union of Germany" visited the former adversaries in France and vice versa. "Hitler's Youth" and "Youth of France" spent vacations camping together. During the Olympics of 1936 in Berlin, the French team marched in front of Hitler with raised hands and was greeted with a great jubilation like no others by a hundred thousand people.

When in the spring of 1938, German troops marched into Austria in disrespect of the Versailles Treaty accord, but in the fulfilment of Article 1 of their Constitution of March 12, 1919, stating that the "Germanic Austria is a part of the German Republic", soldiers of the Reich were showered with flowers. Out of the deep Alps came peasants to great them. All of the country fell into an indescribable excitement. When the man, who fled Vienna twenty five years earlier, appeared there and from the balcony of "Vienna's Hofburg" announced to hundreds of thousands of people that: "On this occasion and at this greatest hour of my life, I, as the Fuehrer and Chancellor of the German Nation and of the Reich, solemnly pray to the German people, that this historical Union of my Austrian Homeland with Germany has been now accomplished and it is an irrevocable act."

In the fall of 1938, the German Armed Forces moved into the Sudetenland, and so the three and a half million Germans living in that border region of Czechoslovakia also joined the German Reich. In the Godesberg's "Hotel Dreesen", owned by the War Comrade Dreesen, Hitler and the British Prime Minister Chamberlain agreed to the sovereign rights of the German people. The French Prime Minister Daladier, and the Duce of Italy Mussolini, had no objections. The "Agreement of Munich" of September 29, 1938, rose hope in Chamberlain, who after his return to London stated that the peace of this century has been secured. Poland and Hungary, with the acceptance of all involved, also annexed bordering regions where, under the Czechoslovakian rule, lived people of their nationality and culture for twenty years.

In the summer of 1933, Hans Frank, a long ago acquainted lawyer, under special circumstances reported himself to the Berghof, near Berchtesgaden, where Hitler set up his headquarters after the first few months in the Reich's Chancellery. "I wish", Hitler started without any hesitation, "that all dealings with the Jewish question should be anchored in the law, so that the foreign countries and the International Jewry will not have any excuse to do any horrible things to us. It came to my knowledge, that your Jewish father has been kicked out of the lawyer's profession because of embezzlement of his clients money. The point is that he was not kicked out by us, for that happened many years ago. So I do agree, my Dear Party Comrade Frank, that in recognition of your achievements your father should be reinstated. But based on your own observation, you know just how necessary it is for us to free ourselves of this Jewish burden by sending these people back to where they came from - to the desert. You must have read my argumentation, which I presented during the Harzburg Conference in 1931 before the writer Hans Grimm. He popularized it widely. At that time I said: 'When we will seize power, we will do our best for the Jews so that they will have their own State. That is how it shall be. I don't want to think about differentiation, which the propagandist Goebbels makes between Western Capitalistic Jews and the Eastern Bolshevist Jews even though, of course, all of us make such a differentiation. Propaganda has to be simple, otherwise people will not understand us.'" Hitler rose and walked through the hall with long steps. "My dear Frank" he continued, "The possibility of being a quarter-Jew is not my 'dark spot' which makes me furious. I want everything to be clear. So I order you, as my Attorney General of the German Reich, to solve this question legally. Do not forget one thing - the will of the Jews to migrate to Palestine is of the highest priority in the wealth of our power. So let them leave our country, and you take care of the legality."

Dr.Frank understood his Fuehrer very well, and on the Reich's Party Day in the Fall of 1933, he said: "Without damaging our will of coming to terms with the Jews in Germany, their security and life judicially or governmentally is not in danger. The Jewish question can be solved rightfully only if one deals with this question in terms of a Jewish State."

The "Law of Reestablishment of Professional Civil Services", which removed Jews from public jobs, existed since the spring of 1933. Henceforth a new law was issued recalling naturalization and adjudication of German citizens. In effect, thousands of Eastern Jews, who immigrated after the end of the First World War, left Germany. Thousands of them moved to Palestine under the British Mandate. In 1917, this land was promised to these wanderers of this Globe by the British Minister Balfour.

The so called "Nuremberg Laws" were completed shortly before the Reich's Party Day in 1935. On September 15, in Nuremberg, the German Parliament had convened. It agreed unanimously on the "Law to Protect the German Blood and Dignity." Hermann Goering, the President of Parliament announced the enforcement of this Law in a powerful voice: "Marriages between Jews and German citizens of Germanic blood are prohibited. Out of wedlock sexual intercourse between these two national groups will be punished". Members of the Parliament roared with laughter at Section 4 of this Law: "Jews are not allowed to hoist the National and the Reich's Flag nor to exhibit Colors of the Reich. They are allowed to exhibit Jewish colors. Execution of this Law is assigned to the State."

Seriousness of the moment caused Hitler to issue this appeal: "Gentle Party Members! You just accepted the Law which significance and its very meaning will be fully recognized many centuries from now. Please be confident that the

Nation itself will change the way this Law will be working. And please make sure, that this Law will gain an extended nobility through an unheard of yet discipline of all the German people, for which YOU will be responsible."[57]

The ancestors' passports were required of anyone who wanted advance to a higher position, and it was good for the public interest. The Nation started searching for its ancestors. Sometimes it happened that a young man, beaming with National Socialism, suddenly received a document from a far away Office showing that he carries a Jewish blood. Quite often such a man committed suicide in a nearby forest. The introduction to an official document was not comforting enough, though it read: "The National Socialist thinking, honors every other nations' sovereignty and justice. It is not about a racial struggle less or more intense, but about influx of a strange race. The person of an Aryan origin is the one who is free of foreign blood. This is how the German Nation sees this matter. First and foremost of foreign kind is the blood of Jews and Gypsies who live in European enclaves. Next is the blood of an Asian or African race, including Aborigines of Australia and Indians of both Americas. However, an individual from England or Sweden, France or Czechoslovakia, Poland or Italy, which countries are almost free of racially impure elements, such an individual has to be treated as related, that is, as being an Aryan, irrespective whether this person lives in his Homeland, in East Asia or in Americas."[58]

The National Socialism's racial doctrine, which was recognized as a Science and found its place in the Universities, did not make any distinction between the religious, Sabbath-Jews, and the baptized Sunday-Jews. The doctrine acquiesced to a statement of the "Jewish World", which was published in London: "The Jew remains a Jew, even if he changes religion; a Christian who accepts Jewish religion does not turn himself into a Jew, because the word 'Jew' does not mean a religion, but a race. So, a free thinking or a godless Jew, is a Jew, just as well as any Rabbi."

Since the issuance of Nuremberg's Laws (1935), German Jews, who had not emigrated yet, lived in an invisible ghetto. Anyone, who came out of it, was that someone who was promoted for his own benefit to the title of the "Honorary Aryan". One such individual was the famous physicist Philipp von Lenard, son of a Jewish merchant of Pressburg, David Lenard. In 1936, he was honored by Hitler with the National Award for Arts and Sciences, and also with the NSDAP's Golden Sign of Honor. In the same year, the Olympic Games were supervised by Theodor Lewald, a talented organizer who was assigned the title of the Reich's Commissar of the Games. Previously he was a Secretary of the State, known also as the "Honorary Aryan". Another one, Erhard Milch, who during the combat times was Director of the Airlines League (Lufthansa) and to whom in the past Hermann Goering (a Workmanship Representative) was selling parachutes and other flight accessories, throughout the years advanced to the post of General Field Marshall.

In 1935, Gerald Kessler, in his scientific dissertation "Family Names of Jews in Germany" (in 1933, he abstained from searching on "Judaism of King's Courts"), pointed out with a candor to the Jewish origin of Reich's Ministers names, who were closest to Hitler. His findings for instance were: "Hess" (derived from an "immigrant"); "Rosenberg" (derived from the German Eastern colonies among Slavs); "Frank" (derived from an "immigrant"); "Ley" (was a polished form of the Israeli Tribe called Levi or of Levy (tribute).

Maiden name of the Honorable Wife of the Reich's Marshall Goering was "Sonneman", which derived from a distorted by Germans Hebrew name "Simson". So the same with Hitler's later wife Braun, which means a "physical characteristic" (or "Brown", for Moses' wife was brown).

This cautious researcher, at that time living in Istanbul, but able to publish in Leipzig, at the end of his investigation remarkably stated: "Germans also honor the great and rich history of Jewry, as well as Jewish names. Jews, however, in respect to their Forefathers should refrain from deploring, or even slightly changing their names. Blessed be those, who remember their Fathers!"

The very resolute Jewish Lady Friedlaender, mother-in-law of Goebbels, then Reich's Propaganda Minister, stirred by the vulgar propaganda rubbish which accompanied persecutions, always had threatened to "...tell my son-in-law everything about this." Until 1945, she still lived with him in the same household.

At the Sport Palace in Berlin Goebbels roared in scorn: "It has been said that our SA -men have laid their violent hands on Jewish women", and waited until thousands of protesting voices subsided, and then continued: "Now, I wish to know the SA -man, who would want to do such a nasty deed!" Everyone laughed at this unruly. Even Goebbels did. "Who is this guy?" asked a newspaper in Geneva, displaying a picture of the little, limping, dark haired Goebbels when he arrived there at the National Union meeting. And next to it, it answered for itself: "This is the Representative of the tall, healthy, blond, and blue eyed Nordic race."

Reinhard Heydrich, the Security and Police General, who was preoccupied with control of the Jews, discovered a Catholic Jew who was born near Haifa, spoke Hebrew, Yiddish and German, and who as a child landed with his father in Solingen, and later in Linz. Long before the annexation of Austria he was fighting there for the Fuehrer. For this reason Adolf Eichmann had to flee to Germany and join the SS. Adolf Hitler's anti-Jewish teacher Professor Leopold Poetsch taught history at the Linz High School in Linz, and Eichmann, full of hope and in the future efficient SS-man of the lower rank, was also his student. Hitler, who once attended the same school as Eichmann, met with him, and as they went on a walk through a forest, Hitler kept Eichmann firmly in his arms and looked long into his eyes. Afterwards everything was taken care of by Heydrich and in Solingen a birth certificate was fabricated for this new comrade, who later was extensively trained under supervision of Heydrich. Further he was trained by Leopold von Mildenstein, a Jewish SS Officer and an admirer of Zionism, who was promoting a plan of awakening in Jews the need of going to Palestine willingly. After overcoming all the surprises created by Eichmann's extremely semitic nose, which looked as if it was a "key to a synagogue sticking out in the middle of his face", the noble circle of his SS colleagues could only say: "Shut up! This is an order of the Fuehrer!" and to everybody everything was obvious because, the Fuehrer was always right. Thus Eichmann was prepared to start work at his Office in Berlin, the work for which in the sixties his defense lawyer Servatius in the Jerusalem Court demanded a medal, obviously for Eichmann's blessed deeds resulting in settlement of the Jews in Palestine.

The names interpreter Gerhard Kessler, in 1935, found that the unknown name "Eichmann" first appeared at the beginning of nineteenth century as a result of changes to the names of Jewish origin. The name changes were made for reasons of bond breaking with fore-fathers and their national history.

The cooperation which existed between Heydrich's Gestapo and the Jewish Self-defense organization in Palestine, the militant "Hagana", would not have been closer if it was not for Eichmann who made it public: "All Parties and Unions, which have been consolidated around the World by the Zionist Organization controlled by the Central Defense and Control Board, play an extremely important role in the politics of the Jews. This Board bears a Hebrew compound word "Hagana", which means "Self Defense". One of the Palestine Zionists, who was dealing in Berlin with Heydrich's Security Service, was Schkolnik, and behind him Levi Eschkol, the future Premier of Israel, who in the summer of 1965, before the "Spiegel" magazine confessed: "At the beginning of Hitler's regime I stayed within for a while."

The commander of "Hagana" was Feivel Polkes, born in Poland, with whom in February 1937, the SD Troops Leader Adolf Eichmann met in Berlin. In a wine restaurant "Traube" ("Grape") near the ZOO, these two Jews made a brotherly agreement. Polkes, the underground fighter got in writing this assurance from Eichmann: "A body, representing Jews in Germany, will exert pressure on those leaving Germany to emigrate only to Palestine. Such a policy is in the interest of Germany and will be executed by the Gestapo."

Feivel Polkes invited his "brother" Eichmann to their ancestor's land. On October 2, 1937, Eichmann, as the Editor of the "Berliner Tagblatt" ("Berlin's Daily Gazette") stepped down from the gangway of the ship "Romania" in Haifa. The Editor wanted to be a little busy, so he wandered from here to there, conversed with people and saw a lot. After returning home he reported: "People of Jewish national circles are very excited about the radical German politics toward the Jews, because this has increased Jewish population in Palestine many-fold. In a short time they will become the majority among the Arabs."[59]

Jewish communities in Berlin, and in all large cities of the Reich materialized the new "Hebrew course" and prepared their boys for "Aliyah" ("Ascent" - immigration of Jews into Palestine). A "Central Committee for Help and Construction" restructured itself into the "Reich's Representation of the German Jews" and later renamed itself into "Reich's Union of Jews in Germany". Together with Eichmann's Office, this "Reich's Union" led the emigration in a nice harmony. Bad words were not heard on either side. Raaman Melitz (in Jerusalem) decided about the numbers to be send out from the Niederschoenhausen regrouping place as follows: "82 percent will go to Palestine, nine percent to Brazil, seven percent to South Africa, and one percent each to USA and Argentina."

Eva Braun, who dyed her hair blond, here in front with her also half Jewish sisters, who too were working for Jewish employers. Hitler's future wife lost her Jewish maiden name through her marriage. According to the name researcher Kessler, her maiden name meant "a dark physical characteristic."

Die blondgefärbte Eva Braun (vorn) mit ihren ebenfalls teiljüdischen Schwestern, die gleichfalls bei jüdischen Arbeitgebern arbeiteten. Die spätere Frau Hitlers verlor mit der Heirat ihren ursprünglich jüdischen Mädchennamen, der laut Namensforscher Kessler bei der Namensgebung an «dunkle körperliche Eigentümlichkeiten» anknüpfte.

The leader of the semi - Union, the "German Workers Front", Dr. Robert Ley (above), was a grandchild of Mr. Levy. The half-Jewish owner of a photo shop in Munich, Heinrich Hoffman (below) is the man who was nominated by Hitler to a Professor because of his photo - retouching abilities. By beautifying Fuehrer's pictures he became a multimillionaire. In Hofmann's photo shop Hitler met the seventeen year old Eva Braun.

Der Leiter der gewerkschaftsähnlichen «Deutschen Arbeitsfront», Dr. Robert Ley, Enkel eines Levy (oben), und der ebenfalls teiljüdische Besitzer eines Münchener Photoladens, Heinrich Hoffmann (unten), den Hitler aufgrund seiner Retuschenkünste zum Professor ernannte und der mit verschönerten Führer-Bildern vielfacher Millionär wurde. Im Hoffmann-Photo-Laden stiess Parteiführer Hitler auf die damals siebzehnjährige Eva Braun.

With the Government's support young Jews were prepared for their new life in Palestine, with agricultural and handicraft courses in Waidhofen at the River Ybbs, in Altenfelden of Austria, in Ruednitz by Berlin, and in Schwiebisch/ Schlesien.

From Rexingen in Wuerttemberg, all 262 Jews emigrated to Palestine and only one returned after the war. Here is how many Jews the German Reich lost to emigration before the War: 300,000 Jewish citizens out of 500,000, mostly the efficient and young.

For the sake of this move to the "Holy Land", Mr.Streicher with his "Stuermer" paper did his best. He insulted, as much as possible, all the Western Democracies which were willing to take the Jews in and in this way hinder emigration to Palestine.

The nationalist and journalist, a Palestinian-Arab, Mr.Younis Bahry, hoped for an "Arabian State of Palestine". At the "Kaiserhof" in Berlin he once saw a young girl dressed in a shoulder-free, long white cloth. She was helping Hoffmann, a fat photographer, who was taking pictures of the Fuehrer from all angles. "Who is this cute doll?" Bahry with all his innocence asked the sitting next to him Dr.von Brauchitsch of the Reich's Radio Station, and a brother of General von Brauchitsch. Dr.Brauchitsch looked around cautiously, put his hands in front of his mouth and answered numbly: "Keep your hands off. She is the Fuehrer's lover. Eva Braun is this child's name." Then he looked around once more and sighed: "She is a quarter-Jew like all the others Hitler had. But nothing came out of the relationship with the daughter of his half-Jewish photographer Henny. Neither with Gretl Slezak, an actress, with whom Goebbels wanted to set up Hitler. He is attached to this one over there..." Dr.von Brauchitsch moved his head in the direction of the photographer and finished his introduction: "All of them are of Jewish blood. Who knows why. Same with the 'Arabian Palestine' my Dear Bahry. So, get it out of your head!"

Adolf Eichmann, who was rich in experiences, had proven himself and in the meantime was promoted to the rank of SS Officer. He moved into the Rothshild's Palace in Vienna after the annexation of Austria. With Jewish co-workers he installed the "Central Station for Jewish Emigrants", and only after a short time 200,000 Jews of Austria were melted down to a handful.

And the work continued. Half a year later annexation of the Sudetenland and the rape of Czechoslovakia had occurred. Then Eichmann, the specialist in foreign matters, moved into the building of the "Israelites Cultural Council" in Prague. There he set up a Center with 32 Departments, which was called "Central Council for the Solution of the Jewish Problem in Boehmen and Maehren". And here too he employed mainly Jews. Their task was to send abroad 300 Jews daily. Eichmann was so clever, that the travel expenses Jews covered themselves.

On April 26, 1961, at the "Trial of the Century" in Jerusalem, Dr.Franz Elieser Mayer, the leader of the Palestine Office of the "Zionist Union of German Jews", said this about Eichmann in the thirties: "Generally speaking it was always possible to communicate with him. I had an impression of him as a rather quiet person, who did what he did and he was very normal, not obliging but correct."[60]

In 1933 the Jewish population in Palestine was so small, that the World hardly had noticed its presence in this Biblical Land, until it substantially increased shortly before the War. Until then Eichmann's businesses were running smoothly so the masses of German Jews were out of danger. In this way after 2000 years of Jewish praying: "The following year in Jerusalem" brother Polkes with his "Hagana" came much closer to the goal of establishing a Jewish Nation in Palestine.

PERSONAL PHYSICIAN MORELL AND THE CONSEQUENCES

Whatever belonged to Hitler's privacy, came out of the "Hoffmann-Stable" - of the "Augean" one. This metaphor refers to Eva Braun and Dr.Morell. All three were of Jewish origin, so the people closest to Hitler were abhorred by Morell's "characteristic way of running business and of his oriental physiognomy", as it was said by Christa Schroeder, a Secretary to Hitler. When travelling, Hitler's Assistants allowed this man, who often was coming late, to ride in their luggage car until Fuehrer harshly put an end to this practice. Before that, Mr.Morell was a ship-physician for one year. During the First World War he practiced in Dietzenbach of Hessen. In 1919 he became famous as a doctor for Sexually Transmitted Diseases at a fashionable Health Resort Kurfuerstendamm in Berlin, where with all kinds of magical remedies he tried to cure aristocrats and ladies of lowest esteem. Once Morell drove to Hoffman, the private photographer of Hitler in Berchtesgaden, who had gonorrhoea. Morell injected him with something and the thankful Hofmann recommended this venereal disease doctor to his friend Hitler, who suspected to have the same kind of illness. This was the way the fate had started. These two slyly businessmen, Hoffmann and Morell, came to terms immediately. Morell's occasional violations of abortion restrictions impinged on his reputation. He belonged to the so called "March Martyrs", who in January 1933, after Hitler seized power joined the NSDAP.

Until 1936, Hitler was praised by everyone, especially by Churchill. But this, however, changed, first slowly, then faster after nomination of Dr.Morell as Hitler's private physician. After application of boycotting measures, which should have resulted in chasing Jews "back to the desert", came pogroms and manslaughters. Thus the German Reich became an enemy of the God and of the World. Upon taking his post of a physician, Dr.Morell did two things at once: first he began poisoning Hitler slowly with strychnine injections, and then made Hitler dependent on him by application of a drug "Pervitine". Pictures, which were taken of Hitler after Morell's eight year care, speak for themselves.

While doing his job he snatched up a few million marks and should be honored as Germany's war profiteer or swindler number one. On letters with the letterhead: "The Fuehrer and Reich's Chancellor", he issued orders; he took part in the Jewish pharmaceutical enterprise Katz & Co. in Budapest; he produced tons of multi-vitamin candies and sold them to the Chief of the German Workers Front, Dr.Ley, who looked like Morell. The same Ley, whose grand grandfather on his father's side removed the letter "v" from his name. Professor Schenk, an Executive Officer with the Chief of the Department of Public Health within the Reich's Ministry for Nutrition and Agriculture, estimated Morell's income from this factory alone to about 20 million marks.

Every doctor who knew Morell, called him a quack or a charlatan, and the English historian Trevor-Roper, after being acquainted with him a little closer during an internment, called him a "plump and an old man with creepy manners, speaking chaotically and with a hygiene habit of a pig." When Hitler's personal servant Krause had a cold and was advised to go to Morell for a shot, Krause answered: "I wouldn't allow Dr.Morell to give me a shot for then I would have to go to him forever." Hitler's advice turned into the order but Krause disobeyed. Pretty soon this Soldier of the Navy was replaced by the SS-man Linge.

When the Prince von Schaumburg-Lippe advised Reich's Propaganda Minister Dr.Goebbels to get treated by Dr.Morell, irritated Goebbels replied: "This criminal will not enter my house." Sometimes Dr.Morell treated local or foreign guests of the Fuehrer. In March 1939, while talking with Goering and Ribbentrop, Czechoslovakian President Hàcha became ill, so the "Wunderbar" ("Miraculous") Morell gave him a shot in a hurry. Strengthened by this, President Hàcha entered Hitler's Office and wrote down that: "From now the destiny of the Czechoslovakian Nation lies in the Fuehrer's hands."

In the middle of the War, Chief of the SS Heinrich Himmler had noticed that Hitler's health worsened constantly and that his personality changed due to this drug abuse. He cautiously tried to explain to the Fuehrer the bad effects of addiction, but Hitler flared up and the Chief gave up. Hitler wants to be a drug addict, so he can scream "VICTORY!!" in a war, which he knew was already lost.

Professor Schenk reported about this to his boss, SS Group Chief Leader Pohl: "The Fuehrer is being doped by Morell to a high degree." And later reported the same to Himmler. In effect after a few days Prof.Schenk received an order "to keep silent about this matter."[(61)]

Also Prof.Dr.Brandt, who said courageously to his Fuehrer: "With these injections you are being slowly but progressively poisoned", was forced out of Hitler's elite and became unpopular. It is needless to say that a few months later Prof.Brandt was under threat of execution. However, Judges of the War Court were unwilling to indict him, so Dr.Brandt survived as Hitler's private prisoner until the end of the War. In an extremely informative book written by the Administrative Functionary Physician Dr.Roehrs, the author proved that Morell's drugs had poisonous effects, bordering on "destruction of human personality." All together Morell administered thousands of injections, with which he handicapped freedom of actions of his protégé Hitler. An Israeli newspaper trivially asked: "After the myth of stabbing the Germany with a dagger in her back, came another myth of a miraculous medicine?" And so no one living in the three partitions of the Great Germany paid any attention to Dr.Roehrs.

Morell was promoted to a professor and with his "Merit of War", a medal, left Berlin on April 21, 1945, after Hitler realized that "Drugs cannot help me anymore." Morell surrendered to Americans and during the war criminals' trial he introduced himself as a hero of resistance against the Nazis. But the historian Trevor-Roper allowed the cat to get out of the sac a little bit in this way: "With all the Hitler's doctors removed, Morell could look forward comfortably to the last and most spectacular of his medical monopolies." ("Nach der Entfernung aller frueheren Aerzte konnte Morell also in aller Seelenruhe an das von ihm monopolisierte aerztliche Werk gehen.")

One of those former physicians, Dr.Giesing, in "Stern" magazine praised himself because he once experimented on how to poison Hitler but at that moment his personal servant, Linge, stepped into the bunker. After the investigation by an appropriate Public Prosecutor in Krefeld it became obvious that Giesing's testimony was a hoax. Dr.Porschen of the Northern Rhein Physicians Association said, that it is hard "to imagine" that such a break of the "Hippocratic Oath" could be treated seriously."[62]

Americans decided that Morell could not be held accountable and so they let him keep his wealth of millions, which he hoarded during the war. They set him free, but hung the vigilant Professor Brandt for he started talking about Morell's medical practices inefficient in application of necessary care. Years after the War Americans returned the "Morell Files", but because they were about Hitler's illnesses and treatments, the files disappeared. But the papers did not disappear from the collection which contained information about Morell's lice powder branded "Russla" ("Russia"), which he was selling to the soldiers fighting in the East, and who were laughing at it for it was useless.

Physician Morell who pumped into Hitler and thus poisoned him throughout the years with strychnine, pervitin and other drugs. After war before the Americans he presented himself for this reason as a resistance fighter. His fortune of millions which he piled up with the help of Mr. Ley stayed untouched.

«Leibarzt» Morell, der Hitler mit Strychnin, Pervitin und Drogen durch Jahre aufputschte und vergiftete und sich daher nach Kriegsende bei den US-Amerikanern als Widerstandskämpfer aufbaute. Sein mit Hilfe von Ley zusammengerafftes Millionenvermögen blieb unangetastet.

Adolf Hitler in 1936 before injections by Morell and after eight years of treatment. The renown physician Professor Brandt warned: "My Fuehrer, by Morell's injections you are systematically poisoned to death." Hitler ordered execution of Brandt but no judge was found for indictment, so the inconvenient man was finally hung by the Americans.

Adolf Hitler vor Morells Spritzen im Jahre 1936

und nach achtjähriger Behandlung im Jahre 1944.

Der tüchtige Arzt, Professor Brandt, warnte: «Mein Führer, Sie werden durch Morells Injektionen systematisch vergiftet.» Hitler verlangte Brandts Erschiessung, es fend sich kein Richter, und schliesslich hängten die US-Amerikaner den Unbequemen.

NOBODY WANTS TO TAKE HITLER'S JEWS

The English, as well as the Third Reich Government, in the official declarations promised that the land in Palestine will belong to the Jews as their National Homeland. While the British Mandate rulers broke said promise with patrol boats, destroyers and airplanes, Hitler's helpers and helpers' helpers did everything possible by confiscation, fire and murder in order to satisfy the agreements made with Zionists. Almost all immigrants were settled in this land of Palestine involuntarily, which was bare in the thirties.

The Britons were torn between the Balfour Declaration of 1917 and their needs for oil from the Arabian world. Finally they permitted the Jews to enter the Palestine land but under the condition that each one will pay 1,000 pound sterling. For the Jews without money they set a monthly quota of 1,500 people. Delegates of the "Jewish Agency" in Berlin competed with the SS in falsifying Palestine Passports and foreign citizenship. Through these tricks the number of Jewish immigrants to Palestine doubled.

The SS newspaper "Das Schwarze Korps" ("That Black SS's Corps") was frank and open, as were the Zionist's papers writing: "The time is near when the Palestine will be taken again by its sons, who through the past one thousand years were lost all over the World. Let our good wishes accompany them." But the majority of the German Jews was not drawn there, where the Zionists, as well as the National Socialists wanted them to go - to the frontier of the Orient. Deviating from the "Palestine Solution" policy, Leopold Mildenstein, a Jewish SS Officer departed Heydrich's Bureau and in search of a solution knocked on the doors of other countries. Most of the German Jews had chosen far away countries, if possible, on the other side of the Atlantic. President of the United States of America, Roosevelt, who remembered his Jewish ancestors from Italy by the name of Rossocampos, was also asked for help. In the summer of 1938, after five years of Jewish oppression, Roosevelt chaired the Conference on the sunny banks of Lake Geneva. Everything looked promising, even the French health resort Evian.

Out of the fifty invited countries, only thirty sent their delegates. The Soviet Union did not, although since the "October Revolution" among People's Commissars 42 were of Jewish origin. The Soviets did not give any reason for the non attendance because their Marxism/ Leninism was so perfect that it had nothing to explain. The Vatican sent an observer, and many Jewish organizations of the World, too. One of them was Mrs. Golda Meir. When the page of the "Hotel Royal" obstructed a beautiful view of the Lake with heavy window curtains, the Conference began. More Jews than diplomats attended. The tension was immense.

A representative of Colombia spoke about the future: "Everything depends on the refugee quota which has to be established, or on the 'ad theorem' declaration of good will at adjourning." So the Conference, as it was feared, as any other conference adjourned with proper sub-Committees and declarations of good will. Every country had its excuse: Australians feared that on their people-empty continent the wages would be restricted, and their workers' unions would not be pleased. A Chilean spoke at the Conference (held in French) in a Spanish-Chilean variation, so only a few could understand what this man philosophized: "The question of these people's intake is a question of production and unemployment. It would be careless and not in the interest of workers to increase the quantity of workers and thus the production, especially when goods will not find buyers." A short, slightly bent historian from Peru spoke about the history of his country where Indians "converged around the Spanish seeds. So it has to be kept Catholic and Latino". As he continued the Vatican observer nodded silently. At the end a diplomat, skilled in history, forced the United States' representation, which up to this moment did not make any comment pertaining the solution of the refugee problem, to respond: "As always, the U.S.A. is the example of wisdom and caution. Until 1890, with a great spirit and without any worry or objections, the U.S. opened its gates to plenty of refugees without any objections. Since then consecutive administrations held back the stream of immigrants. First in 1921 and then in 1924. What was the U.S. anticipating by these limitations? First of all out of concern for safety and welfare of the immigrants, then also out of concern for its Northern Heritage and purity of the Anglo-Saxon race." Roosevelt, who summoned the Conference, probably thought very little of the "Northern Heritage". Rather he thought much more about the "Palestine Solution" which was advocated by Zionists and had to be resolved by "Evian" (Inset: but not by the Soviets' "BIROBIDZHAN". See the REFERENCE to POSTSCRIPT No.114).

The Swiss delegate from the other side of the Geneva Lake was a Chief of Police. Therefore his argumentation was not one of a diplomat: "Has it been forgotten that during the First World War Switzerland took in 150,000 children? Now we are poor with heavy unemployment. No more than 40 franks per year every citizen contributes to our people in need. Many had to emigrate because of this bad situation. So we cannot afford the stay of these refugees in our country."

Nicaragua, Costa Rica, Honduras and Panama have put it more simply with the unanimous declaration: "None of our countries would like to be held responsible for financial obligations stemming from re-settlement of any refugees. We are saturated with merchants and intellectuals. We have to treat similar ones as 'UNWANTED'."

As the Conference progressed, the Arabs have shown to a scared World that they do not want any more Jews in Palestine. On July 7, there was a commotion at the Transjordanian border. Two British cruisers were shipped to Haifa and on July 9, British 11th Hussarian Regiment intervened. In the evening 12 Jews and 52 Arabs were dead. 24 Jews and 145 Arabs were badly wounded.

Shortly before the final touches at the Conference, the "British Medical Association" threatened with a dawdle strike: "No member of our medical profession wants to see our country overfilled with immigrants." At that time in England there were three registered refugee-physicians for every one thousand practicing British physicians.[63]

The final resolution of the Evian Conference concluded that the "involuntary emigration is so immense that it will disrupt international relations and increase general discomfort." The assembled parties thanked the President of the United States for his initiation of the Conference and the Government of France for its managerial function; then packed their suitcases and before travelling home, enjoyed one or two nights of splendor in Geneva.

The German and the foreign press reported pretty much the same way about the Jewish first degree misfortune. The "People's Observer" was satisfied that the "Palestine Solution" remained unsolved and rejoiced: "The effect of the Conference - A FIASCO !" In Hitler's guts the Evian Conference was a "Jewish Conference", and "this has to be said with an honor to the governmental delegates that they, with deep concern, avoided any polemics against Germany as the country of origin of those Jewish emigrants. Precautions were taken, which protected them from the stream of Jewish elements, because the disadvantages of their influence were clear". "The New York Times" desperately complained: "When thirty two nations, who call themselves 'democratic' cannot agree to a plan of helping a few hundred thousand refugees, then all the hope is diminished as to whether they ever together will be able to decide on anything."

Only Colombia, whose delegates were optimistic since the beginning, had opened its borders narrowly. When Mr.Kaul arrived there (today he is called a "Star Attorney" of the German Democratic Republic), shortly thereafter Colombians put him in prison because of a fraudulent bankruptcy. After leaving Colombia this Jewish jurist has up to this day a horrible feeling about the Americans.

Several months went by when in Paris, on Nov. 7, 1938, a young Jew, Herschel Gruenspan, got an idea to kill Ernst von Rath, the First Secretary of the German Embassy. Two days after the shooting von Rath died from the inflicted wounds. To the Court of Justice Gruenspan explained that the French Police attempted to get rid of him what caused his financial misfortune, and that his homosexual partner von Rath disappointed his expectations. For this un-political murder Gruenspan was not harmed much, not even by the Heydrich's Police which caught him and by the end of the War set him free.[64]

Such developments made Hitler even more serious about the Jews still living in Germany. Hence he decided to take the advantage of this situation, just like he did five years earlier when he attacked the Communists for burning the German Parliament down to ashes.

In memory of the 1923 riot, a celebration party was held in the Munich's "Citizen's Brewery Cellar" with participation of the veterans of the Hitler's movement. It was in the afternoon of November 9, when the information about the assassination of the unknown diplomat reached Hitler and Goebbels, both present at the party. They immediately put the things together. According to the SS Group Leader Baron von Eberstein, they "conversed extremely intensely" inclined closely to each other. When the Fuehrer withdrew from the conversation, Goebbels started to lie freely: "I just reported to the Fuehrer that in some regions of the country it came to the anti-Jewish excesses. So we concluded that if they are spontaneous, we will not intervene."

After short telephone calls made by the present regional leaders, those "spontaneous excesses" exploded everywhere a few hours later. Only one among the one thousand SA-men wore civil clothes, and that one incited destruction of the Jewish houses, stores and synagogues by setting them on fire. The mob on the streets howled and plundered.

In his private residence at Munich's Prinzregentenplatz, Hitler received reports about those incidents, and to the gathered artists and officers he showed how "extremely stirred up and confounded" he was. Only when he received a report that some major cities were burning, he ordered the Police to intervene.

Goering, who was responsible for the "Four Year Plan" said that he is "sick of these filthy demonstrations which he will tolerate for the last time." The man of the "Plan" tolerated them anyway, such that the Jews were ordered to pay one billion marks for the destruction, which was provoked by Gruenspan.

The German people did not interfere with these "pogroms". They were only mockering and calling them: "The Reich's Crystal Night", for the broken windows of the Jewish stores. A Jewish merchant in Holland, when his business friend Dederstedt paid him a visit, praised the Germans for they are "neat and good mannered. They were free to plunder without any consequences, but they still wouldn't do it."[65] The Chief of the Security Police, Heydrich, reported to Goering in a military style - shortly and concisely: "In the numerous cities looting of Jewish ordinary and department stores had taken place. To avoid further commotions hard measures have been applied. One hundred seventy four (174) looters were arrested. One hundred ninety one (191) synagogues were set on fire. Seventy six were destroyed completely. About twenty thousand (20,000) Jews were arrested. Thirty six (36) dead and also thirty six (36) seriously wounded. They all were Jews. One Jew is missing."

Dr.Hjalmar Schacht, President of the German Reichsbank, was truly outraged and appeared in Obersaltzberg before Hitler saying: "These activities of the Party on November 9, were reprehensible." At lunch he developed a plan to take one and a half billion marks from the confiscated properties and transfer them to the International Committee combined with a Jewish partnership. To secure the fund, the "International Jewry" should be given a loan, proceeds of which would finance emigration of the German Jews to the Western countries.

Hitler, knowing much about Zionism (International Judaism) got excited and the credulous Schacht went to London to bargain with the Bank of Samuel & Samuel. Lord Bearsted, previously known as Marcus Samuel, asked for a few more days to rethink all of this because first he has to negotiate with Chaim Weizman, the President of the Zionist's World Congress. "Meshuge" ("Crazy" - he thought in Hebrew) - replied the Zionist Leader, while listening to the plan. "Who, I have to ask, will go to Palestine? I would rather see the destruction of the German Jews than the ruin of the State of Israel because of them."

As if having been hit on the head, Schacht drove back to Berlin, and during the Nuremberg Trial of the War criminals, he was still irritated: "Not a single German Jew would have died, if my plan had been accepted."

The illegal immigration to Palestine swelled enormously. The old paddle-steamers or river freighters of less than 500 tons with "slave dealers" on board of the worst kind, came at night to the beaches of Palestine. And before the British troops in the morning could block off the landing spot, masses of the illegals disappeared over the hills and valleys with the help of Jewish residents. Therefore the British Chief Commissar of Palestine cancelled the legal immigration. On July 20, 1939, the Minister of Colonies, Sir MacDonald, explained to the British Lower House the need for hard measures: "The illegal immigration increased dramatically. Thousands of people are waiting in harbors for ships."

On the waiting ships epidemics broke out and the Captains of "Breslau" and "Thessaly" received from the French Mandate of Lebanon a permission to land in Beirut. The Britons were merciless and during the War were not any softer either.

Storfer, Eichmann's agent, chartered old ships wherever he could get them. And the "Hagana", which (after the "Reich's Crystal Night") sent its best agents, Pino Ginzburg and Moshe Auerbach, to support Eichmann, supervised the last part of the Jewish journey and their landing. The "Mossad" (see POST. r.126), "Hagana's" illegal organization for smuggling people was in charge. The Britons guided these old ships whenever they could as far as Haifa. In November 1940, they loaded all the captured refugees onto the large ship "Patria" with the intention of deporting them for duration of the War somewhere to the South Pacific Ocean. But the ship exploded in the harbor and sank within fifteen minutes with two hundred sixty (260) Jews on board who just fled from Europe.

The previous day an old wheel-steamer "Atlantic" with 1,880 refugees, among them women and children from Danzig, from Austria and Czechoslovakia, was brought to Haifa. Because, on the Cyprus Island epidemics of typhus ensued, fifteen passengers on that ship died, before reaching their destination. When the still healthy 1,600 passengers at the beginning of December landed in Haifa, they brutally were forced to board another ship and deported to Mauritius, close to Madagascar, where they lived until August 1945.

In Germany, a Gentleman, whose Jewish-Greek nativity was noticeable a hundred meters against the wind, was especially cruel. He was Admiral Canaris, Chief of the Military Defense and Foreign Espionage. At that time he was involved in domestic politics and recommended that all Jews, living on the German territory should wear a yellow star, as it was practiced by many countries during the Middle Ages.[66] He got this glorious idea on a Sunday afternoon while visiting a neighbor in his garden. This neighbor was once his comrade, with whom in 1923 he was at sea, and who also found his destination in the dirty work of a Secret Agent. The neighbor's name, residing at the Berlin's Augustastrasse, was Reinhard Heydrich, who enthusiastically agreed to the idea. At the beginning of war with Russia it was put into practice for the convenience of Heydrich's Police. But it was improved slightly by ordering the display on park benches of a sign "Only For Jews".

Both Chiefs, Canaris and Heydrich, knew that they are competitors in keeping their dossiers, which could reveal their Jewishness, deep in a safe. At this neighbor's party they were not in conflict with each other, so in the evening Canaris cooked a stew a la marine for both families and Heydrich played on a violin the "Eine Kleine Nacht Music" ("A Little Night Music") of Mozart, very humble for this occasion. And the unwanted and marked with the yellow star fugitives hid in the corners of the cable cars, movie theaters and grocery stores. It was very rare now that a German dared to pad someone's shoulder, even if that someone was recognized as a former friend when he or she wear the star "like the Iron Cross First Class for bravery."

Especially unwanted and marked (even before the yellow star was implemented) were the Jews in Switzerland. In 1935, the need of marking was already explained by Swiss like this: "The rescue boat is full". By orders from Bern the Swiss Consulates in Germany stamped a red "J" on the first page of a passport when a Jew applied for immigration. In this way Jews were identified and their journey kept under control. Even during the War, when people were talking about annihilation of the Jews, the Swiss issued an order for the Border Police to check luggage of those who crept over the border from France or Germany. Only those, whose luggage contained 100,000 franks or an equivalent value in jewelry, were allowed to stay in Switzerland. Many of them returned back to "their home in the Reich" while the Border Police were mockering: "Pas de l'argent - pas de Suisse", a saying which has not lost its meaning: "No money - no Switzerland."

A few years ago (in the sixties) a Swiss newspaper wrote of the old man, who lived his last days from tutoring. During the War he was a Police Officer, who falsified identification documents and thus helped over 3,000 refugees to survive. When this scheme was discovered, he was fired. A quarter century later the Swiss Government offered him a compensation but the "Brave One" did not accept.

On May 13, 1939, Captain Gustav Schroeder left with his motorboat "St. Louis" the harbor of Hamburg. The boat was loaded with 900 Jews who bought Cuban passports delivered by a Cuban for $1,000 each. "You have to understand the price," explained the man, "there is a whole mafia I have to bribe." In Havana, Captain Schroeder talked to the Officials until his mouth went dry. But it didn't help any. Nobody got off the boat. The passports were false. To Havana came the lawyer Berenson from a Jewish "Help Agency" in New York with a $450,000 gift for the President of Cuba Laredo Bru, but he refused to accept it, for the law had to be observed. Then Berenson asked President Roosevelt for a permission to enter these desperate people into the United States, who at that moment were waiting on the open Ocean. President Roosevelt referred their case to his Good Offices without any results whatsoever. In other words, the President refused. So these poor people, who at that moment had a great hope, only saw the Statue of Liberty from a distance at the entrance to the New York's harbor. And they were lucky - for they did not understand what the inscription on the Statue read: "Give me your tired, your poor.... Send these homeless, tempest-tost to me." Having no choice Schroeder turned the "St. Louis" with its people, tired of Europe, onto the Eastern course, back to where they came from, for they could not set their feet on land in America.

Before the War Germans tried to push the immigrants from Poland over their Eastern border. But Poland for a while declined to take them in by using a bureaucratic trick. Passports of all Polish citizens living abroad were invalidated. They had to be renewed. When Polish citizens of Mosaic persuasion went full of hope to the Polish Consulates in Germany, their disappointment was enormous for their passports would not be extended. And so they became "Stateless", and as such their deportation by the Heydrich's Police was imminent. But the Polish Government knew how to defend its borders, simply with the extradition threat of German citizens from their country.

Almost one year later Poland was conquered. Its warfare with the Germans lasted only a few weeks. According to an agreement, which was made shortly before the War, Poland was divided between the Soviet Union and the German Reich. The "Star Attorney" Hans Frank, a half-Jewish searcher of his Fuehrer's ancestors, moved into the Cracow's Castle of the Polish Kings and acted as if he was a Vice-King. His new title was: "Governor General and Reich's Minister". Others called him a "Polish Butcher." Then Heydrich and Eichmann forced their way into his domain of the "General Guberniya (Province) of Poland" with an attempt to create a State within a State - the Jewish State within the Polish body, the Guberniya. They chose the District of Radom as Eichmann postulated: "We told ourselves, that it was given to us, so again we said, why not resettle the Poles for not too many settlements are there anyway. So to the Jews will be given a big territory, especially for the Eastern Jews, who are extremely talented artisans, needing only a source of work. Also, this will be a territory for the Jews from Austria, Germany, Czechoslovakia/ Boehmen, and from the Protectorate of Maehren, and with a developed agriculture, such will be a solution for a while."[67] "For a while", meant, "until Palestine will be ready to take them in."

Those, who arrived there were scared, first by Eichmann, and later by other "Founders" of this remarkable "State within a State". They were told: "Here the Fuehrer gave the Jews a new Homeland. There are no apartments, no houses. If you will build them, then you will have a roof over your head. The wells in this entire region are contaminated. There is an epidemic of cholera, dysentery, and typhoid. If you will drill deep into the ground and find water, you will have water."

After such a fearful introduction, which nota bene did not reflect the reality, to the half-prisoners was shown a new nearby border with Russia. Following shots from the machine guns into the air underscored the seriousness of their situation. So, after a first or second night, some healthy people went deep into Russia. First they had to make their journey through the part of Poland occupied by the Soviets. A few weeks later they found each other in Siberian camps under a suspicion of espionage or other crimes. After the War, the German Prisoners of War, together with those Jewish survivors from Vienna or Boehmen, had a lot of opportunity to think about the past events.

In the spring of 1940, the General Governor Frank found out what was going on at the border and yelled out with an outrage: "The General Guberniya has to be just as free of the Jews as the Reich." Recklessly he chased them back to where they came from. And Jews, who just built houses out of wood and rocks, and who previously with the refugee-helper Eichmann fled from Poland to Vienna, at that crazy time went back to Vienna.

It was much easier to deal with the Jews living in regions along the Rhein, as for example Saarpfalzen or Baden. After the conquest of Northern France, Eichmann loaded them onto the transport trains and shoved them across the border to the un-occupied France. But there they also were not welcome. And everywhere locals were happy when these wanderers took the next opportunity and embarked on ships leaving to Algeria or Casablanca and then disappeared somewhere in the North-Western Africa. There only a few German Officers were present, who were rather more interested in the advantages offered by the War than in controlling the movement of the Jews they were supposed to supervise.

Despite the objections stemming from a fear that eventually Jews would pass some military secrets to the enemy, the Reich's Government allowed those who were willing (even during the Winter of 1941-42), to flee to the Russian combat zones in the East.

Still, in October 1941, a ship ferried the Jews to Lisbon, Portugal. By then the roads from Poland over Slovakia and Hungary into Italian or Yugoslavian harbors were already blocked. The fleeing to the Mediterranean Sea basin was possible only trough Romania and Dardanelle. The German Navy controlled the Black Sea and chased Soviet submarines, which were interrupting free passage of the ships. There they escorted those ships through the mine fields. The Grand Rabbi, Dr.Isaak Goldstein of Berlin, who lived in Romania during the War, recalled: "I owe it to the Truth to tell, that we transported to Constantinople more than 30,000 Jews with a permission of the German Supreme Command on ships under the supervision of the International Red Cross. From there, disrespecting the laws of the English Government, the Jews in great numbers were smuggled through Syria into the Holy Land."[68]

The "Struma", a Bulgarian ship, which transported Jews into the Mediterranean Sea, was in distress because of an engine failure. Then its Captain Gorbatenko asked the harbor Authorities of Istanbul for a permission to dock, but they refused, even after getting a message that the dysentery had taken its toll on the ship's passengers. So, on February 24, 1942, North of Bosporus, this drifting ship became an easy target for the Russian torpedoes, and with 763 Jews aboard was sunk on the Black Sea. Of the four people that were saved, only one survived and lived to see the end of the War.[69]

Throughout the entire year 1942, advertisements were printed in the Romanian newspapers by various agencies, which offered to emigrants ship accommodations. In the capital city of Romania, Bucharest, a "Jewish Emigration Office" and a Governmental Emigration Bureau were cooperating in the same building and on the same floor.

In a report by the Reich's Foreign Minister it was said: "It should be left up to the Ambassador von Papen in Ankara (as far as he thinks it is necessary), to inform the Turkish Foreign Minister Mr.Numan, that according to what we know, the steamer 'Tarix' has not been chartered for one transport only, but for several more to carry up to 5,000 Jews. And that at the same time, on the Jewish part, the negotiations are taking place concerning preparation of rooms on the Swedish and other ships for transportation of 10,000 more."

After sinking of the "Struma", the Turks were still not inclined to make the human life easier. The Government in Ankara, having been asked whether it will permit 20,000 Jews to pass through their country by train from Bulgaria, answered in short: "Turkey has no sufficient means of transportation."

On August 3, 1944, the three ships "Morina", "Bulbul", and "Mefkure", sailed out of Constance into the Black Sea with Jewish refugees on board. They were accompanied by the German security boats until the end of the flank mine barriers. One hour after midnight Soviet submarines attacked them and set the "Mefkure" (which stayed behind because of a damaged engine) on fire. The people, who jumped over board, were shot at with the machine guns. The burning ship sunk in flames together with several hundred Jews.

When on November 28, 1941, in Berlin, Grand Mufti of Jerusalem, Hadj Emin el Husseini proposed to the Fuehrer of Great Germany that in case of war the Arabian world "should not only be supported in actions of sabotage and instigation of uprisings, but also in forming an 'Arabian Legion', Hitler responded evasively: "Any German declaration in this respect might be interpreted as an attempt to dissolve the French Colonial Empire." Hitler remained an anti-Semite, that meant anti-Semitic-Arab, too. He was not concerned much with the French interest in the Mediterranean basin, but more with the Italian "Mare Nostrum" of Mussolini. Hitler did not want his influence over the "Palestine Solution" to spoil and to give up the issue to the millions of Arabs who were driven toward independence by their young leader Balafrej and later danced to his tune. Younis Bahry in his "Ici Berlin" ("Here is the Berlin") published in Beirut, had written much about the Arabian hopes which were ruined by Hitler.

Very terrible things were done by the Germans. The horror entailed entire country sites and cities where the European Jews still lived. Many of them went into exile. Those in the Eastern Europe, who did not reach Romania, or did not want to travel by ship through the Black Sea, moved to Hungary. At the beginning of War, there lived only 400,00 Jews. In 1944, the Jewish population in this country was over one million. In March of the same year Eichmann came to Budapest and got in touch with "Waadah", a Jewish organization helping refugees with the counterfeited Identification Documents. Out of the three leaders of this underground organization, engineer Komoly, publisher Kastner, and a merchant of the knitted goods Joel Brand, Eichmann chose Brand, an old friend of the SS, who in 1933, after the fire of Parliament got to know the German prisons from within.

"I will sell you the Jews of Hungary," offered Eichmann and started bragging about how many countries he had freed of Jews. Joel Brand remembered at the Eichmann's May 29, 1961 trial in Jerusalem, as follows: "He said that he called me to offer a deal. He was willing to sell one million Jews on one term: 'Goods for blood'. Such was his proposal. Then he asked me the following, but made a mistake, which is still ringing in my ears: 'What do you want? Men who are able to produce offspring?' He did not say: 'capable of begetting.' 'What do you want?' he continued, 'Children or old people? Say now!' I could not act diplomatically. I was shocked by this offer. I said that I am not in a position to say who should stay alive and who shouldn't. I wanted all of them to be saved. Then Eichmann said: 'So, what do you want? Goods or blood? I cannot give more than one million. Maybe more later.' I was ordered to go to a foreign country and to get in touch with my own people. He asked me where I want to go. I thought quickly - Switzerland or Turkey. I decided Turkey, because I knew that there were delegations of various 'Pioneer' groups and the Jewish Agency. Then he said: 'Yes', but he could not tell me yet what kind of goods he wanted to get. First he had to go to Berlin for instructions. In the meantime I was thinking about the kind of goods I might offer him. Then he asked me (actually he knew what to ask but only wanted to get a confirmation): 'You have here a wife and children and a mother, who, of course, will have to stay as hostages until your return. Nothing will happen to them. I will take care of them. This will make me sure that you will come back.' A few days later the discussion about the transaction continued. Eichmann said: 'So, you want one million Jews?' I answered that I want them all. So we may bargain about this one million. Then he answered: 'Ten thousand trucks, that means one hundred Jews for each truck, and that is cheap. But the trucks have to be brand new, straight from the factory with trailers and accessories, properly equipped and ready for use in the winter'. Further he said that he would appreciate it much if I could load some trucks with several tons of coffee, chocolate, tea, soap and things like that. He also said, that he may promise to my allies, that the trucks would not be used at the Western Front, but only at the Eastern. I was surprised and shocked, frustrated and happy, everything at the same time. So I stammered like this: 'Who would believe me? Who would give me 10,000 trucks?' Happy, unhappy, all these feelings came over me. I cannot describe it."

As a sign of good will, Eichmann let 1,700 Jews, which Kastner picked out, travel from Hungary to Switzerland, and before the first trucks were to be delivered and Brand were to return, more Jews in the amount of 100,000 would be driven to the Spanish border and left there. As a matter of fact they were put onto six trains and taken out of Hungary, most of them to Strasshof in Austria, where they survived the War.

On the next assignment Brand flew to Vienna, where he received from the SS a passport and a false name of Eugen Band, a German Engineer from Erfurt. Next on a special courier plane Brand landed in Constantinople. From a report, written on May 30, 1961 at the Jerusalem "Trial of the Century" we know how the truck deal had ended:

Asks Public Prosecutor:	"Were you arrested in Turkey?"
Answers Brand:	"Yes, when I drove into the city."
Prosecutor:	"Then you went to Aleppo to meet with Moshe Sharett?" (Moshe Sharett,

	occasionally called Moshe Shertok, later became Premier of Israel. Info by the author.)
Brand:	"No, I drove towards Jerusalem, towards Israel, to meet Moshe Sharett, since he did not get a visa to Turkey."
Prosecutor:	"When you crossed the border of Turkey and Syria, were you arrested by the British authorities?
Brand:	"Yes, after I crossed the Syrian border and arrived in Aleppo, then I was arrested by the British Military Police."
Prosecutor:	"Where did they take you then?"
Brand:	"To Cairo."
Prosecutor:	"How long they held you in Cairo?"
Brand:	"Four and half months."
Prosecutor:	"That was the end of your mission?"
Brand:	"No, no - unfortunately for me. This was not the end of it.".
Prosecutor:	"But you conveyed the proposal you were supposed to, and never returned to Hungary?"
Brand:	"Yes, I conveyed it, but was not allowed to return."[70]

The answer of the British Chief Commissar for Palestine, to whom in Cairo Joel Brand was delivered, and which could clear up this matter, out of the diplomatic politeness was circumvented by the Prosecutor. Lord Moyne, the Commissar, literally asked Brand: "What are you thinking Mr.Brand? What shall I do with one million Jews? Where I shall put them? Who would take care of them?"

Because of this Lord's position, two young Jews shot him on an open street in Cairo. After making his statement, the courageous and betrayed Joel Brand had a heart attack and died, certainly because of his failed mission.

To a Democrat (inset: Author of this book) there is no "taboo" nor a hot iron. So after an in depth analysis of the whole matter, he came to a conclusion that in the "Case of Palestine", Hitler, Heydrich, Eichmann and Zionists were acting shoulder to shoulder, and Chamberlain, Churchill and later Bevin with the Arabs (who were the suppliers of oil), also shoulder to shoulder.

THEY MISCALCULATED AND IT RICOCHETED

Just like the First World War had become unavoidable because France broke the treaty with Algeria and made Morocco her "Protectorate", so it happened with the Second World War when Germany violated the Munich Pact and transformed Czechoslovakia into the "Reich's Protectorate of Bohemia and Moravia."

What the English and French signatories of the "Munich Pact" felt because of the German entry into Prague in March of 1939, is best expressed by the note, which the Jewish Soviet Foreign Minister Litvinov-Finkelstein handed to the German Ambassador in Moscow (March 18): "The occupation of Czechoslovakia by German troops and the following actions of the German Government have to be viewed as arbitrary, violent and aggressive."

The shock of Hitler's betrayal of ideals of the National Socialism embraced the whole German Nation, down to the Squad Leader of Hitler's Youth. Germans believed in the National Socialism as a best devise for their own country, just like the Fuehrer claimed in dozens of his speeches: "As a National Socialist on behalf of the National Government and the National Uplifting, in full consciousness I am announcing that, especially in us, the young Germans, there is a deeply imbedded understanding of the same feelings and sentiments characteristic of other nations. The new generation of this Young Germany, which until now only experienced distress, the misery, and the pity for its own people, and suffered so much under these circumstances, is far from a wish of inflicting the same upon the others. Being permeated with endless love and loyalty to our own Nationalhood, out of our deepest conviction we also respect similar rights of other nations, and from within our hearts we want to live with them in peace and friendship. They should also know that we don't honor any concept of Germanization."[71]

The murmuring of the people drowned the Reich's Propaganda Minister Dr.Goebbels in an ocean of outspoken advices and newspaper articles filled with arguments about a "strategic necessity." "Does anyone want Czechoslovakia (just having been included in the German sphere of influence), to become the 'Soviet's aircraft carrier'?" Goebbels beamed. After receiving such a brainwash, people boasted like before: "Fuehrer commanded and we will follow!"

Britons had a different opinion: "You can't do business with Hitler." A few days after occupation of Czechoslovakia, they guaranteed the security of Poland's borders, for despite of the German-Polish Pact of Non-Aggression they did not believe in its inviolability. A few months after these guarantees, the Second World War broke out which took almost 50 million lives.

Hitler's opinion was to be prepared for everything - just in case. First through an accelerated build-up of the most modern military machine in the world, using the Spanish Civil War as a testing ground area for the newly developed tanks and dive-bombers. Next, through maneuvers of the unscrupulous Reinhard Heydrich who, in those years without the use of any of his own bullets, destroyed the military leadership of the most powerful opponent, the Soviet Union.

When Ernst Roehm, the main opponent of an offensive, but supporter of a defensive army was by Heydrich eliminated, Heydrich introduced a journey man's art of intrigues and falsifications. As the masterpiece of this "polit-gangster", these techniques resulted in a slaughter of the Soviet military elite. He called in a trustworthy artisan from Hamburg, Alfred Naujocks, who did not know what the fear means, but knew very well how to falsify identification documents. He also distinguished himself during a bloody liquidation of Otto Strasser, who illegally run a broadcasting station near Prague. This selected team dug up notes, letters and documents as specimens of writing styles and signatures of the Soviet Generals in the twenties. At that time Reich's Army of General von Seeckt's and Stalin's Red Army were working closely together. The watchful eyes of these two Secret Service men were concentrated on those Red Army Generals, who occupied highest positions in the military hierarchy of the Soviet Union. In the Russian military language of 1937, the documents were prepared which evidenced understandings made between Soviet and German Generals involved in a conspiracy to overthrow Stalin. With the Hitler's explicit permission and with a help of the deceived Czechoslovakian President Benes, these false documents somehow landed on the Stalin desk.

What happened next, is known by the synonym "Marshall Tukhachevsky's plot". In the span of one year of 1937, it took a heavy toll on 90% of the Soviet Marshalls and Generals, on 80% of the high ranking and 35,000 low ranking army officers who were accused of taking part in the plot and in many instances executed because of it. Under those circumstances, the German communists who fled from Hitler with Herbert Whener, left their hotel accommodations in Moscow for safer locations, because they feared the suspicious man from Caucasus (Georgia), who, through cunning and brutal actions became Lenin's successor, and who could make out of them a "tabula rasa" ("a blank paper"). Khrushchev, later on in his secret speech condemning Stalin, had confirmed these events (see POST. r.132 - "Twentieth Party Congress of 1956").

Out of the guarantees given by the Great Britain pertaining Poland, it became apparent that the Imperium did not care much about Hitler's offer of allocating the "Eastern Europe to the Great Germany, under a promise of not taking over England's possessions overseas by the German Army", for England's one hundred year old policy of "balance of power" would not tolerate another strong power on the European continent. This divergence of opinions, in August 1939, caused Hitler's Foreign Minister von Ribbentrop to travel to Moscow. Stalin and his new non-Jewish Foreign Minister Molotov welcomed the German very warmly. After returning to Berlin, Ribbentrop reported that he felt as if he was among old party comrades. In a pleasant atmosphere Stalin toasted to Hitler's health with Crimean champagne and said: "I know how much German people love their Fuehrer."[72]

After a few days these Gentlemen came to a mutual understanding, and on August 23, 1939 they signed the "German-Soviet Pact of Non-Aggression", which in reality was a German-Soviet pact of division of Poland. On September 28, 1939, the comrades Stalin and Ribbentrop put their signatures energetically on a map of conquered Poland (This map solidifies the Pact with the blood of the Polish Nation. The map shows the Eastern half of Poland assigned to one comrade, and the Western half to another - inset by the Publisher).

In Nuremberg, after the War, when the Court of Victors was in session, the dark side of the "WAR OF ATTRITION" (Inset: In the original text it is the "War of Aggression") was too a delicate issue, as was the matter of "WAR CRIMES". The judges knew how to conduct themselves, and so they prohibited all the explanations or arguments using the term "tu-quoque" ("you too"). Simply, they did not want to hear this in the Holy Halls of Justice.

It did not come to an agreement with Poland. After all not because of the English guarantees in a matter of the "Free City of Danzig" or the "Polish Corridor" (Inset: Giving Poland access to the Baltic Sea), to which Hitler waived claims several times, or to a land route from Germany to East Prussia. To Hitler's warlike preparations against this Poland, reborn after the First World War, was more important the fact that there lived the largest population of Jews in the world, and just across the Great Germany's border.

Hitler planned expulsion of about four million Jews from Poland. Polish Government even sent a commission to Madagascar which after its return complained about the bad climate there. Foreign Minister of France, George Bonnet, acquiesced. Polish Foreign Minister, Józef Beck, recognized that this question in the German-Polish relations is very important and decided at the right moment to make public the details of negotiations concerning the Jews. However, only on page 42 of the London's "Polish White Book" one might find a little mention of this matter.

The day after the acceptance of the Non-Aggression Pact between Germany and the Soviet Union, the Statesman Hitler called the three-quarter Jew Heydrich to his side for, in Hitler's conviction, history never questions the victor. In effect Heydrich ordered Naujocks to appear at his command post at the Prinz-Albrechtstrasse in Berlin, for Naujock was always ready to commit any misdeed. In the meantime Naujocks was promoted to the rank of SS Battalion Commander. They had a talk about the "CONSERVES", what meant, dead prisoners of a concentration camp.

In the evening of August 31, 1939, Chief of the Security Services Heydrich ordered an attack on the German radio station in Gleiwitz (Gliwice) of Upper Silesia (Oberschlesien). This started the Second World War with the help of the "CONSERVES", Naujocks and some SS-men. They dressed freshly killed "CONSERVES" into uniforms of the Polish soldiers, delivered them to the broadcasting station and then Naujocks reported into the microphone: "We fired with our guns a few warning shots into the ceiling of the station and are transmitting this message through."

Naujocks broadcasted in Polish a lot of unscrupulous threats and announced that the Polish occupation of Berlin was already prepared. When the SS-men departed, they left behind the "CONSERVES" with bullet holes in their backs. The next morning Adolf Hitler, the Fuehrer and the Reich's Chancellor in the middle of a session of the German Parliament reported about this event: "Last night regular Polish soldiers were firing on our territory. At 5:45 A.M. their fire ricocheted."[73]

In the confusion Hitler made a mistake, for accordingly to the orders German soldiers actually got up early that morning and with their faithful hearts at 4:45 A.M. already marched against the disturbers of peace on the dusty roads of Poland.

Again the noble Swede Birger Dahlerus, in the past Goering's friend, tried to save the peace. Dahlerus flew back and forth between Berlin and London but it was hopeless: on September 3, 1939, England and shortly thereafter France declared war on the Great German Reich. When the surprised Hitler heard about Dahlerus' efforts, and that nobody believed in his assurances, he put his left hand onto his chest and roared: "Idiots! Have I ever lied in my life?"

Two days later Chaim Weizman, President of the Jewish Agency, as it was known then, declared the Jewish war on Germany: "In my statement I wish to put a strong emphasis on the will of the Jews to be on the side of Great Britain in the fight for democracy. The Jewish Agency is willing to enter immediately into any agreement in order to put into use all its human power, techniques, remedies and talents."

A lot has been said about why the English and the French in those first days of September 1939 did not march into Germany. Hitler feared such a possibility for then the whole war might have been finished within a few weeks. The German defense fortifications, the so called "WEST WALL", were only halfway built and manned with thirty unprepared divisions consisting of old and badly trained soldiers. Tank and Air Force units were tied in Poland. Against these forces France had at her disposal hundred ten (110) well trained and fully equipped divisions. England had already transported many divisions of professional soldiers over the English Channel into France. The day the War was declared, Churchill appealed to them on the radio: "This war is England's war. Her goal is a destruction of Germany. Go ahead Soldiers of Christ!"

But none of them marched forward across the Rhein. The English war historian Liddell Hart later wrote: "German Generals were astonished and relieved that this did not happen." One explanation given for this puzzling seating-war was that in those days in Western Europe all the war cries were not founded on a national fervor. The French asked: "Mourir pour Dantzig?" ("To die for Danzig?") Certainly, they did not wish to die for this far away city. And neither did the Britons warm up their feelings towards the fulfilment of guarantees given to Poland, or at least to her dictatorial regime.

The expected "campaign of 18 days" against Poland ended after about four weeks with capitulation of Warsaw. And when on the seventeenth day of September the Soviet Army marched into Poland, England and France did not declare war on the Soviet Union.

At the end of the Polish campaign, Hitler offered peace and on October 6th in his speech before the German Parliament he asked the Western Powers: "Why should now the war take place in the West? To re-establish Poland? The 'Versailles Treaty Poland' will never be formed again. Two of the largest states

Ziemlich hellseherisch sah im Jahre 1919 der «Daily Herald» nach dem Friedensdiktat von Versailles den nächsten Krieg fur 1940 voraus: das hinter der Marmorsäule weinende Kind, das die gerade geborene europäische Nachkriegsjugend verkörpert, halt sich vor den Gewaltigen der kriegsverursachenden sogenannten Friedenskonferenz versteckt.

After the Versailles "Peace-Dictate" in 1919, the "Daily Herald" prophesied the next war in 1940. Here is seen a child who embodies just after the war born European youngsters. The child is crying behind a marble column and is hiding itself from the so called "Peace Conference".

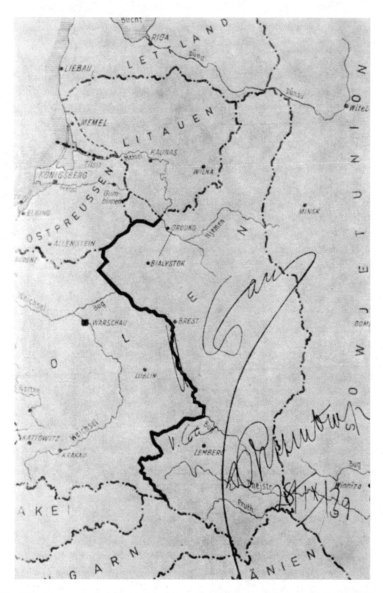

Fünf Wochen nach dem deutsch-sowjetischen Nichtangriffspakt, der in Wahrheit ein Angriffspakt war, signierten am 28. September 1939 die Genossen Stalin und Ribbentrop schwungvoll diese Karte des von beiden zusammengeschlagenen und nunmehr geteilten Polen.

Five weeks after the German-Soviet Non-Aggression Pact, which in fact was an Aggression Pact, on September 28,1939 the comrades Stalin and Ribbentrop put their signatures on the map which shows Poland being sized by both of them and then divided.

in the world will guarantee that." And with the last two sentences Hitler was right.

Western part of Poland became German General Guberniya (Province) where Hitler's former advisor, half-Jew Hans Frank, became the Governor. Before the year came to an end, 300,000 Jews were expelled from the West/ East Prussia previously called the "Corridor" (of Poland). Mixed SS-Soviet commissions on the territory occupied by Russians, searched for ethnic-Germans and settled them in the "Corridor".

In order to wage war, ore and oil are needed. In August 1941, the English won the race to the Persian oil. In a three day fight they overcame a small Iranian Army, and the fond of Germany Shah Riza Pahlavi was exiled to South Africa where soon he died. And Germans won the race to the Scandinavian ore which mainly came from Sweden.

On April 8, 1940, a great portion of the British fleet sailed out for Norway in order to stop delivery of the ore to Germany. Next day German troops crossed the border of Denmark and this country surrendered at noon. Its King and the Government were kept intact. Thus the Danish North Schleswig-Holstein, which existed since the Versailles Treaty, was not annexed to the German Reich. After strong resistance by the Norwegian army and the allied British troops, which lasted only a few weeks, Norway fell into the German hands for the War's duration. Soviet Union expressed no concern about those developments. The reason was revealed in a report, which German Ambassador Count von Schulenburg on April 11, 1940 sent from Moscow to Berlin: "Our Scandinavian action has brought an immense relief to the Soviet Union for the so called 'rock has been pushed off their chest.' The Soviets have already noticed presence of the English and French troops on the shores of the Baltic Sea and - according to Lord Halifax - Finland's question has resurfaced. The long article, which was printed today in the Party's newspaper 'Izviestia' ('News') about our Scandinavian action sounds like a cry of relief."[74]

While in the Northern Norway, General Dietl's mountain troops were fighting fiercely with the freshly landed Englishmen, Hitler gave an order to start the war in the West. At dawn on May 10, the diving-bombers and a larger part of Germany's 135 divisions rolled over the borders of Holland, Belgium and Luxemburg on the way to France.

One of the most knowledgeable English military historians Liddell Hart, commented about the assault plainly: "Hitler's armor was not superior as it is credited with. In numbers it was inferior to the armies that it encountered. But the tank advancements made the difference though they were weaker than the tanks of their adversaries. Only in the air Germans had their superiority and this, as it has been proven, was a decisive factor." To this comment the Air Force General Student added about the parachute units and heavy sailing vessels combined under Captain Koch : "The action at the Albert Channel was Hitler's own idea. Among the other ideas of this man it was probably the most original. The surprise attack on Fort Emael was carried out by a tiny section of the 78th parachute unit under Lieutenant Witzig. This small section undertook a totally unexpected landing on top of the Fort and blew-up armored doors and gun turrets with new and powerful explosives, which until then were kept secret."

In 1940, the successful Ardennes offensive, which opened the way to France, Hitler credited to himself: "Of all the generals I talked to about the assault plan on the West, only Manstein understood me." Liddel Hart noted: "It was a bold undertaking to send tanks and motor vehicles through such a difficult terrain, which traditional strategists considered impassable. Therefore it was a big surprise, and the dense forest helped in blurring strength of the attack."

Hitler's behavior towards Dunkerque, where he gave an order to let the British expedition corps escape, becomes only understandable when looking at his phraseology about the enemy during the thirties: "Similar nation," "German nation" and "German races have to stick together." The Commander-in-Chief Hitler explained to his astonished generals that the British Empire can only be compared to the Roman Catholic Church, for they are both indispensable entities of great persistency and stability.

While Hitler philosophized, over 300,000 English soldiers were shipped by yachts, fish boats and excursion steamers back to their beloved old England and the Goering's Air Force did not harm them.

Some less prominent historian speculated that Hitler only wanted to give his Army a three day rest, which was not his custom while his warfare decisions were at stake. Liddell Hart came much closer to the truth: "Many people, who got away, asked themselves many times, how was this possible? The only answer is that Hitler's philosophy rescued them for nothing else could have prevented the tragedy. Only Hitler's order stopped the armada when it was approaching Dunkerque and idled until Britons reached the harbor on their way home."[75]

In 1937, Hitler let the commanders of his armed forces know that the Great Germany is just a prelude to the Great Germanic Reich.

On June 10, 1940, Mussolini's Italy declared war on the already defeated France. Thirty two (32) Italian divisions were not enough to overcome resistance of the three French divisions which were situated at the Alpine front. This, among other things, did not prevent the Duce to demand the whole French fleet, part of Algeria, all of Tunis, Island Corse (Corsica), and as the occupation zone an area up to the River Rhone.

It was said that during the war Hitler was only the Chief of the Army and not a Statesman. Nevertheless he convinced his partner Mussolini to abandon such a wishful thinking. The German Fuehrer did not let anyone know in the Western Europe (which was almost free of Eastern Jews and therefore unimportant to him) about his plans to conquer the continent. The Italian Foreign Minister Ciano stated: "I have no suspicion, but only subtle feeling concerning Hitler for he speaks with a moderation and clarity, which is very amazing after all his victories".

In the forest of Compiègne the Commander-in-Chief Hitler assigned to his Chief of the Supreme Command General Keitel a presentation of the armistice conditions. They were: "France has been defeated after her heroic resistance in the bloody battles. For this reason Germany has no intention to condition or negotiate the armistice from the stand point of abuse or defamation. The purpose of the German demands is firstly to prevent further fighting; secondly to obtain the guarantees of protection in case of the continuation of fighting with England, which so far has been forced on Germany, and thirdly to create conditions guaranteeing a long lasting peace, which main tenet should be the well-being of Germany, which suffered in the past from the deprivation and injustice."

The war against England found its expression in the renewed peace offering. In this new attempt the fact, that the Soviet Union in disrespect of the agreements made with Germany, assaulted three Baltic countries of Estonia, Latvia and Lithuania, played a role. Soviet Union took over Romania's Bessarabia in the South, and by that threatened German oil supplies from Romania.

But Churchill persuaded his bomber pilots to "take off the gloves" and continue the War, which started shortly thereafter against the women and children. And as the answer to the peace appeal, the British Warlord ordered bombardment of the French fleet stationed in Oran, Algeria. In this way sending yesterday's brothers-in-arms into the depths of the Mediterranean Sea.

The German armies in the French campaign did not lose as much as the Soviet garrison from Leningrad against Finland during the winter campaign of 1939/ 1940. Thus the German armies in a military order moved to conquer more or less prepared England.

While at that time the German generality demanded capture of England (which seemed to be easy), the Commander-in-Chief Hitler was sitting in the Berchtesgaden Villa in a glory of the VICTOR and relaxed. Eva Braun, the young girl who was working in a photo-shop in Munich, had no reason not to be content. Hoffman, the owner of the shop and Hitler's friend, was promoted to a status of the Professor. And the unfatigable Eichmann in the conquered France pushed Jews to the South into the Independent French State under Marshall Petain. Through Marseille they journeyed to North Africa finding there a secure place as if in the "Abraham's Bosom".

Hitler did not like the operation "Sea Lion", a plan to invade and eliminate England. Even during the victory speech after the French campaign he mentioned that "It was never my intention to destroy or to damage the English Empire." The amazement of Britons that nothing has happened to them reverberated, and the historian Liddell Hart acclaimed about this with these words: "When the British army escaped the trap in France, it still was not in a position to defend England. They left the biggest part of weaponry behind while their supply stores in the homeland were almost empty. In the following months England's small, poorly armed military forces faced the powerful conquerors of France. They were separated only by a strip of water. But the invasion did not take place."

Hitler looked toward the East. And it is probably true that his distraction from the operation "Sea Lion" was not only due to his infatuation with the Germanic England, but also due to his fear that the Eastern neighbor, Russia, which was becoming more powerful, could invade his country. So he travelled in search of allies from whom he could expect help in the oncoming "WAR OF

IDEOLOGIES."

In October 1940, after meeting with Generalissimo Franco, the Spanish Caudillo (Leader/ Chief) at Hendays (the Pyrenees border train station), Hitler repugnantly said that he would rather have "three or four teeth pulled out before going through such a meeting again."[76]

He could not even convince the aging Marshall Pétain, Chief of the unoccupied, independent France, to join in the march with him.

The Soviet Foreign Minister Molotov, who knew about Hitler's English-complex, came to Berlin in the following month and in public presented further Russian demands: interest in Finland; interest in Romania; sending Russian troops to Bulgaria and to the military bases in the Dardanelles. Hitler, who expected oil from Romania as an important factor in waging war, sensed danger and got scared. He couldn't believe what he just heard. Thus the German-Soviet alliance, which lasted about one year, came to an end. Probably it is true, that after Molotov left for Moscow, the operation "Sea Lion" was eradicated from Hitler's mind, and that the operation "Barbarossa", an attack of the Soviet Union, began to occupy his mind.

After all this Hitler made a further attempt to come to an agreement with Franco. Since the beginning of the Spanish Civil War (Inset: Also a "WAR OF IDEOLOGIES"), he knew about Franco's Western Jewish origin and about him being financed by the Belearic Islands' Jew[77]. So he chose a delegate, who was of Greek-Jewish descent, the Intelligence Services Chief Admiral Canaris, who had good relations with Caudillo through his blood affinities. They both did not necessarily agree with the Hitler's plans to get rid of the Jews from the Eastern Europe with the help of a small elite of the Western Jews. When killing of the Jews began, Spain accepted only those refugees who could prove their Western Jewish origin.

So these two Gentlemen bet on the English card. And on December 7, 1940, in Madrid, Canaris conjured the indecisive Franco not to grant Hitler his wish to let the German troops march through Spain and attack Gibraltar. By this England had free hands in the Mediterranean Sea, and in the course of the War Germans lost their momentum first in North Africa and later in Italy. This chain of events is supported by the "memories" of the diplomat Ernst von Weizenaecker, who in 1950 testified in Munich. And if someone wants to get the proof of this, please listen to the historian Liddell Hart again: "We know that the Admiral Canaris, the Chief of the German Intelligence Services, who later was executed, took several clandestine operations interfering with Hitler's goals. We also know that Canaris used mysterious ways to hide his trails."

Very late, by the end of the War, Hitler realized that the Italian entry into it was going to be the main cause of the German defeat. In his ideologic stubbornness and because he did not discern Italians from Romans, the Commander-in-Chief of the German Army overlooked the history lessons telling that this country changes fronts in almost every war. More than that, it occasionally changes fronts if the war is lasting too long just for the sake of its first ally. So Germany's tanks drove and Germany's infantrymen marched through the North African sand (where they had no business to be) when the front, erected there in December 1940 by Mussolini, began to sway. Much more importantly, however, was the loss of time in attacking the Soviet Union, what probably led to the loss of the War and in fact it came to that because Italians again opened a new front, this time in Greece.

When the Italians, accordingly with their custom began to withdraw from Greece, operation "Barbarossa" lagged behind in time four important weeks. And when the 1941 winter came four weeks earlier, the "God of War" turned his back on Germany and went to the other camp as General Jodl had anticipated.[78]

In the spring of 1941, the German troops positioned in the Balkans against the Soviet Union had to clean up the mess created by Italy. To make matters worse, Italy's attack against Greece pulled the British troops onto the stage. Bulgaria was taken by the Germans peacefully. Yugoslavia experienced a rebellion of her army officers. This changed the friendly relations with the German Reich into hostilities. The country was overrun by the guerilla warfare. The capitulation of Greece and the withdrawal of the British Expedition Corps was a matter of days. But those valuable weeks were lost forever. It was well known that Russia's roads in autumn become muddy. So, when the great march to the East started on June 22, skeptics discussed the possibility of a "DEATH VICTORY". Hitler too, knew about this danger.

In the summer of 1941, the Politician and the Warlord Hitler found himself in a situation of a chess player who with each next move inevitably hears from an adversary the merciless word "Check". Two moves at once are not allowed and would be impossible anyway. His strength only lasted while overpowering neighboring enemies in the East, North and West, and finally in the South of Europe - however, only one at a time.

Hitler knew very well that the time is working against him so he was pressing ahead to the fullest. In the East the adversaries began to mobilize their huge human reserves and in the West their huge materiel reserves.

Once it came to a grannie (babushka) and her folkish jokes. She asked a suburb's NSDAP group leader standing in front of a map of the world. "What does the homogeneous green field mean?" "Russia" - was his answer. "What do light-red and the light-green colors show, which are covering large parts of the map?" "England's Empire and the U.S.A." - he replied unhesitant. Then the grannie wanted to know where on the map is Germany. When the finger of the suburb group leader pointed to the little blue dot in the middle of Europe, she asked in astonishment: "Well, does the Fuehrer know about this?"

He knew it, of course. He also knew that he missed the operation "Sea Lion."

England recovered quickly, and in addition through the Lend-Lease agreement with the U.S.A. she was well armed with plenty of fighter-bombers, 50 destroyers and some submarines. For protection of armament shipments to England, the supposedly neutral U.S.A. set its foot in Iceland and therefrom its destroyers hunted for the German submarines which on the open ocean attacked British convoys.

"The German Air Force with all its available means must destroy the English

Air Force as quickly as possible", was the call of that time. So this alternative turned into an air battle over England which ended with the German heavy losses, although the German Air Force came out of this battle as a Secondary Victor. Since then the British bombers had their own days and flew over Germany to kill women and children "without gloves", just as the Prime Minister Churchill had prayed.

Hitler's vacillation between the "Sea Lion" and "Barbarossa", the first as his grandeur Germanic feeling with the lack of interest in the conquest of the West, and the second not any less critical, but with his hunger for the land in the East accompanied by the fight against the "SUB-HUMANS", which ruled him since his Vienna days, was at last overcome by the second, for: "As long as Stalin is alive with his wisdom and carefulness, there is no danger. But if he disappears, then the Jews, which are marching now in the second van, will advance forward into the first one." Thus this matter was settled in the Hitler's mind and has guided him into the near future.

If he attacks England, Hitler speculated, then Russia will stab him in the back. If he attacks Russia, England will return to the Continent. So the decision to attack the Soviet Union was the "most difficult decision of my life," he said.

At this time of Hitler's consternation, Rudolf Hess, the "Deputy of the Fuehrer" and a faithful comrade had to come forward. Born to an English-Jewish mother, and educated by the British in Egypt, later on the W.W.II pilot, he had good connections with the English aristocracy. If no one could, he was the one who might convince Churchill to the peace terms, especially since Churchill also had an American-Jewish mother and was anti-communist deep in his bones.

On the World scale the historical peace flight of Hess into Scotland began with a letter written by the founder of the "Geo-Politic", Professor Haushofer. It was addressed to the Duke von Hamilton. Hess explained this historical mission to his adjutant Karlheinz Pintsch like this: "As you know, I am one of the oldest party comrades with my thoughts integrated into the 'Mein Kampf'. I think that you will agree with me if I say: I know more about Adolf Hitler's mind than anyone else in his proximity. Adolf Hitler wants a strong England, and he wants peace with her. That's the reason why he did not invade England. Back then we could have done this easily. We have been trying to reach an agreement. At this moment our enemy is not in the West. It is in the East. That's were the danger is. And that's where the Fuehrer's thoughts are concentrated. I can crash into the sea. I can be shot down. I can be even killed after the landing. But if I would be successful, my journey will save millions of human lives and besides - the future of Germany." Stalin on May 5, 1941, in front of 500 graduates of a military academy gave the secret speech, which could not remain secret and hence reached Hitler and Hess. Probably that speech was taken seriously by them as Stalin said: "If it works out (an attempt to postpone an armed conflict with Germany until autumn), then the war with Germany will inevitably break out under much better conditions than now, for the Red Army will be better trained and equipped."[79]

Five days after this speech, in the dark night of May 10, 1941, an almost fifty year old Rudolf Hess parachuted down next to a farm house close to Dungavel, the Scottish domicile of the Nobleman (Duke) von Hamilton. The airplane ME-110 crashed in the mountains. The next morning, when the Duke appeared at the hospital bed (Hess hurt his leg while jumping), he heard quietly spoken words: "I am a missionary for the humanity. The Fuehrer does not want to destroy England. He wants to end the fight."

The mission failed. Churchill was not willing to negotiate and since then, for over 30 years, Hess is in prison.

Let it be permitted to draw the conclusion based on the fact, that despite the collective German liability nothing bad happened to the Professor Haushofer nor to the Deputy's wife. Quite the opposite - on Hitler's instructions Mrs.Ilse Hess received a pension of the Minister who became the Prisoner of War.

Due to this failed peace mission the German rear guard in the West was not freed of its burdens. Despite of this, following month the German military strength was put in line on the Eastern frontier to "overcome the Soviet Russia by a blitz campaign", named accordingly with the Fuehrer's Order No. 21, the "Fall Barbarossa" ("Striking Red Beard", or "Striking Red Barbarians")

Because the emphasis was put on the synonym "Blitz" ("Fast" or "Lightning"), the Chief Commander Darius on September 11, 1941, at 11:30 A.M., telegraphed to Berlin: "I see Petersburg and the Sea." - he meant Leningrad. The Darius' Army Corps North and a tank Company fought in Lithuania, Latvia and Estonia.

In the morning of October 13, Secretary of the Central Committee of the Russian Communist Party, Shcherbakov, when everyone already has heard cannonades of the German Army Corps Middle, said at the Party meeting in Moscow: "We don't want to close our eyes. Moscow is in danger."

And the Army Corps South in the battle of Kiev alone took 665,000 prisoners, and in November the Corps captured the City of Kharkov in the Soviet "Ruhr Basin".

In the first days of the attack the Soviet Air Force was totally eliminated. The Russians lost thousands of their tanks. In the first fourteen days more than one million Soviet soldiers were taken into German captivity. On the twelfth day the Chief of General Staff, Senior General Halder, noted in his diary: "It would not be an exaggeration if I were to state, that the campaign against Russia has been won within fourteen days."[80] Churchill also expected a quick fall of Russia. So on October 28, 1941, he wrote to the Ambassador Sir Stafford Cripps, who in the meantime was evacuated to Kuybyshev: "Because of your difficult situation and Russia's misery I express my deepest sympathy. But the Russians have no right to blame us. They decided alone about their destiny by letting Hitler march against Poland as the Pact with Ribbentrop provided."[81]

And suddenly winter came with such low temperatures which Russia experienced only once in a hundred years. And this happened many weeks too early. Engines of the German tanks, which previously dug in the mud, now wallowed with their automatic weapons frozen. At minus 45 degrees Celsius, the soldiers wore unpadded winter coats; had no gloves and no felted boots, so that their hands and feet chilblained.

Many questions arose as to why the supplies of winter clothes were insufficient. It came to a point that in the homeland women's fur coats were collected and sent to the front. The tension was so high that the Reich's Attorney, Loellke (after the war he became a Political Attorney of the State in Hamburg), sentenced a milk car driver to death because he purchased a few stolen gloves. The answer to this overall confusion was simple: the prolongation of the campaign in the Balkans by carelessly acting Hitler and his Generals hoping, that the "Blitz" assault in the East would be finished quickly, as it was the case with previous "Blitzes".

The General Staff and the Counter-Intelligence Services in comparison to the German soldiers, were not the same as they were before. Through the political intrigue and false accusations of prostitution and homosexuality masterminded by Heydrich in 1938, the Commander-in-Chief of the Armed Forces and Minister of War Field Marshall von Blomberg and next to him the Commander-in-Chief of the Army Colonel-General Fritsch, who contradicted Hitler, were drummed out of their posts. But the Counter-Intelligence was not able to uncover in time the routinized hard communist, Soviet spy Dr.Sorge, who was often seen as a guest at the German Embassy in Tokyo, and who advised Stalin that without apprehension he can withdraw two million soldiers from the Eastern Siberia because Japan will not attack Russia. Because of this, in the first days of December 1941, Siberian forces were positioned at Moscow. This sealed the fate of the Eastern campaign and of the War, as well. Three Siberian armies (1st; 10th and 20th) were engaged in the battle for Moscow. On December 5th, dressed in warm winter clothes they attacked, pushed to the West, and within forty eight hours reached the German Battle Corps' headquarters of General Schaal. Later he recalled: "The discipline started to weaken. Deserters multiplied and by foot, without weapons or commanders, they were moving towards the West, pulling a calf by the rope or a sledge with potatoes. A panic set in at the supply columns, which previously were used only for the military advances. Without the provisions, frozen and mindless, everyone retreated."

Hitler, who in those days had to think about Napoleon's withdrawal from Moscow, stayed calm. General Dr.Renudilc after the War wrote: "The highest commanders of the army considered a complete withdrawal from the Eastern Front. Hitler refused to discuss the matter for forty eight hours. Then he gathered his staff and ordered: 'The Army must keep its positions and only go back step by step but fighting.' I am convinced with others, who took part in the campaign, that Hitler saved the Army from a complete destruction. He made this decision against the suggestions of his advisors."

Things got worse in those important days of the war: President of the U.S., who was called by Hitler a "blasphemer", a "warmonger", a "super rascal" and the "greatest war criminal of all times", found a back door to the war. Roosevelt's promise to the American mothers of October 30, 1940: "I already said it and I will say it again and again: Your boys shall not go and fight in a foreign war!" was already questionable when his war ships accompanied the British convoys, and when on September 11, 1941, he announced that the "U.S. Navy will exercise a firing test on the Atlantic Ocean." At the time the Siberian Armies destroyed the German divisions at Moscow, Roosevelt sacrificed the Pacific Fleet so that he could enter into the W.W.II against the will of the American people.

About the Pearl Harbor in the Pacific Ocean, Charles Callan Tansill in his book "The Back Door To The War" wrote: "Within one minute 154 Japanese dive-bombers in a low-level flight above the harbor basin, dropped bombs on the proud American Pacific Fleet and destroyed the entire American Air Force in the Far East. Within three minutes four battle ships sunk, a fifth one was severely damaged and three others lightly."[82]

The American Admiral Kimmel, who was in charge of Pearl Harbor, never doubted Roosevelt's intentions and that he is responsible for the death of 3,000 mariners there. He reported to Roosevelt's son-in-law, Colonel Curtis B. Dall: "On top of this, in the late autumn of 1941, shortly before the attack, the U.S. Navy Department (Ministry) in Washington, D.C. commissioned my three aircraft carriers off. One to Wake Islands (half way between Guam and Midway), the second to Midway Islands (1,150 miles west-northwest of Hawaii) and the third into the homeland waters. In this way my decisive forces were dismembered and on December 7, 1941, were unprepared to neither defend the fleet nor to counter-attack. What I will say next, will surprise you more, Dear Colonel Dall. Later on I found out that while approaching the Pearl Harbor, the Japanese forces had special orders to turn back to their waters in case the Americans were to discover their presence. What happened there next, explains why this an extremely important info, which was intercepted and decoded into English and radioed to Washington, was kept intentionally secret from the Hawaiian commanders."[83]

With this manifestation of hostility on December 11, 1941, the U.S.A. entered into the war with Japan and by the same token with Germany, which was in alliance with this distant island-country. By this action the similar coalition was created as this one during the W.W.I, which by future historians will probably be referred to as the twentieth century's "THIRTY YEAR WAR OF IDEOLOGIES".

To Hitler it was certain that by the American entry into the War, the struggle which encompassed the globe was lost for Germany. His conviction was confirmed in Nuremberg by General Jodl, the Operation Chief of Staff of the Highest Command of the Army, who during the war years was always in touch with the Fuehrer: "When the catastrophe of the 1941 winter happened, Hitler did not believe in the victory anymore."

Before Christmas of that winter twelve countries declared war on the Great German Reich. Among them China, and to this abundance of adversaries should be added the defeat of Rommel's North Africa Corps. In a short time Britons seized the whole Cyrenaica in Libya.

On the day of American entry into the war, Hitler reasoned in front of the German Parliament about the defeat at Moscow in the following way: "Like the Greeks against the Karthageans not only defended Rome; like the Romans and Teutons against the Huns not only defended the Occident; like the German Emperors against the Mongols not only defended Germany; like the Spanish heroes against the Africans (Arabs) not only defended Spain, but all of them defended Europe, so does the Germany of today not fight for herself, but for the entire European Continent."

About the U.S.' entry into the war Hitler explained: "Roosevelt is supported by the circle of Jews, who through the Old Testament's greed want to see the U.S. as an instrument, which they may use for a second "PURIM" against the European nations, which are becoming more and more anti-Semitic. But this man also reached out to them."

For Hitler it was "the goal of the Galilean, to free his country of the Jewish oppression." He strived alike this Man who wandered around the earth two thousand years ago, and two days after his Parliament speech, while still considering his loss of the war effort, believed to come through as the New Messiah: "Christ was an Aryan. But Apostle Paul used his teachings to mobilize the 'underworld' and to organize pre-Bolshevism. (Inset: With the teachings of ESSENES. See POST. r.32) If there is God, then He gave not only life, but also the knowledge. And I do manage my life with the insight given to me by God. This could lead me wrong, but nevertheless straight forward and without lies."[84]

At a Christmas party of the NSDAP in the Citizen's Brewery Cellar in Munich on December 18, 1926, Hitler presented himself as a follower of God's Son: "The birth of the man, which is celebrated on Christmas, has the greatest meaning to us, the National Socialists. Christ was the greatest protagonist of a struggle against the worldwide Jewish enemy. (POST. r.46) He had the nature of the most superb fighter who ever lived on this Earth. I will conclude the work of Christ which he could not finish."

As if the battle for Berlin has not yet waged, Rosenberg was still planning to install a Ministry of the Reich for the Occupied Eastern Territories, and when he was in Nuremberg's prison he wrote about the differences between him and his comrade Hitler: "It was noticeable in what this Messiah believed after his return from the Landsberg Fortress. And his beliefs escalated after the seizure of power. At the end of the War these beliefs became embarrassing." The racial researcher Professor Hans F.K. Guenther summarized his divagations: "Hitler emanates the consciousness of an Oriental strength. This consciousness enabled him to perform at a level that hardly anyone could live up to."

So, at least the Europe ruled by Hitler, from the Arctic Ocean down to Sicily, from the Atlantic Ocean to the River Volga shall be free of Jews.

Heydrich also saw in his Fuehrer the New Savior. Wasn't he himself and the Fuehrer partially Jewish, just like Jesus? And have not all three overcome the "JEWISHNESS WITHIN THEMSELVES" in the struggle against the "Breed of Vipers"?

Early on Heydrich's religious and racial mania came to an outburst when in a conversation with Hans Bernd Gisevius he argued that within a short period of time Adolf Hitler will be that, which the Jesus Christ was.

Heydrich, right after the catastrophic month of December 1941, in order to find solution to the Jewish problem, called a conference held at Wannsee in Berlin. According to Hitler this was one of "the most important assignments".

For Hitler from that moment on holding back the front lines had only one purpose, that is: To fulfill the provisions of the Wannsee conference as the "Work intended by God."

Heydrich took command over the "Einsatzgruppen" ("Operational Groups") and when he was assassinated in Prague, the Fuehrer and his friends talked about the "Lost Battle". When Hitler said these two words, his men saw him crying. Irrespective pitiless and murderous acts against the Jews were to continue.

After the war numerous German generals declared that winning of the war with Russia was possible if only their advices were considered. The author of this work has the opinion, that the defeat in the war with Russia may be attributed to Adolf Hitler's brutal willpower. In Vienna, he turned himself into a hater and the proof of this is the fact that three more years he was able to fight against the worldly enemies. The Minister of Elucidation of People and of Propaganda Dr.Goebbels, and the Minister of Mobilization Albert Speer, were most influential helpers in this matter. Dr.Goebbels always came up with new sufficiently convincing slogans for the people. Out of the bombed factories Adolf Speer had pressed more tanks, guns, cannons, airplanes, shells and grenades, and delivered them via destroyed railroad tracks and bridges to the front lines.

Hermann Goering, called in public "Steward Hermann" ("Hermann Meier"), was satisfied which such a reviled name, and led in the middle of the war a happy life. When he became Reich's Marshall he gave the Nation a promise that never ever would an enemy airplane fly over the Great Reich. And Heinrich Himmler, in distaste for his SS-concentration camps in the rears, was called the "Reich's Idiot" by the brave men of the SS-Weapon tank divisions.

Believing in a creation of the United Europe through the struggle with the Bolshevism, several thousands volunteers from the Scandinavian countries, from Holland, Belgium and France, joined the German warriors at the Eastern Front. Even Spain, under orders of Muñoz Grande, later a second man in that country, sent about 20,000 people to the front at Leningrad. Also the SS-Weapon soldiers were fighting side by side with the soldiers from the Balkan Peninsula, among them regiments consisting of Moslems in the German field uniforms with the red fez on their heads. Without the huge deliveries of materiel from the U.S. and England to Murmansk at the Barentsevo Sea, and to Vladivostok of the Far East, and also through Persia in the South, the Red Army would have been defeated. The U.S. delivered weapons, munitions and food, all to be repaid after the War, for war means business too. With about 15,000 airplanes, 13,000 tanks, 4,000 canons and over 400,000 motor vehicles, which in a due course reached the Soviet Union with five million tons of various nutrients and other provisions, the German advances of summer 1942 on Stalingrad and on Caucasus, turned into a proverbial: "Return ticket please to the Health Spa in Caucasus." And the marching soldiers said: "Fuehrer commands, but for the outcome we are responsible." The German Army was in a constant need of oil. So the march on Baku was a must. "If I will not have the oil, I will end the war," so justified Hitler his orders. But when the German tanks reached the oil fields at Baku, each of them was set on fire.

The withdrawing Army from the Causasus joined men, women and children of various nations. Among them were the Cossacks of Caucasus who fought on the German side. Because they fought arm in arm with the Germans against Stalin, the Georgian man from the Caucasus never forgave them for such a treachery.

After the war a large number of these people were pushed by Britons into the Austrian River Drau and the rest, if they had not committed suicide, were sent to their deaths in the Soviet Union.

Discovery of the enemies by General Gehlen behind his desk in the "Office for Foreign Armies East" and far away from the place of subversion, never led to a clear picture of those enemies, nor to an exposure of traitors moled in the Fuehrer's headquarters. Thanks to Gehlen's book "Service" ("Dienst") it was discovered that this man believed in ghosts. Years after an officially admitted death of Martin Bormann, confirmed by the finding of his body, Gehlen was "certain" that the perfectly camouflaged Hitler's First Secretary and advisor Bormann lives in the Soviet Union.

The summer battle of Kursk, seen in sheer numbers, was the largest battle in the world's history. Thousands of tanks advanced from both sides and thousands of airplanes were waiting to take off at the airports. 500,000 train wagons loaded with war materiel already were rolling for three months from the interior of Russia towards Kursk. So the offensive failed, but not due to a strong resistance of the Red Army, but because of the lack of information about its regrouping. The German tanks "Tigers" and "Panthers" burned like torches and after one week of heavy fighting the battle was called off.

The objective of Stalingrad's capture was to eliminate the basic Soviet center of armor and to cut off the most important River Volga from the supply sources of American war materiel, as well as those flowing in via the Caspian Sea from Persia.

In August 1942, the spearhead of the 6th Army under orders of General Paulus reached Volga River banks at Stalingrad. When the Italian and Romanian corps at the wings of Paulus' Army were broken down, and the Army was encircled, Hitler issued orders as if he was still believing in his two year old boasting: "Wherever a German soldier stands, no other will replace him!" But the German army was destroyed and about 100,000 German prisoners of war died from hunger and diseases alike the millions of Soviet prisoners died in Germany. During the first months of the war a great number of Russians, as well as Ukrainians joined the Germans, believing that better times are to come.

In the Ukraine; in the White Russia and in the Baltic countries the people greeted incoming German soldiers warmly. In almost every Ukrainian village, alongside roads stood women with bread, salt and milk. Hundreds of thousands of their men asked for weapons to march with Germans against the communism. The Soviet Marshall Vlasov became a German prisoner of war. After a while he formed the Russian volunteer division ready to fight on the German side. But everything went wrong due to the racial policy of Hitler; of Rosenberg, his Minister for the Occupied East, and of the "GOLDEN PHEASANTS", as

Officials of the Nazi Party dressed in brown uniforms were called by the German soldiers.

The warlike acts of the Soviet partisans, who shot German soldiers in constantly escalating numbers at the outskirts of forests; who for days and weeks put the whole railroad tracks out of order; who blew up Generals and Party Officials in their quarters, were carried out by "SUBHUMANS" created by the teachings of those "Golden Pheasants". The German soldiers did not pay much attention to such ill-teachings and never obeyed their own "Brown Commissars" orders to shoot the Red Commissars, albeit Jews, on the battle field.

Thanks to the elimination of an extensive bureaucracy in the thirties, the economic progress in Germany was possible. But due to this new situation the German soldiers paid with blood because of the formation of a new bureaucracy. This new bureaucracy brought laborers into Germany by force, whereas it could have won hundreds of thousands of them in a voluntary way. Exceptions were rare, like the one of Joachim Nehring, a District Official of Galicia. In 1950 he was questioned by the Chairman Mosich of the Denazification Tribunal in Munich: "When you, the one concerned, acted humanly with the people of Ukraine in contradiction to the usual habit of the NS-regime, certainly you did this out of your righteousness. Did you think at that time that by a sensible dealing with those people it might be much easier to reach the National Socialist goal?" Because this faithful National Socialist believed in a clean idea, he protected the Jews from the "Einsatzkommandos" / Operational Troops/ orders, and answered: "Of course, throughout the war I was dominated by the thought of helping the Great Reich to win, whenever I could. Testimonies of the witnesses prove, that I did this in accord with humanity."[85]

After destruction of the Sixth Army at Stalingrad (February 1943), the German combat troops in North Africa were also eliminated from the front arena. Soon afterwards followed a successful landing of the Western Allies in Italy and the withdrawal of Italy from the Pact with Germany in effect of the negotiations which took place in Tanger ever since the Americans landed in Morocco.

And throughout the entire year of 1943, the Red Army marched toward the West. It captured the Kuban's bridge head and Donec area, next the Ukraine with Kiev. In the beginning of 1944 from Leningrad, which was never fully encircled, about one million Soviet soldiers commenced a counter-attack and within eighty minutes a drum shelling completely flattened German ditches and bunkers at the front line. Even at Verdun during the W.W.I, the soldiers did not experience such a vicious attack. The rest of the German divisions continued to defend themselves at the Estonia's border. The Army Corps Middle moved to the Northern borderline of the Pripet Swamp. In the South soon Russians reached the Romanian border and Czechoslovakia.

At night of June 6, 1944, the hostile paratroopers landed at two o'clock in the morning, east of the French River Orne. From the British and American war ships and transporters, anchored at night in the Bay de la Seine, at dawn, after a heavy shelling by their ships and airplane bombings, 18,000 soldiers stepped on land to set bridgeheads. On this day Hitler in his Berchtesgaden's Villa slept like a dummy until noon. Invasion of the Continent, which Stalin demanded during the past three years begun. For Hitler it was the "Second Front" opened by his, confused by Roosevelt, "Germanic Brothers" - the Britons. Opened by this "Aging Gangster" and by Churchill, that "Crazy Drinker." Soon the combined Anglo-American forces landed on the Mediterranean Coast of Southern France, which was previously occupied by the German troops.

From the colonel's ranks down to a single one military person, everyone knew that the War was lost. On July 20, 1944, in the Hitler's East Prussian headquarters, Colonel von Stauffenberg placed a briefcase with a bomb next to Hitler, under a cart table and walked away.

Stauffenberg's bomb killed and wounded several of his comrades, who were, like him, Hitler's opponents. But the Commander-in-Chief Hitler got away from this calamity almost unhurt. There was no gun in the briefcase, with which the full of illusions Hitler might be killed. This failed attempt made him despicable. "These revolutionaries, these traitors are worthless to me" Hitler told his valet Linge. "They are not even rebels. If Stauffenberg had pulled a gun and shot me, then he would be a man. What he did, was a cowardice!"

In the midst of rubble, Hitler's certainty that he has been chosen by God prevailed. Sitting on a box, Hitler thought: "By analyzing what just happened here I come to a conclusion, that since I was so amazingly saved, nothing more disastrous will happen to me again. More than ever I am convinced that it is ME, who is destined to bring the great Work of MINE to a Happy End."

The war went on and in its last nine months demanded just as many victims as it did in the previous fifty nine months.

The Army Front Middle fell apart and the Russians were excited that this German defeat was worse than that at Stalingrad. Twenty five divisions were lost and dozens of German generals were taken prisoner. It was said that soon thereafter they were converted into the resistance combatants with the instructions of the German communists acting under the auspices of the "National Committee of a Free Germany".

In August 1944, the Red Amy stopped the offensive in East Prussia at the border with the Great German Reich, and the Western Allies reached the River Rhein. Then it became clear to men like Goebbels, Speer and Himmler that the war was lost. To Goebbels, once again from the old socialist struggle times, returned his EGO: "Now it is enough. Now we must see how to get out of this mess in a sensible way. I tend to think more and more that we can make an agreement with Russia, but not with Churchill because he is a blind hater. This is proven by his speeches which contained the meanest and most cynical insults against us. Stalin, however, as a matter-of-fact, is a realistic politician."

Goebbels, to whom the leadership of the "Total War" was assigned in Berlin's Sport Palace, had discovered that at most every tenth German soldier was fighting. Less and less of the soldiers were at the front lines. The shrinking numbers of the warriors are now more and more interested in talking about an overall situation than about "wearing the uniform". And Goebbels wailed: "We were missing the main point - the simplicity and coherence between our law-giving and executive branches. Instead of a Constitution we have a great number of regulations, commands of the Fuehrer, and ordinances ,which often contradict or even cancel each other. For the sake of understanding them, a great deal of wisdom is necessary."[86]

Minister of Armament, Speer, who with the help of hungry and aging German workers and forced foreign laborers, still managed to produce in the ruined plants tanks and fighter planes in the growing numbers, did not want to materialize his own idea of injecting poisonous gas into the Fuehrer's bunker.

And Heinrich Himmler of conservative breed, who de facto was the ruler of the entire police system, tried to come to terms with the Western Powers. But he declined to join the efforts of the SS General Schellenberg, Chief of the Foreign Intelligence Services, who already commenced negotiations with the Jews in Switzerland, and who constantly pushed Himmler to a more "fruitful deeds", like what will happen in case the Chief of the Army and of the Great Reich Adolf Hitler would be overthrown or killed, or a Civil War were to breakout. Such was the evident dilemma of the opposition which failed to act.

Romanians, Finns, Bulgarians and Hungarians, who formed the alliance with Germany abandoned it. Even worse: only a few days after their capitulation before the Red Army, they formed new governments and declared war against the German Reich. In the Balkan countries the confusion was out of control, while the Finnish soldiers with warm gestures and sad looks showed the German soldiers roads leading to their Fatherland.

The Allies' two wrong decisions should be credited for the fact, that although Germany's soldiers, workers and women were tired of war, they started again to believe in the Fuehrer and his promise of victory by use of the "Wonder Weapon" ("Atomic Bomb" - inset by Publisher).

To the first decision belonged a secret order given to General Harris of the British Bombers' Fleet, the same Harris to whom the English Queen after the War did not want to be married to. This order was justified: "The main goal of your bombardments is to break the high morale of the enemy's population." But the order and the tactic of "carpeting with bombs" of the workers' districts created the opposite effect. It ignited a new wave of resistance of the entire German Nation with its soldiers combined.

The second decision, in 1943, persuaded by President Roosevelt at the Casablanca Conference, demanded of Germany to "capitulate unconditionally". This demand caused almost every German to believe, that the German Reich is the only foe of the enemy camp but not the National Socialism.

The last German protest took place in December 1944, when in the Ardennes three German Armies ran over the American front and 10,000 U.S. soldiers rose their hands. The Allied Armies' Staffs in Brussels and Paris made preparations for evacuation. But then the fuel shortage brought the enthusiastic attack to an end. The German tanks got stuck and the fighter planes could not take off anymore. An admirer of the Allied Powers, Liddell Hart, noted this about the December battles: "The concept, the decision and the strategic plan were the mental possession of Hitler. It was a glorious idea and could have led to a great success if he had enough forces and reserves in storage."

The British Prime Minister Churchill had similar thoughts, and in January of 1945 wired to Stalin: "The battle in the West is very difficult and at any moment the highest command might demand a serious decision. I would appreciate it, if you would let me know, if in January we could count on a larger Russian offensive at the River Vistula in Poland or somewhere else. I consider this matter very urgent."

Stalin did not wait for three years with the offensive like Churchill did before, but only one week. On January 12, 1945, the Red Army from the Baltic Sea down to the Hungarian border stepped into its last thunderous attack, which ended three months later in Berlin. It was not a real war. Young German soldiers were bleeding to death, killed in the Russian forests and in fields. Soviets pushed against the badly trained, fifteen year old boys and against sixty year or older men, who were called to battle by Dr.Goebbels. About two million German aging men, women and children fled from the Eastern parts of Germany to the West. They were milled by the caterpillars of the Soviet tanks, torn apart on the country roads by the artillery shells, by the airplane bombs, by the grenades of the advancing armies, or drowned under the broken ice of the rivers or of the Baltic Sea.

The horror in East Prussia, for instance, was heated up by a poem of the Jewish admirer of Stalin, Ilja Ehrenburg, who after the war dissented from its authorship: "Kill, kill the Read Army warriors, kill! Kill the German child in its mother's womb!"

The author of this book, in February 1945, was wounded in East Prussia and fell into the Russian hands. He asked a Soviet General of Asian descent, in his thirties, at a dinner table: "How could all this be possible?" "You see," the General answered, "in every army there is a certain percentage of criminals. Only those, who get a promise to do whatever they wish along their way in any village, town etc., are eager for sacrifices. The others, who follow behind, are better mannered and wish to enjoy their lives in peace. Soon we will be in Berlin."

Soviet Marshall Sokolowskij excused his criminals more plainly: "Our soldiers felt a certain satisfaction when they could show "it" to those women of the Noble Nation. And besides, it is not true that all German women are virgins."[87]

The murders and rapes were stopped by G.F. Alexandrow, the chief ideologist of the Central Committee of the Soviet Union Communist Party, whose essay appeared in the Party's newspaper "Pravda ("The Truth") under the headline: "Comrade Ehrenburg simplifies too much."

The Americans also wanted to show what they can do. So in February of 1945 they bombarded the City of Dresden, which was packed to the brim with the refugees and wounded. The bombardment was carried out by their "Flying Fortresses". Their first wave turned this City of Art into an ocean of flames. The second and third waves prevented the extinguishing of flames because of use of the explosive bombs and air mines. Finally, the accompanying fighter planes shot women and children with the machine guns, who tried to rescue themselves

Die Kraft der Deutschen Wehrmacht, trier im Herbst 1941 bei einem Panzerangriff auf das brennende Leningrad, zerbrach im Dezember 1941 vor dem tiefverschneiten Moskau, als drei sibirische Armeen zu stürmen begannen. Die USA traten in den Krieg ein und damn' wusste Hitler, class der Krieg fur Deutschland verloren war.

Strength of the German Army was weakened by the tank assault on the burning city of Leningrad in the autumn of 1941, and in December of that year in front of the deeply snowed Moscow by three Siberian Armies which commenced counter-offensive. At the same time U.S.A. entered into the war and with that Hitler knew that the war has been lost.

When Hitler realized that the has been lost, in the beginning of 1942 he called the "Wannsee Conference" with a task of resolving the "Final Solution of the Jewish Question". And still for three and half years he kept the German men and women on the battle fields because his Messianic illusions urged him to finish the "Work of the Lord."

Die Wannsee-Konferenz zur «Endlösung der Judenfrage» fend Anfang 1942 stats, als Hitler erkannt haste, class der Krieg nicht mehr zu gewinnen war. Noch dreieinhalb Jahre hielten deutsche Männer und Jungen aus, weil der im Messias-Wahn lebende Hitler das «Werk des Herrn» zu vollenden trachtete.

in the waters of the River Elbe. The cautious estimate is documenting that the quarter of a million people had died.

In March of the same year, the Western Allies crossed the River Rhein. In April the Red Army entered Vienna and encountered there the American troops, white, yellow and brown skinned, all mixed together.

On April 25, in Torgau at the River Elbe, American and Soviet troops united in presence of many photographers, and three days later in Italy German Generals signed the armistice truce. On May 7, 1945, in Reims, France, the German Army capitulated unconditionally before the American General Eisenhower, and on May 8, before the Soviet Marshall Zhukov in Berlin. And the Victors decided to divide the Great German Reich.

One week before the unconditional capitulation, in the ruins of the Reich's Chancellery, Adolf Hitler, who, because of the Morell's poisons and the waged war in his fifties became a trembling man, finally took a gun into his hand. But first, a few hours before, he dictated his last political will: "I do oblige the Leadership of the Nation and its followers to strictly observe the racial laws and to a full hearted resistance against the poisoners of all the people in the World, the International Jewry."

ACTION OF THE TEUTONIC HOLY ORDER LEAD BY THE JEWISH MONGRELS

Shortly after the turning point of the War, the December 1941 catastrophe at Moscow, on January 20, 1942, in a Villa of the Berlin's suburb Wannsee, a conference was held on the "Final Solution of the Jewish Question", presided over by the proudly chest bearing Commander-in-Chief of the German Security Police, half-Jew Reinhard Heydrich, who declared that he is in charge of the whole operation. In addition to Eichmann were present representatives of Rosenberg's Ministry of the Occupied Territories, of Frank's General Guberniya in Poland, as well as of the Interior and Foreign Ministries. The task of the operation was outlined by Heydrich:

"(a.) to prepare for an increasing emigration of Jews;

(b.) to guide the stream of moving emigrants;

(c.) in certain cases to accelerate the emigration process."

He called this "the goal of cleaning the German living space of Jews in legal ways." On that day Heydrich did not talk about the extermination of Jews.

During the Nuremberg's Trial the obese Reich's Marshall Hermann Goering lost a lot of weight in his prison cell, but in the reverse process he gained back then aggressive spirit of his youth, especially when he referred to the "Wannsee Conference". He argued with his defense lawyer Jackson, that a translation of the conference's outline was full of mistakes. At this point Jackson agreed: "Okay, I do accept that. But how about what you said one time ago, as follows: 'In supplementation of the assignment, which you received January 24, 1939 concerning emigration and evacuation as a solution of the Jewish problem in a positive way, I do instruct you to meet all the necessary preparations within the German sphere of influence in Europe pertaining organization and financing of the whole operation.'"

And the dispute between Goering and Jackson continued:

"Goering: 'I don't think this is correct.'

Jackson: 'Okay, please give your version.'

Goering: 'I will read it exactly like it is written here: In supplementation of the assignment by the decree of January 24, 1939, which ordered you to solve the Jewish problem by emigration or evacuation in circumstances of the time that would be operationally most feasible. Therefore, I instruct you to meet all the demands of preparation on organizational, practical and material levels.' And now comes the most critical phrase which was translated wrong. It says: 'for a complete solution' and not 'for a final solution', i.e. '...for a complete solution of the Jewish question in the German sphere of influence in Europe.'"[88]

In the meantime, the Jew Eichmann became a Commander of the SS

Battalion. When in 1937 he finalized his assignment in Palestine, he reported cheerily that soon the Jewish population there will outnumber the local one. Right after the "Wannsee Conference" Eichmann enjoyed an "evening at the fire place" at Heydrich's house. Since then, in letters to various Ministries, Heydrich introduced Eichmann as his acting consultant.

For several months killing of the Jews by Heydrich's "Operational Groups" in Russia, had already been taking place. Therefore, Eichmann's testimony during his trial in Jerusalem, that he did not converse about this matter at the "fire place", is not trustworthy. Heydrich justified his actions with Hitler's "Special Order" of 1941, establishing the "Operational Groups". Therefore , he instigated vigorously his Policemen to go to the East, "because the Eastern Jewry is a reservoir of Bolshevism and by the will of Fuehrer must be destroyed."

SS General Ohlendorf remembered that Heydrich passed onto commanders of the operational groups Fuehrer's order stating that "communist functionaries, activists, Jews, gypsies, saboteurs and other agents shall be always considered as elements, who by their sheer existence endanger overall security. Therefore they shall be eliminated without any due process of law."

It was a wide open definition under which each Eastern Jew could have fallen.

The German army combat troops, who never carried out this "Special Order", suspected more than they really knew about what was going on behind their backs. They just welcomed the fact that their rears were kept clear. Thus in 1941, between the Baltic Sea and the Black Sea, with all their strength they marched ahead as fast and as far as possible.

This investigative work does not concentrate on the number of Jews ordered by Hitler to be destroyed. Suffice it to say that one murdered person is already too much, but it is of no use to the historians who are still walking in the dark.

In 1952, in an U.S.' newspaper, a Jewish statistician estimated 350,000 victims. Thus far this estimate rose to six million. "If we Jews declare that it was six million, then this would be a shameful lie" said the statistician.[89]

The number "six million" was born in speeches at the beginning of the Nuremberg Trial and was supported by the reports of the SS-Officer who was in charge of gassing Jews with Zyklon B. He was Kurt Gerstein of Jewish origin, almost like everyone with this kind of a name, as for example earlier mentioned names of Finkelstein, Bronstein, Mildenstein, Bechstein and Einstein.

The data which contained Gerstein's documents and after the war was delivered by this SS murderer to the French Intelligence Service, were so unbelievable that even at the Nuremberg trial, being posed to search for the truth, this data was not permitted to be taken into account.

However, the weekly magazine "Der Spiegel" ("The Mirror") had no reservation in using the number of "six million" taken from the Gerstein's documents. Hence it assessed: "With a measurement stick and a stop-watch it has been proven that in the gas chambers the size of 25 square meters and 45 cubic meters, 700 to 800 Jews were crowded together and gassed."

The director of the famous Youth Village in Dortmund listened to the questions of his pupils pertaining "Spiegel's" assessment and requested an explanation. On February 21, 1967 appeared a reply: "You are absolutely right that Gerstein made a mistake in his computation."

This reply did not prevent the "Mirror" (which usually is exact with numbers) to spread Gerstein's doubtful numbers, so in the series of articles written in 1968 by a Jewish professor Saul Friedlaender, it repeated them: "700 to 800 in a room of 25 square meters and of 45 cubic meters."[(90)]

This December of 1968, the author of this book travelled by train from Amsterdam to France and then to Switzerland with an Export Director of a Dutch Natural Gas Company, a Jew. At the sight of the covered by snow Ardennen, war memories awakened my companion for during the winter 1944-45 he was fighting there as a Commander of Canadian Artillery. When he opened the "Mirror" and came to page 100, I asked him: "You are certainly good in computation. So, what do you think about "Spiegel's" assessment regarding the gassing?" After an in depth thought he answered: "Sooner or later these lies will hurt our necks."

The next day in Geneva, we once again discussed the subject matter with Professor Friedlaender, a Citizen of Israel. The author of the "Mirror's" series was appalled: "This magazine publicized my presentation omitting the footnote which states that Gerstein's numbers are wrong." To this, on January 21, 1969, from "Spiegel" came forth a remarkable comment: "It is conceivable that Gerstein, in the face of cruelty, could not solve a math problem. So there was no need to explain this to a reader in the footnote."

Next to the Friedlaender's presentations of the "Gerstein's Numbers": "In four chambers four times 750 people in four times 45 cubic meters", the weekly put a picture with the subtitle: "Preparation Zyklon B. It liquidated 25,000 Jews daily."

The historical investigation cannot be made with a "wooden hammer on a judge's pulpit". To the readers' surprise, the "Mirror" lowered his estimate down to five million.

In the Thorwald's (Thunder God of the Forest) series of the "Spiegel", the number dropped even more: "Despite the real or mimicked feeling of guilt or sorrow about the killing of more than four million Jews during Hitler's era. (Jewish circles always claim there were 'six million')...."

The feelings and falsifications are still playing a role in this sad chapter of humanity. And that's why in Joachim Fest's series of reports, the photo-trickeries were made, which later were recognized as falsifications. Such were also made much earlier by other independent experts playing with shadow formations and retouching. (Falsifications or not, in his book which appeared on the U.S. market in 1996 under the title "Plotting Hitler's Death: The Story of the German Resistance", Joachim Fest came to a conclusion that "Lessons of failed resistance is that it is virtually impossible to overthrow a totalitarian regime from within." - inset by the Publisher).

While extermination of the Jews was going on, German people chose rather to go and fight at the front lines than to take part in it. This dirty job was more and more taken over by Latvians, Poles, Ukrainians, and even by Jews. The Jewish professor Hannah Arendt in her book "Eichmann in Jerusalem", printed in 1964, wrote that the Jewish leaders' participation in the extermination of their own kind, without any doubt is the darkest chapter in the Jewish history.

That in Amsterdam as in Warsaw, that in Berlin as in Bucharest etc., the Nazis could rely on Jewish functionaries who prepared lists of persons and their wealth; who collected from them money to cover costs of deportation and extermination; who kept an eye on victims' apartments; who created their own police to capture other Jews so to bring them to the deportation trains and then assist them to their bitter end, as well as that in the death camps extermination acts were performed by the Jews, all of that was confirmed by the witnesses at the Jerusalem Trial. And these facts, as above, were very well known. The witnesses also confirmed, that the Jewish "Special Squads" worked in gas chambers and crematoriums; that they pulled gold teeth from the dead; cut their hair off; dug graves for the victims and later opened them in order to remove traces of the mass murder; that Jewish technicians built the gas chambers in the "Autonomous" Theresienstadt in Czechoslovakia, although none were there but only a Jewish hangman.

Hitler, thanks to his association with the Vienna Jews and his teacher Lanz von Liebenfels, knew about the extreme hatred of the cast-off Jews towards their kinsmen. Just like he made use of this hatred in the struggle for power by employing the Jews in his decisive "body and stomach" gazettes: "People's Observer" and the "Stormman" ("Stuermer"), so during the War he made use of it for destruction of the Jews.

The first time the "gasser" SS-man Gerstein, got in contact with the Gestapo, was on September 27, 1936, when he was arrested for the "subversive operation." He admitted then that he distributed 8,500 anti-Nazi brochures to the important government officials. On July 14, 1938 he was arrested again but this time he landed in a concentration camp in Welzheim. After a discharge, this "opposition fighter" changed his mind and joined the SS. Pretty soon he advanced to a rank of the Commander and during the War he was a supplier of the poisonous gas, thus playing a terrible role in the mass killings of the Jews. Gerstein was the person who informed the Swedish and Swiss authorities and later the Western Allies about these gassings. The Dutch engineer Ubbink passed Gerstein's report to London. After the war the Swedes made an "Aide-Memoire" ("Memoirs") of the Baron von Otter public. This revealed the Baron's conversation with Gerstein about the gassing. The gas murderer Gerstein was eagerly reporting to the foreign countries about his top secret actions. He also appeared before the Apostolic Nunciature in Berlin. He asked the Suffragan to Arch Bishop Count Preysing to alarm the Pope. He also was informing about the gassing Dutch forced laborers in Berlin. The same evening, when he met the penitentiary's priest Buchholz, he told him about his secret actions. Later in a letter Buchholz stated: "He reported to me about this all openly and frankly. He counted names and locations of the death camps. He talked about the 'daily efficiency' of various incinerators and gas chambers..., about the daily profits from gold teeth, fillings etc., and told me that the number of victims came up to ten million, which was not known to us and was so terrible, that it was absolutely unbelievable."[91]

Priest Mochalski described a similar incident: "After the Mass Services an unknown gentleman entered my Sacristy in civilian clothes and handed me a document in a red cover with the inscription on top: 'Secret Matters of the Reich'. It was addressed to the Head Commander of the SS. He introduced himself to me as 'Gerstein'."

In short, just like his supervisor Eichmann, Gerstein also made an effort to come up with the numbers in millions ("far over ten million"). Without any scruples, without a minimal caution, he presented his reports to strangers, talked with dozens of foreigners who were the enemies of the Regime or belonged to a neutral or occupied countries. Later Gerstein reported that once, when he was present at a speech: "I was asked to leave His Holiness' Embassy. Nevertheless I did tell about all of this to hundreds of personalities."[92]

At that time, under the strict control of the Regime, it was impossible to say even one word about the top secret on top of another top secret without an order, and essentially to "hundreds of personalities". Such a person would have been arrested many times over.

The main purpose of spreading these horror stories was to get rid of the European Jews through Denmark, Italy, the Balkan Peninsula and so forth across the Seas into the Orient. "Are you getting tired of Europe?" was said by the Jewish foes. "We would like to get your affirmation."

And at the borders' escape routes the military personnel did not pay any attention to them, but even offered escorts, like it was the case on the Black Sea, or with the human cargo in trains escorted by the SS over the Spanish or Swiss borders. Another purpose of the Gerstein's mission was to make for the Germany's war-chest a splendid business with the Western World by the exchange of millions of hostages for certain products. Those were the reasons why Gerstein operated with the number of "25 million gassed", which are today not cheerily quoted, but are proving the goal which was clearly outlined by the "Coulisses' Men" of Gerstein.

The French drew a similar conclusion and imprisoned the man who claimed to be the opponent of gassing. On July 25, 1945, Gerstein was found dead in his prison cell in Paris. Next to his body was found an unfinished letter. Gerstein's widow does not believe that it was a suicide. Neither she nor her or his relatives or friends ever saw Gerstein's tombstone, so the cause of his death remains unknown. Hitler's plan and the plan of the Jewish exterminators did not work out. They thought that by talking about those horrors the whole World would be shocked so deeply, that it will take care of the Jewish nation and England will open the gates to Palestine widely. Eichmann's efforts to shove off the Jewry, under German control into the Near East, failed. During the business deal with the Jewish agent Joel Brand in Budapest, Eichmann assured him that the one million Jews offered is only the beginning. If the willingness to take the Jews would be manifested, he will immediately explode all the gas chambers.

On May 25, 1944, the U.S. Ambassador Steinhardt reported to his Government: "Two days ago a certain Joel Brand, who claimed to be a delegate of the Jewish community in Budapest, arrived in Istanbul and submitted to Mr.Barlas of the Jewish Palestine Bureau a proposal which apparently came from the Jewish Affairs Commissioner, Eichmann. This proposal suggested that Eichmann will end the deportation and wiping out of the Jews from all the territories occupied by Germany, including Romania, in exchange for two million pieces of soap, two hundred tons of cacao, eight hundred tons of coffee, two hundred tons of tea and ten thousands trucks."[93]

To the so called Free Western World which was not interested in such a business "The idea that the Jews would stream into Palestine disturbed the White House more than the idea of Jews being gassed to death," complained after the war an American author Arthur D. Morse in his book "The Waters (Inset: of the Red Sea) Were Not Divided."

The exterminators in Eastern Europe gave up the extermination. It hasn't been determined yet what was true about Eichmann's "millions" and whether they were only the propaganda of horror. Years ago a Judge of Hamburg, Dr.Wilhelm Staeglich, (Inset: He was in service close to Auschwitz) testified: "None of the prisoners acted as if they were scared, mistreated or under a threat of death. In the Dachau Concentration Camp's Museum there is a picture with the subtitle 'burning ovens of Auschwitz.' On this picture I recognized a bakery oven which was shown to us by a prisoner working during the baking process."

And the Suffragan Dr.Neuhaeusler, who was exiled from 1941 until 1945 to the concentration camps in Sachsenhausen and Dachau, in his brochure "That's how it was in Dachau" corrected the newspaper report that 238,000 people were gassed and burned there, for in the Dachau concentration camp weren't any gassing devices. After the appearance of Neuhaeusler's correction, the fascia, which for many years was displaying the wrong message, was removed from the memorial building.

The Reich's Leader of the SS, Heinrich Himmler, withdrew the territories designated for a destruction of the Jews from the jurisdiction of the Austrian Kaltenbrunner, Heydrich's successor, and took them over under his command, obviously with a heavy heart: "The Fuehrer put this very difficult task on my shoulders. Nobody can take this responsibility away from me. So I am forbidding everyone to say anything about this matter," wrote Himmler after Heydrich's death to an SS agent in contact with the Reich's Minister for the Occupied Territories, Rosenberg.[94]

To the Reich's and Districts Commanders the Leader of the SS-Holy Order explained that "The Final Solution became the most difficult task of my life."

Finally Heydrich's successor, the SS Weapons Commander-in Chief Kaltenbrunner, received from Himmler the following order: "With immediate effect I prohibit any destruction of the Jews and I am ordering taking care of the weak and ill people. I make you personally responsible, even if this order will not be implemented by the lower rank commanders."[95]

Only after the war the Zionists were able to exaggerate the events which took place during the years 1942 and 1943 in order to put pressure upon the whole world. With this pressure they forced England to honor the Balfour Declaration. Thus the discriminatory actions pursued by Hitler, Heydrich, Eichmann, and Gerstein paid off with the long term reparations as the basis for establishment of the State of Israel. People, who performed the acts of extermination had no doubt that regardless of who wins the war, the "two thousand year wanderers" of this Globe will regain their "Holy Land".

The "Jewish Expressions" newspaper printed in Germany, dated January 15, 1960, had no doubts either as it wrote: "The large emigration waves are caused only by the forcible departure from the domicile country."

It appears from all the Hitler's destructive dealings with the Jews, ever since his Vienna days, that he differentiated Eastern Jews - as said Rathenau: "The Asiatic Hordes", or simply Heydrich: "The Mob" - from the small minority of the Western Jews whom he recognized, because they supported him in seizing the power with millions of dollars.

In 1967 the "Institution On German History After The War" in Tuebingen, published a presentation of the German Deputy in charge of the "Four Year Plan", who in the former Polish Lvov (Lemberg) was supposed to organize work for a quarter million Jews living there. It said: "The negotiations with the 'contract partner' took place in the Office of the Armed Forces Transport commander at Akademicka Street (Academy Street). There, contingencies were made for the "final solution". Sephardic Jews (Inset: i.e., the Western Jews, as the Author sees it) living in Galicia as a minority, were separated and deported by hundreds with the German help and its Allies' airplanes, including entire families. That's how in October 1943, sixteen selected Jews from the Labor Camp in Lublin (the camp was installed on the grounds of a civil airport at Czwartkowa/ Thursday Street) were transported to Spain and from there to the U.S. Among them was a relative of President Roosevelt's advisor Morgenthau."

Most of the Jews captured in the Western Europe immigrated there during the past century from the East and therefore the pitiful people were treated by Himmler as Eastern Jews. Those, who anyway were considered as Western Jews, were sent by Eichmann's men to the Theresienstadt, which didn't look like a concentration camp, nor a hungry Jewish city, for it had its own administration, schools and cultural establishments. Many times the gentlemen of the SS-Imperium, who always were money-hungry, made splendid business deals with its Jewish "citizens". These secret dealings made the SS Chief Leader General Kaltenbrunner furious and about this he testified in Nuremberg: "Himmler did the worst things through Becher which should be revealed here. They consisted of letting the Jews go free after mediation by Becher and the Joint Committee in Hungary and then in Switzerland, firstly in exchange for warfare materials; secondly in exchange for raw materials, and thirdly in exchange for foreign currency. I heard about these deals in the News Center and expressed my opinion immediately, but not to Himmler, because it would have been hopeless, but directly to Hitler." There was no question about the fact, that throughout the whole war the armament and foreign currency came into the German Reich via

Entrance into the Auschwitz camp. The leading author of Nuremberg's Racial Laws, Dr. Hans Josef Maria Globke, gently called their "commentator", made provisions for Auschwitz. After the war he took a major part in formation of the Federal Republic of Germany.

Eingang zu dem Lager Auschwitz. Der Hauptverfasser der Nürnberger Rassengesetze, verniedlichend Kommentator genannt, Dr. Hans Josef Maria Globke, der die Voraussetzungen zu Auschwitz schuf, gestaltete entscheidend die Bundesrepublik Deutschland mit.

The Reich's Leader of the SS, Heinrich Himmler, while visiting concentration camp Mauthausen. After Heydrich's death, he led the attack on Jews by himself and through an undercover agent in Romania, Hungary, Spain, Sweden and Switzerland he pushed the Western Allies towards the "Palestine Solution", and in 1943 ordered to stop destruction of Jews "with an immediate effect."

Der Reichsführer SS Heinrich Himmler bei Besichtigung des Konzentrationslagers Mauthausen. Nach dem Tode Heydrichs leitete er die Judenbekämpfung selbst, drängte durch Unterhändler in Rumänien, Ungarn, Spanien, Schweden und in der Schweiz die West-Alliierten zur Palästina-Lösung und verbot 1943 «mit sofortiger Wirkung jegliche Vernichtung von Juden.»

Switzerland.

With Himmler's order to stop the extermination, the situation completely changed. The Jew Ginsburg, who writes under the cover name Burg, after negotiations with the Britons reported from Hungary, that emigration of the Jews to Palestine failed: "Interior Minister Kovarcz insisted on the liquidation of all Jews in the ghetto. The Police General Winkelmann as the Chief of Police in Budapest, conferred with Himmler and then requested the Hungarian Interior Minister to come to him. Winkelman advised Kovarcz that the 84,000 Jews in the Budapest ghetto are under the German jurisdiction, therefore in the interest of the German Reich he prohibits its destruction."

In the spring of 1944, Himmler, trying to extinguish the rumor of exterminations, in a speech to over two hundred German Generals in the "Holy Order Castle" Sonthofen, announced that the Generals at any time and without notice may inspect any concentration camp and see for themselves that the rumor has no substance.

At that time the SS Judges of War, mainly Storm Leader Dr.Morgen and Dr.Reinicke, were already cleaning up the mess. The lower rank SS Commanders, who sexually abused Jewish women, were degraded and put into the concentration camps. After the war they came forward as "persecuted" by the Nazi Regime. Dr.Morgen alarmed by a Commander of the Security Police in Lublin knew, that the SS Security teams used to play soccer with a selected group of young Jewish Camp Policemen. Also that they celebrated together festivities and among the eleven hundred Jewish wedding guests were members of the Jewish Camp Security in the SS uniforms drinking Martell, a cognac. "With the consumption of delicatessen and alcohol unusual things were happening there," the SS Judges as witnesses testified before the surprised Court in Nuremberg.

The low ranking SS Storm Troopers leader (a lieutenant) was sentenced to death by the SS Justice on the grounds that: "He lowered himself to cruel actions which were unworthy of a German and of the SS Leader." This mentioned above Dr.Morgen, sued also a Commander of the Concentration Camp Buchenwald, Karl Koch, and sent him to the Camp's gallows in front of the mistreated prisoners. The same fate met Hermann Florstedt, a Commander of the Camp in Majdanek, near Lublin. In a short time two hundred verdicts were enforced. Moreover, when the war was over, six hundred trials were in progress. Among them one against Eichmann and another against Commander of the Auschwitz Concentration Camp, Rudolf Hoess.

In 1924 Hoess, because of a murder, together with Martin Bormann (Inset: later the right hand of Hitler) was sentenced by the State Justice Court to ten years in prison. After his release he took revenge in his own way against the "SS Holy Order Under The Scull", which he felt had betrayed him.[96] When imprisoned by the Americans (before his execution in Poland), he confirmed in writing whatever Americans wanted. Among his many testimonies one stated: "In concentration camps slaves were put to work" although the term "slave laborers" was never used by the authorities of the German Reich.

In Hitler's political and operational staff the Jewish element was strong. It was also strong at the level of Jewish baiters as well as exterminators. The SS General Erich von Bach-Zelewski, the Chief of the Antipartisan Units, and the SS General Odilo Globocnik, previously a District Commander of Vienna, known as the "Jewish Exterminator", were also Jewish mongrels.[97]

When one of these perpetrators, the SS General Friedrich-Wilhelm Krueger without any Jewish blood in his veins, moved hundred thousand Jewish defense plant workers under protests of the Armed Forces from the ghettos to the concentration camps, and married a half-Jewish Lady, Himmler consoled him: "Your position in the SS will not be affected in any way, neither by my opinion nor by the whole bad luck of your wife's genealogical tree. I give you my solemn assurance in writing that this could not ever happen to you."[98]

With the victorious feelings the ordinary front soldiers, together with the SS-Weapon Troops returned home. And at this new stage of their careers they could have settled the accounts with the past in a different way than did the so called "denazification" of Germany, for under it the pawns were hanged and the bureaucrats elevated, like Dr.Hans Josef Maria Globke, the main author and not just a commentator of the Nuremberg Racial Law (the basis of all the destructive actions), to one of the highest offices in the German Federal Republic.

THE FINAL SOLUTION: ISRAEL

The war was over. Special Jewish units from the USA landed in Northern Italy. These units received many years of training at American Universities on how to re-educate the Germans. In German families the father made the decisions. The discipline and order were the principles of the German upbringing; Hitler, the Fuehrer, simply transferred that German family system to the State and that is how it worked. But this harmed the other nations.

Those, who came, were highly educated and ethical boys. Do not mistake them with the revenge squads, which at the same time came from Italy across the Alps on the yellow painted military trucks with slogans on their banners: "NO nation, NO reich, NO fuehrer. The Jews Are Coming!"

When on the superhighways a bicyclist was spotted, the right door of the heavy truck was opened abruptly killing the rider. On April 6, 1946 to a large prison camp at Nuremberg, where 36,000 SS-men were detained, the Jews delivered bread poisoned with arsenide. Seven hundred prisoners died instantly and later a few hundred more in agony.[99] (see POST. r.141)

With the other gentlemen on that special assignment, who were educated at the universities, it was easy to communicate. Thus came to an extensive exchange of experiences with the Germans who stayed in Italy in the War Reporters Companies. They were waiting there for new orders and by the way taught the American colleagues how to form or change mind of the other nations. Dark haired, beautiful girls poured red wine into glasses and with these gestures, friendly, international bounds were made. After a few more drinks the conversations led to God and the Whole World, as well as to Hitler's unclear origin and his Messianic illusions and to a strange fact, that the powerful American Air Force with its thousands of "Flying Fortresses" never attempted to destroy any of the camps containing the gas chambers. And that is when one educated young man from the U.S. jumped up with a red face and called across the table to a German propagandist, known among his friends as "Wildente" ("Wild Duck"): "But you have done our work."

Those people, who came across the Atlantic to change human minds, soon managed the key positions in the newspapers and radio stations by themselves or through their trustworthy agents. And their main purpose was to keep the World shocked with thousands of news articles, brochures, books etc., full of stories about the extermination of Jews in the Eastern Europe. In effect the overseas countries opened their gates to the "Made by Europe Tired People." Through the temporary camps of numerous charity organizations they streamed into them. Only England, which wanted to secure her strategic position at the Suez Canal and to keep her Empire, and her influence in the "oil countries", refused to take in those hundreds of thousands of people with tattooed KZ-numbers (Concentration-camp-numbers) on their lower left arms, storming the beaches of Palestine.[100] Thus the "Exodus" began, which derived its name from an old Mississippi Steamer used on the Eastern Mediterranean Sea for the Jewish cargo.

The Jewish terrorist organizations spread fear all around.

They were supplied with the U.S.' money and weapons from the European depots and deserted battle fields. In January of 1947, the underground group "Irgun Zvai Le'umi" ("National Military Organization") declared war on England. British soldiers and officers were kidnapped, hung or shot in the open streets. The British headquarters in Palestine, the British Consulate in Rome, the British quarters in Vienna's Park Hotel were bombed. On July 23, 1947, before the House of Commons in London, the British Prime Minister, Clement R. Attlee, said about the bombing of the British headquarters in the "Kings David Hotel" in Jerusalem: "Honorable Deputies, you must acknowledge these horrifying and brutal murders, which have been committed against us in Jerusalem. Among the many disgraceful conducts, which have been exercised by the Zionists in Palestine, this one was the worst. By this insane action ninety three innocent British officers have perished."

The Palestinians, who at the same time were exiled from their own country, have learned well how a new State is being founded.

During the spring of 1947 Dr.Nahum Goldmann, the future Zionist leader, at the seventh meeting of the Canadian Jewish Congress explained to listeners at the Mont Royal Hotel that "We insisted on Palestine not because of religious, historical or sentimental reasons, but because Palestine is a turning table of three continents and in the military, political, and strategic sense it is the World's Center." "Besides," - added speaker Goldmann, quoting a statement which appeared in the "Congressional Bulletin" - "the oil reserves in this area are much higher than on the whole American continent."[101]

"To establish Israel, we only have twelve months" said Goldman. "After that the interest of the World in our cause will become weaker."

From the German point of view, Adolf Hitler, as the "goodness preacher", was one of the most frustrated leaders in the world's history. At least he was seen as such in the German eyes, but with an exception, millions of war victims, attributed to this "beliefs' protagonist", reached a culmination within a few years, not centuries. But despite of those sacrifices, the "Jewish-Bolshevist Pestilence" set its foot in the heart of Germany. The American Army allocated the Thuringia and Saxony to the Red Army and since then the Soviet Union is keeping guard at the River Elbe. For thirty years in Berlin, the Capital City of the Reich, the military occupying forces have a lot to say, which they wouldn't have if the right of the Nation to self-determination was of concern.

Approaching this entire matter from a different perspective, it can be said that Hitler's life long dream of a Vienna adolescent has been materialized with a splendor: "THE HATRED TOWARDS HIS OWN KINSMEN", combined with the hatred of his Jewish helpers Heydrich, Eichmann and many others, which escalated into the insane extermination (inset: "No one can arrange a mass annihilation without a sanction of the Lord" - see POST. r.5, Chapter 11, Verse 32 and 33), at last has finished the "WORK OF THE LORD" by founding the State for the Jews, who were dogged by the ill fortune for over two millennia.

On May 14, 1948, three years after Adolf Hitler's death, and twelve months

Die letzte Aufnahme des im April 1945 in Wahn und Rauch untergegangenen Hitler. Chefideologe Rosenberg wandte sich kurz vor seiner Hinrichtung in Nürnberg ate: «Hiders Sendungsglaube war merkbar, als er aus der Haft in Landsberg zurückkehrte und steigerte sich, bis dieser Glaube am Schluss des Krieges peinliche Züge annahm.»

The last photo of Hitler taken in April 1945, shortly before his "departure" in illusions and smoke. In Nuremberg Chief Ideologist Rosenberg before his execution had said: "Hitler's belief in a Higher Mission was noticeable when he returned from imprisonment at Landsberg. It escalated and close to the War's end it was embarrassing."

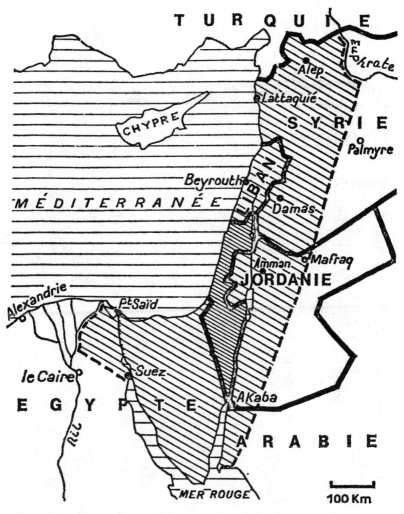

Diese Karte verschickte Dr. Israel Eldat vom staatlich-israelischen Rundfunk im Jahre 1967 nach dem sogenannten Sechs-Tage-Krieg an die Mitglieder der Knesset.

In 1967, after the so called "Six Day War", this map was sent by Dr. Israel Eldat from the State Radio Station of Israel to the Members of the Knesset (Israel's Parliament). (Inset: It shows Israeli objectives of a "BLITZ" combat) after Goldmann's speech in Canada, the British soldiers took down the Union Jack from the flagstaff of the Government Building in Jerusalem. At midnight the British Highest Commissaire of the Palestine laid down his mandate. At two o'clock in the morning President of the United States of America, Harry Truman, acknowledged Israel as a new State.

David Gruen from Poland, who called himself Ben Gurion ("A wounded male dove"), as the first President of this resurrected Jewish State shouted: "A Jew, who does not live in Israel, lives in a sin!"

The years of street battles were gone. The decades of wars over the living space and secure borders have begun.

Hennecke Kardel,
Marva, Genf,
1974

REFERENCES

1. "Der Spiegel" ("The Mirror") magazine, 24/ 73, p.124.
2. Bernt Engelmann, "Deutschland ohne Juden" ("Germany Without Jews") Schneekluth 1970, p.240.
3. Joachim C. Fest, "Hitler", Ullstein 1973, p.1047.
4. Joachim C. Fest, "Hitler", Ullstein 1973, p.1047.
5. Joachim C. Fest, "Hitler", Ullstein 1973, p.1047.
6. Hans Frank, "Im Angesicht des Galgens" ("In the Face of Gallows"), Munich-Graefelfing 1953, p.331.
7. Max Domarus, "Hitler - Reden und Proklamationen" ("Speeches and Proclamations") Süddeutscher Verlag München South German Publisher, Munich) 1965, p.1891.
8. Dietrich Bronder, "Bevor Hitler kam" ("Before Hitler Came"), Hans Pfeiffer Verlag (Publisher) 1964, p.204; 1975, p.211.
9. A change in the Entry of June 7, 1837 of the Census Book of Doellersheim by Pastor Zahnschirm, January 1877.
10. August Kubizek, "Adolf Hitler, mein Jugendfreund" ("Adolf Hitler, My Young Friend"), Leopold Stocker Verlag, Graz 1953, p.79.
11. Wagner's Jewish origin was proven by Leon Stein in "The Racial Thinking of Richard Wagner", New York 1950; by Arnold Zweig in "Bilanz der deutschen Judenheit" ("A Bilance of the German Jewry"), Koeln 1961, and by Dietrich Bronder "Bevor Hitler kam" ("Before Hitler Came"), Hans Pfeiffer Publishing House, Hannover, 1964, p.362 "...seine jüdische Herkunft kaum mehr umstritten" ("...there is any doubt about his Jewish extraction.")
12. "Osservatore Romano", Rom, September 15, 1937; Konrad Heiden, "Hitler", 2nd volume, Europe Publishing House, Zurich 1937, p.200; Dietrich Bronder, "Bevor Hitler kam" ("Before Hitler Came"), Hans Pfeiffer Publishing House, Hannover 1964, p.291.
13. August Kubizek, "A.Hitler, mein Jugendfreund" ("A.Hitler, My Young Friend"), Leopold Stocker Publishing House, Graz 1953, p.289.
14. Josef Greiner, "Das Ende des Hitler-Mythos" ("The End of the Hitler Myth"), Amalthea Publishing House, Vienna 1947, p.39.
15. Josef Greiner, "Das Ende des Hitler-Mythos" ("The End of the Hitler Myth"), Amalthea Publishing House, Vienna 1947, pp.60 and 63.
16. Walther Rathenau, "Reflexionen" ("Reflections"), S. Hirzel Publishing House, Leipzig 1908.
17. Josef Greiner, "Das Ende des Hitler-Mythos" ("The End of the Hitler Myth"), Amalthea Publishing House, Vienna 1947, p.115
18. Gerhard Kessler, "Die Familiennamen der Juden in Deutschland" ("The Family Names of Jews in Germany"), Leipzig 1935, p.51.
19. From the letter Nr. 248 of the Empress and Royal Austrian-Hungarian Consulat of Salzburg, January 23, 1914.
20. Archives of the Republic, Koblenz NS 26/ 17 a.

21. Balthasar Brandmayer, "Zwei Meldegänger" ("Two Messengers"), Franz Walter, Ueberlingen at Bodensee 1932.

22. Archives of the Republic, Koblenz NS 26/ 4.

23. Balthasar Brandmayer, "Zwei Meldegänger" ("Two Messengers"), Franz Walter, Ueberlingen at Bodensee 1932.

24. Georg Franz-Willing, "Die Hitlerbewegung - Ursprung 1919-1922" ("The Roots of the Hitler Movement - 1919-1922"), Decker's Publishing House G. Schenck, Hamburg 1962, pp.25/ 26.

25. Konrad Heiden, "Adolf Hitler", European Publishing House, Zurich 1936, p.118.

26. Philipp W. Fabry, "Mutmassungen über Hitler" ("Conjectures on Hitler"), Droste Publishing House, Duesseldorf 1969, p.24.

27. Georg Franz-Willing, "Die Hitlerbewegung - Ursprung 1919-1922" ("The Roots of the Hitler Movement - 1919-1922"), Decker's Publisher G. Schenck Hamburg 1962, p.113.

28. Dr.Hans Severus Ziegler, "Wer war Hitler?" ("Who Was Hitler?"), Verlag der deutschen Hochschullehrer-Zeitung (Publisher of the German High School Teacher's Newspaper) Tuebingen 1970, p.231.

29. Dr.Ernst Hanfstaengl, "Zwischen Weissem und Braunem Haus" ("Between The White And The Brown House"), R. Piper & Co. Publisher Munich 1970, p.129.

30. R.H. Bruce Lockhart, "Als Diplomat, Bankmann und Journalist im Nachkriegseuropa" ("A Diplomat, Banker, and Journalist in Europe After the War"), German Publisher Agency Stuttgart 1935, p.109.

31. Dietrich Bronder, "Bevor Hitler kam" ("Before Hitler Came"), Hans Pfeiffer Publisher Hanover 1964, p.238: "In 1921 Hitler bought from his Holy Order Master Sebottendorf the 'People's Observer' for 100,000 marks. To this amount contributed 30,000 marks his friend Moses Pinkeles alias Trebitsch-Lincoln and the rest came from other Jewish sources."

32. Dr.Ernst Hanfstaengl, "Zwischen Weissem und Braunem Haus" ("Between The White And The Brown House"), R. Piper & Co. Publisher Munich 1970, p.106.

33. Dr.Ernst Hanfstaengl, "Zwischen Weissem und Braunem Haus" ("Between The White And The Brown House"), R. Piper & Co. Publisher Munich 1970, p.30.

34. Leonard Lyons, "New York Post", November 7, 1966, p.45.

35. Dr.Hans Günther, "Rassenkunde des deutschen Volkes" ("Ethnogeny of the German People"), J.F.Lehmanns Publisher, Munich 1923, p.430.

36. Paul Schmidt, "Statist auf diplomatischer Bühne" ("A Minor Man on a Diplomatic Stage"), Bonn 1950, p.463.

37. A declaration of the Publisher Amann at the Nuremberg Trial.

38. Curtis B. Dall, "Amerikas Kriegspolitik" ("America's War Politic"), Grabert Publisher Tübingen 1972, p.177.

39. "Deutsche Rundschau" ("German News"), Publisher R. Pechel, 70th

year, Volume 7, July 1947, Stuttgart's release, p.22.

40. Severin Reinhard (Sonderegger), "Spanischer Sommer" ("Spanish Summer"), Affoltern/ Switzerland 1948.

41. "Die Weltbuehne" ("The World Stage"), Berlin, Vol.19, May 1948

42. Hans Frank, "Im Angesichts des Galgens" ("In the Face of Gallows"), Munich-Gräfelfing 1953, p.330.

43. Otto Strasser, "Hitler et moi" ("Hitler and Me") Bernard Grasset, Paris 1940, p.218.

44. "Die Weltbuehne" ("The World Stage"), Berlin, March 30,1922, p.309.

45. Philipp W. Fabry, "Mutmassungen über Hitler" ("Conjectures on Hitler"), Droste Publisher Düsseldorf 1969, p.130.

46. Otto Strasser, "Hitler et moi" ("Hitler and Me"), Bernard Grasset, Paris 1940.

47. Newsrelease 35/ 70 of March 4, 1970 by the Lower Saxony Minister of the Interior.

48. Personal remarks to the Publisher.

49. Otto Strasser, "Hitler et moi" ("Hitler and Me"), Bernard Grasset, Paris 1940, p.155.

50. "People's Observer", March 24, 1933.

51. Hjalmar Schacht, "Abrechnung mit Hitler" ("A Reckoning with Hitler"), 1948, p.37.

52. Ernst Forsthoff, "Deutsche Geschichte seit 1918 in Documenten" ("History of Germany since 1918 in Documents"), 1938, p.407.

53. Dietrich Bronder, "Bevor Hitler kam" ("Before Hitler Came"), Hans Pfeiffer Publisher Hanover 1964, p.294: "Chief of the State Secret Police ("Gestapo") Reinhard Heydrich was predominantly Jewish." Source: Riemanns Music Encyclopedia of 1916. It listed father of Reinhard as "Heydrich, Bruno, actually Suess."

54. Gerhard Kessler, "Die Familiennamen der Juden in Deutschland" ("The Family Names of Jews in Germany"), Leipzig 1935, p.107.

55. Heinrich Bennecke, "Die Reichswehr und der Roehm-Putsch" ("The Reich's Army and the Roehm's Revolt"), Olzog-Publisher, Munich 1964, p.52 - An affidavit of the Chief General von Kleist before the International Military Court at Nuremberg 1946 - Attachement 4 IFZ-Archive.

56. Peter Kleist, "Auch Du warst dabei" ("You Were There Too"), 1965, p.122.

57. DNB-Text, September 15, 1935.

58. "Ahnenpass" ("A Pedigree"), Publisher for Census Matters, Berlin SW 61, 1935, p.3.

59. Eichmann. An interrogation report of the Jerusalem Court, 1961, Book I, Columne 90 - Keesing's most recent archive, p.3240 B.

60. Eichmann. A report on the 17th Session of the Jerusalem Court, 1961.

61. Dr.Hans-Dietrich Roehrs, "Hitler, die Zerstoerung einer Persoenlichkeit" ("Hitler, a Devastated Personality"), Kurt Vowinckel

Publisher Neckargemuend 1965, p.111.

62. An information from the Physicians Association of Northern Rhein of March 16, 1970.

63. Arthur D. Morse, "Die Wasser teilen sich nicht" ("The Waters Were Not Divided"), Rütten and Loening Publisher 1967, p.195.

64. Friedrich Karl Kaul, "Der Fall des Herschel Grynszpan" ("The Downfall of Herschel Grynszpan"), Academy Publisher 1965, p.135: "It is necessary to say that no one in the Heydrich's Defense Main Office wanted any trial against Grynszpan. Opposition of this Office against a trial was firm."

65. Erwin Dederstedt "Der Bruder aus dem Ghetto" ("A Brother From The Ghetto"), Blick & Bild Publisher Velbert 1965, p.76.

66. D. Bronder "Before Hitler Came", Hans Pfeiffer Publisher, Hannover 1964, p.347.

67. Eichmann. Jerusalem Trial of 1961. Evidence # T/ 37.

68. Georgette Goldstein-Laczko, "Die Geschichte des Rabbi Goldstein in Berlin" ("A History of the Rabbi Goldstein of Berlin"), Heos-Publisher Tuebingen-Paris 1961, p.142.

69. Juergen Rohwer, "Die Versenkung der juedischen Fluechtlingstransporter Struma und Mefkure im Schwarzen Meer (Februar 1942, August 1944)" ("Sinking of the Jewish Refugee Freighters "Struma" and "Mefkure" in the Black Sea (February 1942, August 1944)"), Bernard and Graefe Publisher on Military Matters, Frankfurt at Main, 1964.

70. Interrogation reports on Joel Brands at the Jerusalem Trial of 1961 (57th Session, May 30, 1961).

71. "People's Observer", Munich, May 18, 1933.

72. Dr.Philipp W. Fabry, "Der Hitler-Stalin-Pakt 1939-1941" ("The Hitler-Stalin Pact 1939-1941"), Fundus Publisher Darmstadt 1962, p.81.

73. DVB-Text, September 1, 1939.

74. Walther Hubatsch, "Weseruebung" ("Practices of a Visier") Goettingen 1960, p.531.

75. B.H. Liddell Hart, "Jetzt duerfen sie reden" ("Now They Should Talk"), Stuttgart Publisher 1948, p.172.

76. "Ciano Diplomatic Papers", London 1948, p.402.

77. A personal message to the Author by Schulze-Lesum, who thanks to a conversation with Hitler in Bayreuth in 1936 managed to get Junker airplanes with which Moroccans of the Caudillo Franco could reach a battle field. (Taken from the "Les Juifs" ("The Jewry") by R. Peyrefitte, Flammarion, Paris '65, p.5.

78. Nuremberg's Evidence C-134.

79. Alexander Werth, "Russland im Kriege 1941-1945" ("Russia In The War of 1941-1945"), Droemersche Verlagsanstalt 1965, p.112.

80. Franz Halder, "Kriegstagebuch III" ("War Diary III"), Stuttgart 1964, p.38.

81. Winston Churchill, "Memoirs", Vol. II, Book I, p.375.

82. Charles Callen Tansill, "Die Hintertuer zum Kriege" ("The Backdoor To The War"), Duesseldorf 1958, p.698.

83. Curtis B. Dall, "Amerikanische Kriegspolitik" ("American War Politics"), Grabert Publisher Tuebingen 1972, p.239.

84. Henry Picker, "Hitlers Tischgespraeche" ("Hitler's Table Speeches"), Seewald-Verlag 1963, pp.38/ 39.

85. "Der Scheinwerfer-Prozess" ("The Show Trial"), Ewald Hippe Munich 1950, p.9.

86. Wilfried von Oven, "Mit Goebbels bis zum Ende" ("With Goebbels to the End"), Duerer Publisher Buenos Aires 1950, Volume II, p.161.

87. Alexander Werth, "Russland im Kriege 1941-1945" ("Russia in the War 1941-1945"), Droemersche Publisher house 1965, p.718.

88. Report of the International Military Tribunal, Vol.IX, p.584.

89. "Deutsche Hochschullehrer-Zeitung" ("German High School Teacher's Newspaper"), Tuebingen, Nr. 3/ 4, 1959, p.12.

90. "Spiegel" Nr. 51, December 16, 1968, p.100.

91. Letter from the Cathedralchapter P. Buchholz of July 10, 1946 - Archive of the Kurt Gerstein House.

92. "Vierteljahreshefte fuer Zeitgeschichte" ("Quarterly Magazine on the History of Time"), 1st year of publication 1953, p.192.

93. Arthur D. Morse, "Die Wasser teilen sich nicht" ("The Waters Were not Divided"), R. & L. Publisher 1967, p.313.

94. Helmut Heiber, "Reichsfuehrer! Briefe an und von Himmler" ("The Reich's Fuehrer! Letters to and from Himmler"). German Paperback Publisher Munich 1970, p.167.

95. "Deutsche Hochschullehrer-Zeitung" ("German High School Teachers Newspaper"), Tuebingen Nr. 3/ 4, 1959, p.27.

96. Heinrich Hannover, "Politische Justiz 1918-1933" ("Political Justice Between 1918-1933"). Fischer Library Frankfurt/ Main 1966, p.159.

97. Dietrich Bronder, "Bevor Hitler kam" ("Before Hitler Came"), Hans Pfeiffer Publisher Hannover 1964, p.204.

98. Helmut Heiber, "Reichsfuehrer! Briefe an und von Himmler" ("The Reich's Fuehrer! Letters to and from Himmler"), German Paperback Publisher, Munich 1970, p.290.

99. Michel Bar-Zohar, "Les vengeurs" ("The Avengers"), Fayard 1968, p.63.

100. Israel's Prime Minister Levi Eschkol in the "Spiegel" Nr. 31/ 1965 to Conrad Ahlers, p.66: "I think that at least hundred thousands of people are still living here with a number by the concentration camp engraved onto their wrists."

101. Adrien Arcand, "A bas la haine" ("A Despicable Hatred"), Edition La Vérité, Montreal 1965, p.48 - "L'Unité Nationale" ("The National Unification"), Montreal, Nr. 4 of December 1953, p.8.

POSTSCRIPT

PASSIONS OF IGNORANCE

Author of the "ADOLF HITLER - FOUNDER OF ISRAEL", in a sarcastic tone and a brief military style, touched on a problem which he encountered within the "SAME TIME" of his life (see PREFACE), but did not exhaust all the possibilities because of something having to do with the "THE MOST PERSECUTED IN OUR TIME - THE TRUTH". This Publisher certainly will not either, for the subject matter needs an in depth study.

Nevertheless, the Author proved that the ideologists of the Nazi movement were unscrupulous one-quarter, one-half or full blooded ISRAELITES, more or less assimilated within the Teutonic society. Kardel's work deals with Jews of the Israelite origin as adversaries of Jews of the Judaite origin. The first group, as a distinction, and symbolically was equipped with the "Death Sculls" and "Swastikas", the latter with "Red Stars" and "Sickles and Hammers", together with the heathen "Magen David". (POST. n. 4 and n. 5)

Author's sarcasticism is well founded for his "SAME TIME" has been entangled in the complexities of the human character influenced by the extremities.

In its own way Hitler's character in search of a spiritual domination over extremities and guided by authorities like Jesus Christ, was entirely squeezed by the narrow time frame of one generation, which overpowered his passion for the search of goodness at the cost of others, a virtue common among idealists of any sort. Hitler character was also squeezed by the so called "Judeo-Christianity" which deals with "Who is Who" nationally, racially and godly.

To better understand Kardel's sarcasticism, as well as the whole issue of the "Judeo-Christianity", one must be an American the way Thomas Jefferson was. Overwhelmed by the immensity of our minuscule planet Earth and grandeousness of America, he set up a "BEACON" for the new Nation - the NATURE'S GOD, which is still in ITS infancy. And IT will be there for as long as a plentitude of other gods does not stop over-flooding America. Among many, one is the most potent - the Yahve, who three millennia before Christ had some importance in the Empire of Ebla (now Middle East). Among Israelites his name appeared during the time of Moses (ca 1500 B.C.) (POST. r. 04), although before him the God of Adamites and Israel was "El" (Genesis 33:20). Yahve (or Israel) was no less important than the Gods of Babylon or Egypt, where ruled the monotheistic religion of Egypt's God Amon, as nine millennia earlier ruled God Horus. (POST. r. 01) And He, Yahve, was very competitive with other God Balaam (Numbers 22). As it will be seen later, "Yahve" and/ or "Israel" were Eblaite's names for Gods. First name was attributed to the "Man" and the second to the "Sun".

With such a plentitude of gods it is necessary to mention that their multitude was conditioned by environmental factors and cultural isolation. This incorrectly creates an overall picture of polytheism (besides animism) although, in fact, there was practiced monotheism confined to specific areas of influence. Local rulers needed the highest authority to explain their positions. Thus it came to a creation of many independent gods of tribes, large or small community groups, cities and countries. Not many of those gods, of course, through economical, cultural or military expansions could become the universal - One God. And as of now, we are still a long way from discovering or inventing such One. But Yahve, certainly was taken from Eblans and has a purpose of dividing the entire world:

> *The whole world spoke the same language. Then the Lord said: While they are one people nothing will stop them from doing whatever they presume to do. Let's then confuse their language, so that one will not understand what another says."* (Gen.11:1-9) (POST.r.84 & n.7)

And the Prophet Isaiah added to this:

> *"Yahve from Jerusalem shall judge and rebuke nations."(Isaiah 2:4) "Israel shall suck the milk of Gentiles and eat the riches of the nations."* (Isaiah 60 and 61; See also Micah 4:3)

What attributes one god should have to become an "Universal God"? The one invented by Moses about 1,500 B.C. certainly does not have them. His god is not less primitive than animistic gods, which still can be found in some isolated areas on this Earth, for he communicated with people through stones (Genesis 28:11-12; 16:18 and Joshua 24:27), through visions (Genesis 15:1 and 46:2), through animals (Numbers 22:28), and so forth. What he has in common with other gods, is his veneration for gold as his people shall make the "GOLDEN CALF" not for THEMSELVES but for him (Exodus 32:8 and 31), and those, who disrespect this god's urge for gold shall be put to death (Exodus 32:28).

As the Bible presents it, Yahve is an imaginary god of lies, greed, hatred and vengeance, creating turbulence in the human characters. This turbulence starts working early among the "chosen-unchosen" when to the newborn of mixed marriages it is said that he/she does not belong to the community of the "chosen". Thus, at that moment a hatred to the "own kind" is implanted. It is not inflicted by violence or abuse (like circumcision), but by the simple word "chosen". This is the phenomenon which Author claims must be overcome by a Jew within, that is the "JEWISHNESS REJECTED WITHIN", which in case of Hitler's Israelo-Jewish collaborators lead to the "Gentile's Unholy Behavior" and mass murders.

Thus this very word "CHOSEN" gave birth to Christianity. Similarly as Yahve's cheating gave birth to Mohammedanism and to the Hitlerite Nazism. Even Americans are affected by this phenomenon, as is seen in front of TV screens. It is visible in distorted families whose children are rebelling against their parents and the society, because they are rejected as "chosen" and display their hatred towards the "chosenness", in the extreme with swastikas tattooed on their chests (about swastika see POST. n.5) To better understand this phenomenon it would be worthwhile to approach it from two sides: its RELIGIOUS and NON-RELIGIOUS aspects.

THE NON-RELIGIOUS ASPECT

This aspect is not new, and it reaches its highs as presented in the POST. r. 127. According to TALMUD Jesus Christ was an illegitimate child conceived by a Roman soldier. Thus in the Judean community he was an outcast and so naturally he rebelled and "OVERCAME HIS JEWISHNESS WITHIN". With such a personality he answered to an appeal among the people who were searching for an "Universal God".

Among other things it should be noted that Jesus claimed, that "My mission is only to the lost sheep of the house of Israel" (Matthew 10:6 and 15:24, and Acts of the Apostles 1:6), as if only through the "House of Israel" people might be liberated. Similar disillusionment overcame Mohammed when he discovered that his "chosenness" was stolen from him by Yahve himself. Yahve cheated an unaware Isaac, so that this patriarch instead of blessing Essau, as a progenitor of Arabs, blessed Jacob - and the "House of Israel" (Gen.27:27-40). Since then Arab nations wage war against descendants of Jacob-Israel. (1 Sam.14:47) (see POST. r. 47)

The Hitlerite Nazism was founded on a similar basis. And founded not only on the lost "birth rights" i.e. the "chosenness", but built upon ideological differences between Israelites and Essenic Jews (POST. r. 32 and 128) who were wrestling among themselves over the "PRIVATE OWNERSHIP", which since the advent of communism (Karl Marx's "Communist Manifesto", 1848) reached its climax in the Bolshevik Revolution.

This hatred creating phenomenon praised by Hitler, undoubtedly Jesus encountered, too. He even was elevated by Hitler to the status of the "Honorary Aryan". The same motive for hatred is also present in the "Song of the Only God" ("Bhagavad-Gita"). At the Holy Battle of Kuruksetra in ca 3000 B.C., God Krishna urged warrior Arjuna to exterminate his relatives and kinsmen for their attachment to the worldly, material goods.

The Author, H. Kardel, by the circumstances is also entangled in a hatred to a point where he curses the "Bolshevik Pestilence". He does it not only for reason of its godlessness, but also for its defiance of the private ownership in which defense he and millions of other German soldiers shed their blood. But he did not take into account, that those "Hordes of Judeo-Bolshevik-Pestilence" were also up to an idea of creating a "Paradise on Earth" without the "Golden Calf" for THEMSELVES. Into such a horrible and very costly entanglement fell not only the Author, for according to him, it consumed 50 million lives.

THE RELIGIOUS ASPECT

Jesus Christ, as Krishna, a God or Son of God, was conceived by the Holy Spirit, as Krishna was, and as such was not accepted by the "chosen people" waiting for a Messiah under the Roman occupation.

By His spiritual birth and his acclamation "Before Abraham came to be, I AM" (John 8:58), Jesus explained to the Judaites (Jews) the lack of Yahve's authenticity invented by the Empire of Ebla, and He broke the continuity of "chosenness" - according to the Bible, the "Davidian Ascendancy". Hence Jesus explained to the Jews, that since He is the Son of God conceived by the God's Spirit, he is not of Jewish origin. In this way Jesus Christ put into motion His "WORD" i.e. the WORD OF GOD of Egyptians, Babylonians, Aryans, Hindus etc. If the Author Kardel by cursing the "Bolshevik Pestilence" had this in mind, so he had the strength to annihilate it as the warrior Arjuna had at the will of Krishna (despite of his humanly objections to killing relatives and kinsmen on the battle field).

As far as the religious aspect is concerned, it is no wonder why SELF HATRED motivated "Israelites" who supported Hitler in his goal of finishing the "THIRTY YEAR WAR OF IDEOLOGIES" with the hands of Gentiles, in effect inflicting HATRED upon the entire Teutonic Nation, as it is said: "I will send many fishermen, says the Lord, to catch them and I will at once repay them double for their crime" (Jeremiah 7:30 and 16:14-19) - as it was the intention of Yahve to punish Israelites by Assyria (Isaiah 10:6).

As if reversing the motion of the "Wheel of History", the Teutonic Nation during its over 500 year relation with the "chosen people" discovered a lack of cohesiveness among them. Hitler used this uncohesiveness to pitch them against each other in a combination of ATAVISM, HATRED and VENGEANCE, the latter for the atrocities committed by the communists, before the Nazis repeated the same alone or with the help of other nations during their campaign of 1941-43 in Eastern Europe (Ukrainians, Russians, Latvians, Lithuanians etc., but not the Poles, as the Author stated erroneously. Poles were "bystanders" and often the sufferers at the hands of all those quoted, including the hordes of the Bolshevik Jews between 1939 and 1941 - see POST r. 135 through 138. In the family of this Publisher survived Poles of Jewish origin by inter-marriage, and some others were harbored elsewhere at the risk of death).

NON - RELIGIOUS AND RELIGIOUS ASPECTS COMBINED WITH HATRED AND ATAVISM

Search for the TRUTH, as it was the goal of the Author, seems not to be a difficult task if one relies on the infallibility of the Torah (Holy Bible), which in the context of the "chosen people" pretends to be a chronicle explaining the history of the World in general, and of Israel in particular. Faced with this problem, the Publisher subtitled Kardel's work with the "ISRAEL IN WAR WITH JEWS", which more correctly should be "The War of Sephardim against Ashkenazim" in fulfilling of Jacob/ Israel testament, which after 3000 years only partially has been materialized. To this subtitle gives credence Jeremiah 16:16, which is about an utter destruction of the Jews in a sort of "holocaust". And if a doer of such a holocaust was destined to be Germany, like Assyrians in the past (Isaiah 10:6), the Author's curiosity has no merit, but only his sufferings. Though still remains an unanswered question - why people, who are deeply believing in the authenticity and authority of the "Chronicle", based on this premise are propagating it, and voluntarily are taking upon themselves all those sufferings coming their way in order to fulfill the lofty promises given to them by their God (see Genesis).

Whatever the title of this book should be, it would not per se explain the whole subject matter completely and so it would only leave this topic unanswered, unbelievable and unsolved. However, any attempt to understand the "Nazi" phenomenon without the Bible would be impossible. If one adds an element of sanctity to those atavistic traits, as desired by Yahve (or Krishna, as quoted), he or she would not have to wonder why even the Jews participated in their own HOLOCAUST having vivid examples of other holocausts inflicted upon people of the non-Adamic stock, as in the biblical times it was of common occurrence (2 Sam. 12:31). The Author has reached his goal of bringing to light such a cruel issue of Judeo/ Israeli participation in the HOLOCAUST because atavism is a quality not only of the Jews (e.g. see "Am I a Murderer?" by Calel Perechodnik, a confession of a Jewish Ghetto Policeman - POST. r. 138 and n. 5 re the HOLOCAUST). When such a quality is sanctified over many generations, no one should expect a quick change in the human character, and especially when it is shaped by the godly axiom: "Let people serve thee (Israel), and nations bow down to thee." (Gen.27:29) and if they will not, they should be exterminated (Deuteronomy 7:16 or Isaiah 10:7)

Serious arguments also come from the monumental work of D. Bronder. Both, Kardel and Bronder, sent a message to the Jews and/ or Israelis, that their predestined efforts in formation of Nazism, as a tool for creation of a JUDEO/ ISRAELI TEUTONIC STATE, fell short due to contradictions of their Bible. D. Bronder explicitly reveals such a drive for a Teutonic State with a common language of Yid-German following the book of Esther, Chapters 9 and 10. These two Chapters set a pattern to be observed throughout millennia.

In the "Mein Kampf" ("The Battle of Mine") Adolf Hitler many times alluded to GOD and/ or to a PROVIDENCE. As a diligent student he obviously was aware that Yahve is the "Only God under the Sun". Knowing the name of this God, Hitler established Division IV B4 within the State's Main Security Office with a task of studying the Bible full of Providence's advises. He also knew about the human shortcomings, as well as precepts of the Bible. To this attests his divagation: "I know people who 'read' immensely, book for book, letter for letter, yet I would not describe them as 'well versed'. True, they posses a mass of 'knowledge', but their brain is unable to organize and register the material they had taken in. They lack the art of sorting what is valuable in a book from that which is without value and retaining forever." (Notice the similarities in his and Krishna's philosophy presented by the Bhagavad-Gita). Through this Bible Study Division Hitler longed to "retain of what is of value" in order to justify his murderous, but providential deeds. Thus he assigned to his faithful Party comrades a servitude to the Providence. How this Providence worked throughout the millennia, the Publisher is shortly presenting below.

PROVIDENCE

When in the year 4003 B.C. the Adam (the "Man" in Hebrew) was created from a hunk of soil (from a clot of blood according to the KORAN) already great civilizations flourished. In the oldest book, known as "Instruction of Ptah-Hotep", written about 4770 B.C., one may find a reference to a "Horus Dynasty" which ruled 13,400 years before that of Menes (2900-2700 B.C.).

The Bible about these civilizations mentions a little (Genesis 6:4). There were civilizations of "Giant Nephilims". About 100 years after Adam's creation, in his place of living - the Paradise, was established a rule of staying away from wisdom. Disobedience of this rule would cause loss of the Paradise. Next, these "first" human beings were put to a test by checking their ability to kill each other. Because Cain acquired this ability, he was appropriately marked and sent to the world of Nephilims (Gen. 4:15).

To this peculiar group of humans the knowledge about the surrounding world was restricted to a belief, that it was created in six days and that it is a center of the entire creation (not of the Universe for its comprehension was incompatible with their imagination). Such a lack of comprehension ensued almost throughout the next six millennia because this group of humans tried persistently to convince descendants of the "Nephilims", that what was revealed to them is T R U E. Noah's short disruption of that process was temporary, for the daughters of the "Nephilims" and their progeny conceived from Japhet, Shem and Ham had resumed it. But despite of those disruptive events an evolutionary process of raising humans from lower levels of conscience to higher continued, as well as from lower instincts of atavism to the higher level of spiritualism.

But any disruption, as it is a Law of Nature, follows a reverse process of creativeness, notwithstanding the initial atavistic programming (Cain). No wonder then, that people under a spell of such a programming could participate in the HOLOCAUST as easily as humans not of their group, the Gentiles. If one adds to this primeval programming the next in line, which Torah inflicted upon said group ever since Abraham's exodus from Babylonia to Egypt and from Egypt to Canaan (Palestine), then it becomes obvious that whoever acquires such a programming cannot think or act in any different way than is required of him by God or by Providence.

Disruption of the evolutionary process enhances vulnerability of humans to reverse it and no one under the spell of Bible is free from this tendency. From the time of Eden, as is evident in the Torah, the atavistic programming is continuing mercilessly. No wonder then that the new group of people (Adamites), foremost inclined to the atavistic programming, could participate in the HOLOCAUST. This primeval pattern of behavior and of restricted knowledge obviously has laid a barrier against evolutionary progress of shaping human spirituality.

After the mythical Exodus from Egypt (POST. n.1) the next set of events, i.e., expulsion of other humans from Canaan (Palestine) in ca 1200 B.C., goes under a short reign of the "House of Israel", which ended with its division into Judah (Judea) and Israel. Four hundred years of constant fighting between Judah and Israel was ended by Persians in ca 700 B.C. This caused a dispersion of Israelites around the Mediterranean Basin. There they acquired different cultures and lost their native language but not the belief in God of their ancestors for whom they fiercely struggled ("Israel" means fighting with or for God - Genesis 32:29). Literally "Israel" has a different meaning: "Is (ransom) - ra (sun) - el (god)", as this name 2500 B.C. was in use in the Empire of Ebla. (POST. r. 04).

Two hundred years later came an assault on Judah by the Babylonians and their dispersion into the Asia Minor, where they mixed with Mongols, ruled over them for about seven hundred years (Khasar's Kingdom). In the thirteenth century A.D. they were conquered by Russians of Nordic-Aryan descent and dispersed again, this time all over Eastern Europe. From there they traded with Germans, acquired their language known as Yiddish (Yid - daytsh, i.e. Jewish-German) and for over 500 years blended into their traditions almost unchanged. (POST. r.100 - "Contents: Three") In Eastern Europe they preserved their differences more drastically.

The last dispersion of the remnants of Judeans occurred under Romans (70 A.D.) and with this the promise of their God to rule the world entered a new phase of realization, lasting, as it is seen, nineteen hundred years with adherence to the biblical precept of secret population explosion, for only Yahve shall know their exact numbers (2 Samuel 24:10-16 - "a small holocaust".)

The "HOUSE OF ISRAEL" consisting of eleven tribes, and the remaining two Judah and Benjamin, formed new identities: ISRAEL and JUDAH, which in their historical annals after a complete dispersion of both, are recognized as Sephardim speaking LADINO, and as Ashkenazim speaking YIDDISH, both guided by two different TESTAMENTS or blessings. According to one, the "House of Israel" is guided by Joseph, son of Jacob (Israel) who obliged the two, just newly created tribes of Efraim and Manasseh, to fulfill it. These two tribes had to consolidate all the thirteen tribes.

The TESTAMENT FOR "THE HOUSE OF ISRAEL" reads:

> *"Shepherd, the Rock of Israel, the God of your father (Jacob), God Almighty blesses you with blessings (which) may rest on the head of Joseph the PRINCE among his brothers." (Genesis 49:22-27) "These shall come upon the head of Joseph and upon the brow of the PRINCE among his brothers, the majestic bull, his father's FIRST BORN, whose horns are those of the wild ox, with which to gore the nations, even those at the ends of the earth."* (Deuteronomy 33:16)

The TESTAMENT (BLESSING) OF MOSES, the man of God, pronounced upon the Israelites before he died, reads:

> *"The Lord hears the cry of Judah; you will bring him to his people. His own hands defend his cause, and you will be his help against his foes." (Deuteronomy 33:7). "You, Judah, shall your brothers praise - your hand on the neck of your enemies; THE SONS of your father (Jacob)*

SHALL BOW DOWN TO YOU. The scepter shall never depart from Judah or the mace from between his legs, while tribute is brought to him, and he receives the people's homage." (Gen.49:4-10)

These contradictory blessings in the first instance are submitting the tribes to the "House of Israel", and in second do not, thus creating a big conflict between the Israelites. Moreover, the first blessing (testament) accepts Egyptian mother of Ephraim and Manasseh and glorifies Egypt with the name of Ephraim, which means: "God has made me fruitful in the land of my affliction", while the name Manasseh is reminding of Joseph's sufferings: "God has made me forget entirely the sufferings I endured at the hands of my family." (Genesis 41:50-53)

Under such biblical conditions it had to come to a secession of Judeans from Israelites and to a quarrel as to who has inherited the "BIRTH RIGHTS" and God's "CHOSENNESS". In other words, the ancient Israel was conceived with imperfections and this lead to a "REJECTION OF ISRAELISM FROM WITHIN" and emergence of Judaism, with all the consequences deriving therefrom and with its phenomenon of "REJECTION OF JEWISHNESS FROM WITHIN", as the Author Kardel discovered it intelligently.

Due to these biblical testaments the drama of these special people unfolds. Up to this day the fighting between Israelites and Judaites (which started at the very beginning of their State, the "House of Israel"), over the fulfillment of these two testaments continues. It is also a daily occurrence in the modern State of Israel where Ashkenazim discriminate Sephardim, and both do the same to Falashas i.e. to the black "Ethiopian Jews" who are the unspoiled descendants of the tribe Dan. (POST. n. 2)

This combination of the biblical drama with the human atavism resulted in many atrocities throughout the history of the "chosen people", from which it is too difficult or impossible to escape. AND ALL THIS WHILE THE GOD YAHVE/ISRAEL IS WATCHING. (POST. n. 6) Therefore it is not surprising that in this testamentary plot the people affiliated with Israelism or Sefardims on one side, and with Judaism or Ashkenazims on the other are involved. The last consolidation attempt of these special people by any means possible has been taking place under the banner of Z I O N I S M (POST. n. 3) as, for example, it is presented in the Book of Esther, Chapters 9 and 10. It is remarkable, that this "Book" emanates throughout the past generations, even in the U.S., glorifying the FEAST OF PURIM, which is teaching about how to deal with Gentiles (POST. r.45). Undoubtedly this is the same method as of the NAZIS, who reinvented crematoriums (brick kilns) of King David, who used them to annihilate his "enemies" under the banner of the heathen's "Shield of David". (POST. n. 4)

Considering that with the advent of Marxism a new "E V I L" took hold of all Europe promising of a new "Paradise on Earth", a counter-EVIL took hold of the German people fighting against Marxism, to whom was also promised a "Teutonic Paradise" lasting 1000 years.

Under such a biblical scenario it would be illogical to expect the VIRTUE to prevail over the human ATAVISM producing fruits of genocide. Of genocides, which were committed many times over within a short time span of this Century (for instance on 1.5 million Armenian Christians by Ottoman Turks), in order to fulfill lofty ideas worthy of no God, whether this God be of Mohammedans, Israelites, Judeans or of any other Nation. Worthy of no God, who is giving his blessings while humans are killing each other on the battle fields or under other circumstances. In this way he is giving a FOOD to the historians counting the number of victims, as it was done perfectly and in a scientific fervor by the author of the "Hitler's Army - Soldiers, Nazis, and War in the Third Reich" (POST. r. 76).

This author (raised in Modern Israel) treats the matter from the point of view of the MARTIAL ART and proves, that the cohesion of the German Army was underlined by self discipline in the face of committed murders without consideration of the ideas to which Kardel and others pay a lot of attention to. However, the author missed a conclusion, that the Second World War was indeed the THIRTY YEAR WAR OF IDEOLOGIES. If the author as modern Israeli looks at history through such a prism, then he pays a lip service to the Israeli Army, which he once was a member of, and which has no resources to wage war on the same scale, as his predecessors did in the SMALL WORLD of the "Holy Land", nor on the Nazis' scale and their opponents. Some other factors must be employed here guaranteeing that if another war were to change the face of the World, it would create not just a new Israel, as Kardel presupposes, but a Kingdom of Yahweh/ Israel instead of a Kingdom of Jesus, Allah or Krishna, as many would wish. It is not difficult to imagine what would happen if those Kingdoms were to be created on the battle fields or outside as was created the modern State of Israel.

Within this "JUDEO-CHRISTIAN" world, as many like to call it, Jesus Christ could not stop genocides, as for example those which were committed 500 years ago on the indigenous people of Mesoamerica. Ever since 620 A.D. Mohammed with his KORAN could not stop them either in other parts of the World. About the genocide of 100,000 year old Australian Aborigines by the Christian Anglicans nobody was concerned, either. Thus the "WHEEL OF HISTORY" turns itself in the biblical style undisturbed.

If the NATURE'S GOD of the American Declaration of Independence, in contrast to the biblical PEOPLE'S GOD will not make a difference, and religionists' or politicians' mania to create a "KINGDOM OF JUSTICE" all over the World will not cease, efforts of Hennecke Kardel and others like him will have been futile. Therefore the Publisher, in more or less sarcastic tone follows the Author's intentions, because the biblical dreams are not worthy of a suicide or of new genocides.

The development of sciences, since Nicolaus Copernicus, leads humanity to the "HEAVENLY SPHERES". These "SPHERES" are imagined by religionists sufficiently enough, so that with little effort by immersing themselves more into the SCIENTIFIC REALMS, they may find, the sought after, and highly desired "UNIVERSAL SPIRIT". If the "Universal Spirit" will not heal the humans of their sanctified dreams, they may perish. (POST. r. 56) It is worthwhile to note, that the "Universal Spirit" is slowly but steadily allowing ITSELF to be recognized, undoubtedly aiming at a "Paradise", which through a physical and mental evolution, as on October 22, 1996 Pope John Paul II put it in a statement to the Plenary Session of the Pontifical Academy of Sciences - people may reach "Paradise" with GOD in it (for IT/HE is the NATURE'S GOD of the Declaration of Independence - claims the Publisher.)

Publisher

FOOTNOTES TO THE POSTSCRIPT

/1/ "Mythical" for as it came to light most recently, the "Exodus" never happened. (Source: Dr.Yehuda Shabatay with a doctorate from the Jewish Theological Seminary of America, New York, 1996).

/2/ "Falashas" - are hardly accepted by Ashkenazims and Sephardims, not because of their black skin, but because they consider the Palestinian and the Babylonian Talmuds as heretical interpretation of the Bible.

/3/ Which in the modern State of Israel are passing through a metamorphosis. (The POST. r. 42 and r. 76 are good examples)

/4/ The "Magen David" ("Shield of David") is a hexagram which has been used by many cultures, among them Arabian, and carries a special mystique important to astrologers. Therefore its establishment in 1917 as a symbol of Zionism was strongly protested. (Source: Bernard S. Baskas, Rabbi Emeritus of the Temple of Aaron, St. Paul, Minnesota, 1996)

/5/ The "Swastika" has its occultic roots in various cultures of the past and as an emblem of the Nazi movement it was established almost at the same time as the Zionists' "Magen David". The swastika in Vedic tongue "svasti" and in its classical Sanskrit's derivative "svastika", has a meaning of a "good luck" or "welfare", and among European Aryans was symbolizing the Viking God Thor ("Thunder" sending fire from the Sun or Heaven). (POST. r. 07) Similar symbol was used by the Jewish magazine "Ostara" with an inscription in the Runic Alphabet invented by the Viking God Odin ("The Only One") and accompanied by a name of "Guido von List", a person who had access to secrets of the runes ("Das Geheimnis der Runen"). (See a respective illustration in this book). The runic alphabet represents both learning and magic lore. Coincidence of "swastikas" in the Lambach's Seminary and the semi-one in the "Ostara" Jewish magazine, brought to Hitler (the artist painter) an idea of using it as the emblem of his Party, and the title "OSTARA" (meaning "An Era of the East") as a propaganda slogan "Drang nach Osten" ("An Urge For-" or "A drive Toward the East"). The same urge which the Caucasian Aryans had in 1500 B.C., and who mixed their blood with Dravidians on the Indian Peninsula. They implanted there their own distinctive culture of Brahminism from the Aryan's God Brahma ("A Gate To Everything") who was ruling the world together with god Agni ("Fire" in Aryan-Russian), god Visnu ("Pink"- younger) and god Siva ("Grau" - older). The names of these gods stem also from the language of Aryans. Their drive towards the East and South gave a beginning to Sumeria, Babylonia, Iran (Persia) and so forth. In the South they encountered nomads of Semitic origin, among them the Khabiru (Hebrews) - POST. r.56. It was a drive towards the Sun curiously rising on the eastern horizon, which was accepted by many as "GOD SUN". And indeed it was a drive towards the "LIGHT GIVING LIFE", as far as to the American Continents (Aztec, Maya and Inca civilizations) from where humans are now sending, also eastwardly, their space ships to the other planets and in the future to the emanating "Light Giving Life" Stars. About the "Light Giving Life" it is recommended to see the SILENT RUNNING on Home Video by Universal Production, 1971, U.S., and as an addendum, the COSMIC VOYAGE, a movie produced by Cosmic Voyage Incorporated, 1996, IMAX, Los Angeles, U.S.

About :

- the European and Caucasian Aryans it is recommended to read:
    (1) "Vedic India" by Zenaide A. Ragozin, Delhi, 1912 and 1961;
    (2) "The Culture and Civilization of Ancient India" by D.D. Kosambi, London, 1965, and
    (3) "Living with the Himalayan Masters" by Swami Rama, Pennsylvania, 1980 where of special interest is the Chapter entitled "Jesus in the Himalayas" meditating there for 18 years.

- the meaning of the Runes (see POST. r.07) it is also recommended to read:
    (1) "Discover runes: understanding and using the power of runes" by Tony Willis, 1993, and
    (2) "Raido: The Runic Journey" by Jennifer Smith, 1994.

- the problem with the HOLOCAUST, read the "AUSTRALIA AND THE HOLOCAUST 1933-1945" (POST. r. 139). There, the Jewish efforts to inflict GUILT FEELINGS upon the entire World for sufferings caused by their MOSAIC ideology, cannot be seen as anything else but an attempt of aggression on the human consciousness to such a degree, that even inhabitants of remote countries, for instance of the Solomon Islands, should feel this guilt and CARRY IT ON WITHIN, so that IT can be easily exploited. Exploited for the same purpose, as in 1938 Calel Perechodnik (in Russian it means a "Transient") believed "in the historical mission of the Jewish people by spreading culture among the nations of the world (also through the French Revolution)", or, as Hennecke Kardel put it, through "NAZIONISM". At the end (1944) of his cruelsome career as a helper of Nazis in Poland, Calel was also OVERCOME BY HATRED TOWARDS HIS KINSMEN (POST. r. 138. page 255). To be a HUMAN, it is not necessary to be a JEW and SUFFER because of the JEWISH RELIGION (page 200). On page 180 Calel revealed a name of a GESTAPO-man, (a Jew), who also contributed to the sufferings. (See also POST. r. 137 - "Hitler's Willing Executioners").

- the NATURE'S GOD, please consider the PREFACE.

/6/ Peculiar enough - but Yahve is observing Goyims through eyes of certain Jews, one of whose under the title "Old - Fashioned Hatred TV" (READER, July 7, 1996) assures that he is tracking their "enemies". Two week later this TV commentator got a reprimand, which is quoted here in full: "CLANDESTINE FORCES - Mr.Abe is advising what pursuers of ideologies advice: 'let your enemies keep talking so you can keep careful track of who and where they are ("As Seen on TV," July 11). Then clandestine forces of fascists, communists, dictators, etc., will do a "cleansing", and afterward people will posthumously decorate their martyrs. Under communists and fascist regimes, where I was happy to live, it was standard policy that if you were not with them, you were against them. As an American, Mr.Abe must rather choose a peaceful persuasion that any ideology (even the biblical one - 'an eye for an eye, a tooth for a tooth') is a scourge for humankind. In order to eradicate it, the Founding Fathers of this great nation created a Constitution which everyone shall obey. Publisher."

/7/ About content of this Footnote, read reproductions at the end of the POSTSCRIPT: "Second language" and "What should America's official language be?"

REFERENCES TO THE POSTSCRIPT
(BIBLIOGRAPHY - WITH COMMENTS AND
RECOMMENDATIONS OF FURTHER READING)

PRIMARY WORKS

01. 1918 (1st Edit.1906) London, Battiscombe Gunn: "The Instruction of Ptah-Hotep and the Instruction of Ke'Gemni - The Oldest Book in the World." (It contains pre-Hammurabi Codices)

02. 1971 (1st Ed.1904) New York/London, Chilperic Edwards: "The Hammurabi Code and the Sinaitic Legislation."

03. 1951 (1st Ed.1888) Russel Frederick Hears: "Eight Decisive Books of Antiquity - The Laws of Hammurabi and the First Bourgeois State."

04. 1981 (2nd Ed.1991) New York, Giovanni Pettinato: "The Archives of Ebla - An Empire (in the Near East) Inscribed in Clay." (These discoveries have been ignored by T.E. Levy - See r. 42.)

05. 1968 (2nd Ed.1972) U.S.A./ India, His Divine Grace A.C. Bhaktivedanta Swami Prabhupada: "Bhagavad-Gita As It Is."

06. 1974 U.S.A., England, Canada, Australia. Troy Wilson Organ: "Hinduism - Its Historical Development."

07. 1964 (1st Ed.) U.S.A. H.R. Ellis Davidson: "Gods and Myths of Northern Europe." (2nd Ed. 1981: "Gods and Myths of the Viking Age.")

08. 1957 (3rd Ed. 1950-1991) U.S.A. English Version by D. Goetz & S.G. Morley: "Popol Vuh - The Sacred Book of the Ancient Quiche Maya." 09. 1968 (1st Ed.) New York. Warwick Bray: "Everyday Life of the Aztecs."

10. 1975 U.S.A. Loren McIntyre by National Geographic Society: "The Incredible Incas and Their Timeless Land."

11. 1990 U.S.A. Linda Schele & David Freidel: "A Forest of Kings - The

Untold Story of the Ancient Maya."

12. 1982   (1st Ed. 1962) U.S.A. The Jewish Publication Society of America: "The Torah - The Five Books of Moses."/ "The Holy Bible." (A distortion of history of mankind. Read also about monotheism in Egypt predating the Moses: "Tutankhamen - Amenism, Atenism and Egyptian Monotheism." by British Museum, New York, 1923.)

13. 1978   U.S.A. The Jewish Publication Society of America: "The Prophets - II SAMUEL 12-31." (A part of the Torah)

14. 1982   U.S.A. The Jewish Publication Society of America: "The Writings - I CHRONICLES 20-3." (A part of the Torah)

15. 1535   London. Myles Coverdale: "The Holy Scriptures - The Olde and Newe Testamente with the Apocripha: Faithfully translated from the Hebrue and Greke."

16. 1972   Muenchen. Dr.Martin Luther: "Die gantze Heilige Schrifft Deudsch, Wittenberg 1545."

17. 1560   Geneva. "The Bible and Holy Scriptures Contained in the Olde and Newe Testament. Translated According to the Ebrue and Greke."

18. 1611   Printed in London, New York, Toronto. The Authorized King James Version by Oxford University Press: "The Holy Bible."

19. 1794   London. Samuel Bagster & Sons Limited: "The Hebrew-English Old Testament from the Bagster Polyglot Bible."

20. 1821   Paris. Par Le Maistre de Sacy: "La Sainte Bible Contenant L'Ancien et le Nouveau Testament."

21. 1870   New York. "Hitchcock's New and Complete Analysis of the Holy Bible or, the Whole of the Old and New Testament, Arranged According to Subjects in Twenty-Seven Books, Chap.IX. Prisoners of War. Sec.88."

22. 1880   New York. Canoniska Boecker: "Bibelen eller den Heliga Skrift."

23. 1893   Leipzig. R. Stier und K.H.W. Theife: "Die historischen Buecher des Alten Testaments."

24. 1896   New York/ London by S. Bahgster and Sons, Ltd.: "The Septuagint Version of the Old Testament with an English Translation."

25. 1901   New York. Thomas Nelso & Sons: "The Holy Bible Containing the Old and New Testament Translated Out of the Original Tongues."

26. 1910   Nueva York. Sociedad Biblica Americana: "La Santa Biblia que nosta del Antiguo y el Nuevo Testamento."

27. 1911   Elberfield. D. Martin Luthers: "Die Bibel oder die ganze Heilige Schrift des Alten und Neuen Testaments."

28. 1948   New York. "The Old Testament, Newly translated from the Vulgate Latin by Msgr. Ronald Knox at the Request of His Eminence The Cardinal Archbishop of Westminster."

29. 1957   Philadelphia. George M. Lamsa: "The Holy Bible from Ancient Eastern Manuscripts Containing the Old and New Testaments."

30. 1968   New York. American Bible Society Edition: "The Holy Bible As Printed by Robert Aitken and Approved & Recommended by the Congress of the United States of America in 1782."

31. 1969   (2nd Ed.) London. Soncino Books of the Bible: "Samuel - Hebrew Text & English Translation with an Introduction and Commentary by the Rev. Dr.S. Goldman, M.A." (see r. 21 - Sec.88).

32. 1969   New York. Charles F. Pfeiffer: "The Dead Sea Scrolls and the Bible"

33. 1882   London. Rev. H.D.M. Spence, M.A.: "Treasures of the Talmud" Being a Series of Classified Subjects in Alphabetical Order from "A" to "L" Compiled from the Babylonian Talmud (compiled between 352-427 A.D.) and Translated by Paul Isaac Hershon: 'For offenses between man and God the Day of Atonement secures pardon.' 'Israelites dwelling outside the land of Israel are unintentional idolaters.' 'A daughter of Israel must not assist at the accouchement of a heathen female, for she would thus be helping the birth of an idolater.' 'A certain man once prayed behind a synagogue and did not turn his face towards it. Elijah passed by ... and appeared to him (incognito) as an Arab merchant and said, 'Thou standest before thy Lord as if there were two (Gods), and he drew his sword and slew him.' 'It is said (Ezek. XXXIV.31):...ye my flock...are men, ye are called men, but the nations of the world are not called men but brutes.' 'Why are idolaters defiled? Because they did not stand on Mount Sinai... when Israel stood at Mount Sinai that defilement was removed; but the Gentiles, who did not stand at Mount Sinai, their defilement was not done away.' 'Seven commandments (given) to Noah's descendants (universal laws binding on all mankind): (1) The prohibition against idolatry; ....(7) The obligation to establish courts of law. A non-Jew who disobeys one of these commandments is liable to the death penalty.' 'A proselyte of Egyptian extraction, whether male of female, may not marry a Jew by birth for two generations (although he may marry another proselyte).'"

34. 1989   New York. Jerusalem. Steinsaltz Edition: "Talmud", Volumes 9.

35. 1970   New York. Arthur Edward Waite, P.M., P.Z. "A New Encyclopaedia of Freemasonry and of Cognate Instituted Mysteries: Their Rites, Literature and History: 'Edwin, a mythical son of Athelstan, presided over a meeting of Masons at York (926 A.D.) and certain charges were agreed upon for the government of the Brotherhood...a connection between Freemasonry and the Jewish sect ESSENES (see r. 81) was advanced from time to time in the past...The living channels of the Secret Tradition in Israel...are Enoch, Abraham, Moses, Solomon and then...Rabbi

Simeon ben Yochai at the beginning of the Christian Dispensation, a Greater Exile for Jewry."

36. 1940   New York. Adolphe Franck: "The Kabbalah" ("Tradition"): "...before the end of the first century of the Christian era, there circulated among the Jews a profoundly venerated science which could be distinguished from the...Talmud and the Sacred Books - a mystic doctrine evidently engendered by the need for reflection and independence as well as philosophy, and which, nevertheless, invoked in its favor the united authority of tradition and scriptures."

37. 1978   U.S.A./India/England. Charles Ponce: "Kabbalah - An Introduction and Illumination for the World Today." ("The Kabbalah, the main compendium of Jewish mystical thought, differs from rabbinical Judaism in proposing that: 1. The creator God of the Bible is a limited God & that he is subordinate to yet a higher, limitless & unknowable God, the En-Sof. The term En-Sof translates into limitless or boundless. 2. The universe is not the result of creation ex nihilo, but the result of a complex operation performed by the emanated attributes of the En-Sof, the Sefiroth. 3. The Sefiroth are a bridge connecting the finite universe with the finite God.")

38. 1927   (5th Ed. after 1st of 1816). George A. Barton, Ph.D.: "Archeology and the Bible, Chap.V. The Patriarchs Before the Flood: It has been known from the writings of Berossos, a Babylonian priest who died about 260 B.C., that the Babylonians had a list of long lived kings who lived before the Flood. (see r. 1: The 'Followers of Horus' are legendary dynasty of demigods believed by the Egyptians to have ruled for about 13,400 years after the reign of Horus.') The (Babylonian) cuneiform text read as follows: 'Column IV. The kingdom of Erech passed to Ur. In Ur Mesannipada was king..... Column VII.....Total 134 kings. Grand total 28,876 years.'"

39. 1950   Vancouver B.C., Canada. Ivan Panin: "Bible Chronology in Three Parts: Part.II. Bible Data. 'Adam Created 4003 B.C.'"

40. 1975   Tennessee, U.S.A. Frank Klassen: "The Chronology of the Bible: 'Adam created on Friday, April 1, 3975 B.C.'"

41. 1988   Chicago and London. Hans J. Nissen: "The Early History of the Ancient Near East, 9000-2000 B.C."

42. 1995   New York. Thomas E. Levy: "The Archaeology of Society in the Holy Land: Chapter II. The First Settled Societas - Natufian (12,500-10,000 B.C.); Chapter III. The Impact of the Sea Peoples (1185-1050 B.C.); The Kingdoms of Israel and Judah (Ca.1000 - 750 B.C.)."

43. 1980   (5th Ed.) Tokyo. Bukkyo Dendo Kyokai: "The Teaching of

Buddha."

44. 1987   New York. Robert C. Lester: "Buddhism - The Path to Nirvana."

45. 1989   Tokyo. Isaiah Ben-Dasan: "The Japanese and the Jews, translated from the Japanese by R. L. Gage." (Seventh printing from 1970).

46. 1988   (4th Ed. from 1956) Advisory Editor Betty Radice: "The Koran" or "Qur'an" ("The Recital","The Book") (622 A.D.) "Mohammed...firmly believed that he was the messenger of God, sent forth to confirm previous Scriptures (the Torah). God revealed His will to the Jews and the Christians through chosen apostles, but they disobeyed God's commandments and divided themselves into schismatic sects. The Koran accuses Jews of corrupting the Scriptures and the Christians of worshiping Jesus as the Son of God, although God had expressly commanded them to worship none but Him. Recites in the name of the Lord who created man from a clot of blood."

47. 1979   (5th Ed.) New York. Fred J. Khouri: "The Arab-Israeli Dilemma."

48. 1977   Utah, U.S.A. Translated by Joseph Smith in 1830: "The Book of Mormon, An Account Written by the Hand of Mormon Upon Plates taken from the Plates of Nephi" (after destruction in 587 B.C. of Jerusalem by the Nebuhadnezar, Ruler of the Old Babylonian Empire, this member of the Israeli tribe Nephi set sail for America.)

49. 1966   Utah. Bruce R. McConkie: "Mormon Doctrine."

50. 1971   (6th Ed. after 1875) Boston. U.S.A. Published by First Church of Christ, Scientist. Author: Mary Baker Eddy: "Science and Health with Key to the Scriptures."

51. 1976   (5th Ed. after 1955) Chicago. Urantia Foundation: THE URANTIA BOOK in four parts: I. The Central and Superuniverses. II. The Local Universe. III. The History of Urantia. IV. The Life and Teaching of Jesus."

52. 1974   Santa Barbara, California. Clyde Bedell: "Concordex of the URANTIA BOOK - Mission of the URANTIA BOOK."

53. 1957   Garden City, New York. William Foxwell Albright: "From the Stone Age to Christianity."

54. 1926   (28 Ed.1975) California. Joseph Lewis: "The Bible Unmasked."

55. 1975   New York. Lloyd Graham: "Deception and Myths of the Bible."

56. 1976   Boston. Julian Jaynes: "The Origin of Consciousness in the Breakdown of the Bicameral Mind. 'O, what a world of unseen visions and heard silences, this insubstantial country of the mind! What ineffable essences, these touchless rememberings and unshowable reveries!....This consciousness that is myself of

selves, that is everything, and yet nothing at all - what is it? And where did it come from? And why?.... Book II. 4. A Change of Mind in Mesopotamia (Babylon). 6. The Moral Consciousness of the Khabiru (Hebrews).'"

SECONDARY WORKS - I

57. 1942 Boston. Anna Seghers: "The Seventh Cross", translated from German.
58. 1944 Boston. Konrad Heiden: "Der Fuehrer - Hitler's Rise to Power."
59. 1948 New York. Louis P. Lochner: "The Goebbels Diaries - 1942/ 1943."
60. 1959 Warszawa. E.Crankshaw: "Gestapo, narzedzie tyranii" (Translation from English by Jerzy Dewitz: "Gestapo, Instrument of Tyranny.")
61. 1960 Connecticut. William Shirer: "The Rise and Fall of the Third Reich - A History of Nazi Germany."
62. 1962 New York. Bantam Books: "The Pictorial History of the Third Reich."
63. 1962 Warszawa. Kazimierz Kakol: "Adolfa Eichmanna droga do bejt haam/ The Road of Adolf Eichmann to the Bejt Haam."
64. 1968 Boston, Toronto. William Manchester: "The Arms of Krupp."
65. 1969 New York. Eugene Davidson: "The Trial of the Germans."
66. 1969 New York. Leo Mosley: "On Borrowed Time - How World War II Began."
67. 1970 New York. G.S. Graber: "History of the SS."
68. 1971 Boston. Adolf Hitler: "Mein Kampf" (Translated by Ralph Manheim)
69. 1973 New York. Robert Payne: "The Life and Death of Adolf Hitler."
70. 1974 France. Jean Mabire: "Les S.S. Francais - La Division Charlemagne."
71. 1975 Genf. Dietrich Bronder: "Bevor Hitler Kam - Eine historishe Studie"
72. 1976 New York. Lucy S. Davidowicz: "The War Against the Jews - 1933/ 45."
73. 1976 New York, John Toland: "Adolf Hitler."
74. 1986 New York. G.L. Posner and J. Ware: "Mengele - The Complete Story."
75. 1986 New York. Bernard Cohen and Luc Rosenzweig: "Waldheim" (Translated from German by Josephine Bacon)
76. 1991 New York. Omer Bartov: "Hitler's Army - Soldiers, Nazis, and War in the Third Reich." (It is a book about the Germans on "Crusade" against the "Communists' Paradise" as presented by the author educated in Israel and also seen by Poles (see r. 135); by a Russian (r. 133); by a Jew (r. 105) and by others (r. 132 & 134).

77. 1992   New York. John Weitz: "Hitler's Diplomat - The Life and Times of Joahim von Ribbentrop."

78. 1996   New York Times News Service (11.19.96): "The British and the U.S. knew in '41 of Nazi massacre of Jews in Belarus and Ukraine: 'Nazis - elite SS units with municipal (local) police units - were executing every Jew (and communists) they could lay hands on."

SECONDARY WORKS - II

79. 1946   New York. Rabbi Elmer Berger: "The Jewish Dilemma."

80. 1953   Chicago. Alfred M. Lilienthal: "What Price Israel."

81. 1956   New York. Melford E. Spiro: "Kibbutz - Venture in Utopia" ("Kibbutz is an agricultural village (in Israel as a dream of Essenes, a sect of Judea) in which all property... is collectively owned, in which work is collectively organized..." - and which served as an example to the Soviet Union in its fight against private ownership.)

82. 1957   Chicago. Nathan Glazer: "American Judaism."

83. 1957   New Haven. Rabbi Elmer Berger: "Judaism or Jewish Nationalism" (of this author: Essay of 1942 "Why I am a Non-Zionist" and more).

84. 1957   U.S.A. William Chomsky: "Hebrew: The Eternal Language."

85. 1959   U.S.A. Will Herberg: "Judaism and Modern Man."

86. 1959   New York. Arthur Hertzberg: "The Zionist Idea."

87. 1960   (9th Ed. 1972) New York. Rabbi Morris N. Kertzer: "What is a Jew?"

88. 1961   New York. Arthur Hertzberg: "Judaism".

89. 1965   New York. Max L. Margolis and Alexander Marx: "A History of the Jewish People."

90. 1965   New York. Elie Wiesel: "The Jews of Silence." (on Soviet Jewry)

91. 1967   New York. Chaim Potok: "The Chosen - A novel."

92. 1968   U.S.A. Abba Eban: "My People - The Story of the Jews."

93. 1969   New York. Joseph Leftwich: "The Way We Think - A collection of Essays from the Yiddish." (Volumes 2)

94. 1970   New York. Hans Habe: "Proud Zion" (Translated by Anthony Vivis)

95. 1971   New Jersey. Rabbi Morrison David Bial: "Liberal Judaism at Home."

96. 1971   New Jersey. Melville Shavelson: "How to Make a Jewish Movie."

97. 1971   Paris. Martin Gray: "For Those I Love." (Translated from French)

98. 1973   Philadelphia. Milton Himmelfarb: "The Jews of Modernity."

99. 1974   New York. A. Foster & B. R. Epstein: "The New Anti-Semitism."

100. 1974   Canada. Marvin Kalb and Bernard Kalb: "Kissinger" (Henry A.)

101. 1975   New York. "My Life" by Golda Meir.

102. 1975   New York. Chaim Potok: "In the Beginning" (A novel)

103.1976	Philadelphia. Stephen M.Poppel: "Zionism in Germany 1897-1933."
104.1976	New York. Irving Hove: "World of Our Fathers."
105.1977	Philadelphia. Lev Kopelev: "To be Preserved Forever "(Translated from Russian)
106.1977	New York. Mark Jay Mirsky: "My Search for the Messiah."
107.1977	U.S.A. Eva Fleischner: "Auschwitz: Beginning of a New Era? - Reflections on the Holocaust."
108.1977	New York. "Abba Eban - An Autobiography."
109.1977	Connecticut. Rabbi Sidney Greenberg and Rabbi Jonathan D. Levine: "The New Mahzor for Rosh Hashanah and Yom Kippur." (A prayer book)
110.1977	London. Simon N. Herman: "Jewish Identity - A Social Psychological Perspective."
111.1978	New Jersey. Hans Ashkenazy: "Are We All Nazis?"
112.1978	New York. Lev Kopelev: "The Education of a True Believer." (Translated from Russian)
113.1981	New York. Elie Wiesel: "The Testament." (A novel, translated from French)
114.1981	Philadelphia. Israel Emiot: "The Birobidzhan Affair - A Yiddish Writer in Siberia." (Birobidzhan - an autonomous Jewish Republic in the Soviet Union in the mid-1930s, hailed as a growing center of Jewish culture)
115.1981	U.S.A., Canada. Sylvia Rothschild: "Voices from the Holocaust."
116.1982	Utah. Victor L. Ludlow: "Isaiah: Prophet, Seer, and Poet."
117.1983	U.S.A. "Amoz Oz in the Land of Israel." (Translated from Hebrew by Maurie Goldberg-Bartura)
118.1985	Boston. J. Neusner: "Israel in America - A Too-Comfortable Exile?"
119.1985	Boston. President of the U.S. J. Carter: "The Blood of Abraham."
120.1985	New York. James Parker: "The Conflict of the Church and the Synagogue - A study of the Origins of Antisemitism."
121.1986	New York. Yair Kotler: "Heil Kahane."
122.1987	Philadelphia, New York, Jerusalem. Abraham Rabinovich: "The Battle for Jerusalem - June 5-7, 1967."
123.1987	Boston, Toronto, London. Alan M. Dershowitz: "Chutzpah."
124.1988	New York. Neal Gabler: "An Empire of their Own - How the Jews Invented Hollywood."
125.1988	Boston. Howard Simons: "Jewish Times - Voices of the American Jewish Experience."
126.1990	New York. Victor Ostrovsky and Claire Hoy: "By Way of Deception" (about "Mossad" - intelligence body of Israel).
127.1991	New York. John P. Meyer: "A Marginal Jew - Rethinking the Historical Jesus. Vol.I: The Roots of the Problem and the Person." (As a man, not as a Son of God)

128.1991   New York. Rabbi J.Telushkin: "Jewish Literacy - The Most Important Things to Know About Jewish Religion, Its People, and Its History."

129.1992   New York. David Biale: "Eros and the Jews - From Biblical Israel to Contemporary America."

130.1994   New York. Eva Fogelman: "Conscience & Courage - Rescuers of Jews During the Holocaust."

131.1995   New York. Roselle K. Chartock and Jack Spencer: "Can It Happen Again? - Chronicles of the Holocaust."

SECONDARY WORKS - III

132.1970   Boston. Toronto. Edward Crankshaw: "Krushchev Remembers." (Translated from Russian)

133.1973   New York, Evanston, San Francisco, London. Aleksandr I. Solzhenitsyn: "The Gulag Archipelago - 1918-1956, Volumes 2." (Translated from Russian by Thomas P. Whitney)

134.1975   New York. Patrick Watson: "Alexander Dolgun's Story - An American in the Gulag" by Alexander Dolgun.

135.1995   Massachusetts, White Eagle (April 16, 1995): "POST HOLO-CAUSTUM". 'Bibliography: (1) 'Stolen Childhood/ Skradzione Dziecinstwo' by L. Królikowski, New York, 1983; (2) 'A Boquet of Thoughts and Reminiscences/ Wiazanka mysli' by Polish Women's League, Wellington, New Zealand, 1991; (3) 'The Invited' (about Polish children, in 1944 invited to New Zealand as refugees from the Soviet Union)/ 'Osiedlenie Mlodziezy Polskiej w Nowej Zelandii w 1944' by Krystyna Skwarko, Wellington, 1974; (4) 'A Boy in the Gulag' by J. Kmiecik, London, 1983: (5) 'Tovarisch (Comrade), I Am not Dead' by G.S. Urban, London, 1980; (6) 'The Long Walk' by S. Rawicz, London, 1956; (7) 'Kwaheri, Africa' by A.A. Zarzycki and S. Buczak Zarzycka; (8) 'The Polish Heart','Travel Without Choice','Sunshine at Last', a Trilogy by L. Kondratowicz-Kordas, Perth, Australia, 1992 (9) 'Living in two Worlds - the Polish Community of Wellington' by Petone Settlers Museum, the Hutt City Council, 1992; (10) 'Isfahan, Miasto Polskich Dzieci/ Isfahan (Iran), City of Polish Children' by I. Beaupre-Stankiewicz, D. Waszczuk-Kamieniecka and J. Lewicka- Howell, London, 1987; (11) 'Losy Polaków w ZSRR w latach 1939- 1986/ The Fate of Poles in the Soviet Union 1939 - 1986' by Polish Combatants Association and J. Siedlecki, Great Britain, 1987; (12) 'Memoirs of Poles in New Zealand deported to the Soviet Union/ Wspomnienia Deportacji do ZSRR' w 40sta Rocznice Deportacji do ZSRR, Wellington, 1980; (13) 'Children of Europe' by D. McCardle, London, 1949; (14) 'The Fate of Polish Children During Last War' by R. Hrabar, Z. Tokaz and J.E.Wilczur, Interpress, Warsaw, 1981; (15) 'W czterdziestym nas Matko na Sybir zeslali/ Mother, they deported us in 1940 to Siberia' by J.T. Gross, London, 1989; (16) 'W okowach tajgi, pamietnik zeslanca/ In the Yoke of Taiga, Memoirs of a Deportee' by E. Debowski, Kielce, Poland, 1992; (17) 'Krystyna's Story' (of a Polish child in the Soviet Union) by Halina Ogonowska-Coates, Wellington, 1992. "The First Journey, a Preamble: This could be my mother's story. It could belong to any one of the t w o m i l l i o n Poles who were deported to the Soviet Union during the Second World War. But in a way it is nobody's story, for who can remember all that happened after the soldiers came and took them away? As a child I loved my mother but she seemed different from other mothers. She didn't know how old she was. She couldn't remember were she was born. I wondered what had happened to her that she could have forgotten such important things. It had something to do with the Second World War. When I grew older I wanted to get to know my mother and to find out about her past. Eventually I learned that she was among the seven hundred and thirty-two Polish children who had survived forced deportation to the Soviet Union and had traveled half way across the world to take refuge in New Zealand in 1944. My mother was reluctant to talk about her past. She said it was too sad, but I kept asking questions. I wanted to know what had happened to my Polish grandmother. I wanted to know about the place where my mother was born. Slowly my mother began to talk to me. We sat together for hours, talking and crying, putting together the tattered fragments that were her memories, but there were many missing pieces. My mother had been a small child when she was taken from her Polish home. I went to visit her Polish friends to find out more. These people had endured similar harrowing experiences, but they took me into their hearts as my mother's daughter and told me stories that will always haunt the corners of my mind. Slowly my mother's childhood came alive to me. I can close my eyes and see her playing in the fields outside Baranowicze, a small girl with blue eyes and blonde hair. This could be her story:....'"

136.1996   New Haven, London, Robert W. Thurston: "Life and Terror in Stalin's Russia, 1934-1941." (See a reproduction at the end of the POST.: "ACHIEVEMENT OF THE U.S.S.R. AFTER 60 YEARS OF EXISTENCE". See also POST. r.106, p.21, similar to "Our country had a piece of BAD LUCK. It got chosen for the Marxist experiment ..." - Boris Yelstin, June 16, 1991).

137.1996   New York, Daniel Jonah Goldhagen: "Hitlers' Willing Executioners."

138.1996   Boulder, Colorado, Calel Perechodnik: "Am I a Murderer?"

139.1994   Melbourne, Paul R. Bartrop: "Australia and the Holocaust 1933-

1945."

140.1975 U.S.A. Austin Flannery, O.P., General Editor. Preface by John Cardinal Wright: "Vatican, Council II. Declaration on the Relation of the Church to Non-Christian Religions. Guidelines on Religious Relations with the Jews. The Dignity of the Human Person."

141.1996 (October) U.S.A., TV DISCOVERY CHANNEL aired a movie "REVENGE" about the "Poison Crusade" of Palestinian and European Jews against the Cities and Prisoners of War in Germany who one year after the Second World War were determined to punish the "Nation of Murderers" for what it had done to their families. At that time the Poles were tried by the Communists for not fighting against the Germans in defense of the Soviet Union.

ACHIEVEMENTS OF THE U.S.S.R. AFTER 60 YEARS OF EXISTENCE

THE HUMAN VICTIMS

The Russian Civil War (1917-1921)	3.000.000
The Ukraine Civil War	2.800.000
War against Finland (1918)	50.000
War against the Baltic countries (1918-19)	410.000
War against Poland (1920)	600.000
War against Georgia (1921-1922)	20.000
War against Poland (1939)	103.000
War against Finland (1939)	400.000
Second World War (according to Khrushchev data)	20.000.000
The Red Terror (1917-1923)	2.290.000
Second wave of Terror of Cheka (1923-1930)	2.000.000
First Famine (1921-1922)	2.000.000
Second artificial Famine in Ukraine (1933)	7.000.000
Killing of "kulaks" (collectivization)	1.000.000
Third wave of Terror by the NKVD (1933-37)	1.600.000
Yezovshchina (1937-1938)	2.500.000
Years of Anti-war and Post-War (1937-47)	2.700.000
In concentration Camps in Siberia	20.000.000

Total to the 60 anniversary of the U.S.S.R.: 68,473.000

Plus:

HUNGARY ?? CZECHOSLOVAKIA ?? KOREA
VIET NAM ?? ANGOLA ?? CAMBODIA ??

TODAY - AFGANISTAN; WHOSE TURN TOMORROW ???

Daily Californian

Serving East San Diego County

P.O. Drawer 1565 El Cajon, CA 92022
Office 613 W. Main St.

Friday, August 11, 1978

Home Edition: 2 Sections, 24 Pages
Mail Edition: 2 Sections, 24 Pages

Second language

Editor:

The mind of a human being is not as sophisticated as it may appear. Man zealously acts to protect the language he learns as a child, which is determined by his place of birth.

Cultural progress requires simplicity of language. But American civilization is a good example of how language has become increasingly complex.

Any living creature is reluctant to give up material goods. Human language is a mental possession, and resignation from it occurs only if one is striving for a sublime purpose.

Capitalism is a system which works for a sublime purpose — to produce plenty of material goods. U.S. capitalism shares its prosperity with others. Culturally and economically, the American nation could go one step further — it could surrender its language for a brighter future for mankind.

What is needed is a pan-tongue, easy to adopt by various national cultures, which could still celebrate their old customs through simplicity of language.

Such a language already exists — Latin, which is on the edge of extinction, or Esperanto, which is still fighting for understanding and application. Everyone knows that Latin has substantially influenced all European languages.

Which one, therefore, should mankind choose? The ancestral and natural one, or the modern but artificial one? These are main questions for future discussion.

The sublime purpose of the unification of mankind cannot be achieved without spiritual sacrifices, resignation of simplified national languages and long-lasting battles reviewed by history.

So let's start to teach people a second language, whichever would be more practical, Latin or Esperanto. If the American nation initiated such a plan, others would follow. Myself, I prefer Latin for its historical traditions.

155

What should America's official language be?

When the Founding Fathers debated about the language of the future American Nation they chose Latin, but selfishness prevailed instead.

People of different cultures setting foot on this land were coerced by Anglo-Saxon traditions, although this civilization was only in name, as 200 years later M. Ghandi exclaimed and has venerated a culture of humanism of competing rather cooperating nations, Sanskrit notwithstanding.

Other thinkers imply that Hebrew was created simultaneously with the world and was employed by God in his conversation with Adam and Eve. Since then, as Rabbinic tradition says, evolved languages of mankind. So we should venerate the Hebrew with its Mount Sinai's expression.

And if in this competitive world (each decade becoming smaller through modern technologies) a communicative tongue could prevail, it does not mean that it has to be English, nor Sanskrit or another.

Just take a look at Australia. People there were coerced to speak pure English although they are still using 140 others. Or at the U.S. where over 320 languages are still in use. In the rest of America it it mostly Spanish.

In such a real world, once again in the history of the U.S., a debate ensues in Congress whether English should be an official tongue of Americans.

But who are Americans? What is their relation to the entire world? Would they strengthen their bonds with it through English?

M. Ghandi was right speaking about competitiveness among nations. L. Zamenhof, 100 years ago, was right by inventing a neutral language ESPERANTO for the sake of the competitiveness. People might live with their cultures in isolation but cooperate through a Pan-tongue.

Proponents of English should consider this, and communicate with the world in a common language thus not infringing on rights of other nations to their traditions. They should advocate bilingualism in every nation with the ESPERANTO, but not the English as a tongue of a new "Roman Empire" for it did vanish.

Maybe then the people of the world will choose the U.S. Constitution as guidance on their way to progress and destroy the proverbial "Tower of Babel." If people really have peace on Earth in mind, the sooner they do this the better.

The 9th Circuit Court of Appeals in Arizona undoubtedly had recently all of this in mind when it declared that making English an official language of the U.S. is unconstitutional.